Kindle Version

Copywright@

All Rights Reserved. No part of this book may be reproduced in any form other than that in which it was purchased, and without the written permission of the author.

Your support of Author's rights is appreciated

Contents

Foreword

I decided to write this story to give to my family and the next generation. It is my own personal view of the hope we held onto during the months from March to May 2020.

On Tuesday the 31st December 2019, we were out with friends celebrating the end of the year, at our local pub called the Alvanley Arms in Cotebrook. There were 16 of us that night enjoying a 3-course meal with wine and dancing afterwards to a band and enjoying the celebration of a New Year 2020 with our friends.

Unknown to us, across the world in the wholesale seafood market in Wuhan, China, The World Health Organisation (WHO) was being alerted to a virus that had appeared within the animal food chain. This virus was thought to have originated from a bat or snake. As a precaution, officials decided to shut the market down on Wednesday 1st January, 2020. When the news reached us, we were fairly complacent.

After all, we have travelled to Asia, Australia and New Zealand in our lives. We have eaten Pad Thai amongst other foods, from market stall vendors in Thailand.

We participated in a special BBQ, where we were able to sample different meats and fish, under the stars and the milky way galaxy. Our gourmet meal was enjoyed at a unique dining experience called the 'Sound of Silence Dinner' at Ayers Rock in Australia. The night sky around us, was pitch black devoid of lights, whilst we ate our food, it was impossible to know whether we were eating crocodile or kangaroo!

The news from China did not make us feel anxious or worried at this point in time. A few years ago, in 2005, we had travelled in transit through Singapore amongst the outbreak of SARS when the wearing of masks was essential. However, as Sars was contained in Asia, and we were going further on to Australia and New Zealand. We were able to travel through the airport safely, but not stay in Singapore as planned.

I started writing this story in my mind, before putting pen to paper as the news escalated across the world in early January, about a serious outbreak of a virus causing deaths in the city of Wuhan in China. I hoped it would go away, but it did not!!

At the time of the outbreak of this new virus, it was believed that it was a type of influenza which is causing serious pneumonia like symptoms with a long dry cough and serious outcomes for the lungs of those infected.

Apparently, the virus had jumped from a bat or snake into humans somehow and mutated with devastating consequences, which unfolded daily before our eyes. The food markets in Wuhan were the place of origin for this virus, where unusual specials of all kinds of animals are part of the food chain.

It took the rest of the world a short while to cotton on to what was happening, before the spread of this disease became so serious, that it eventually caused a worldwide pandemic.

Parallel lines run alongside this book with the stories contained in my book **A LIFE OF HOPE**.

I have described the effects on the world after the Second World War, when thousands of lives were shattered as the bombs fell, families were torn apart, children lost not just their mums and dads, but their safe secure family life.

The effects of the bombs caused many children to grow up in the National Children's Homes and to suffer deep loss, causing long term mental health issues. In writing this second book, I hope to have portrayed that the same devastating effects of the COVID-19 virus that have shattered thousands of lives just the same!!

The COVID-19 virus took hold of human life with catastrophic outcomes and changed the course of human life in 2020.

Families were torn apart just the same as in the Second World War. Children lost not just their mums and dads, grandparents, aunts and uncles and cousins, but their safe secure family life which was literally turned upside down overnight with the implementation of Lockdown!

Mental health and financial hardships will affect not just the current generation, but generations following behind us for many, many years ahead.

On Sunday 5th January, 2020, officials were querying is this a return of **SARS?**

However, on Tuesday 7th January 2020 the WHO identified the disease from the market in China to be a new one and named it 2019-nCOV belonging to the Coronavirus family including SARS and the common cold.

On Saturday 11th January 2020, the first death from this new virus was reported by WHO (World Health Organisation) for a woman who had travelled from the district of Wuhan in China to Thailand.

For the remainder of the months of January, February and the early days of March 2020, all our families and friends were enjoying normal life.

We watched the news and read how rapidly the Coronavirus was spreading out from its beginnings in the market place to infect huge populations of China and Asia very rapidly. Thousands of deaths were occurring, still we thought it would be stopped or curtailed. None of us had grasped the unfolding horrors, that this virus was easily transmittable through the globe by sneezes, coughs and colds the usual form of transmission. We didn't know that it could mutate or become more aggressive in its formation, as it infiltrated slyly into unsuspecting human bodies.

The symptoms described by its victims were sore throats which felt like blades of knives inside the throat, raging temperatures off the scale at 40+ degrees and shortness of breath. The virus attacked the lungs vehemently, to the point that people were dying choking, as they struggled to breathe. Doctors discovered that pneumonia was swelling the lungs of patients with fluid. Respirators were used to try to save lives, but sadly people with other underlying health problems did not have the immunity or strength to fight the illness with their bodies.

As panic started to set in across the globe, life as we knew it began to change. Face masks were being worn, the majority of the workforce where possible were told to stay at home and work from there rather than in the office, hospitals became under pressure, mayhem set in for the whole globe.

My story for the dreadful month of March 2020 begins with the following information to all people living in the UK:-

Everyone is told to start washing their hands properly, using soap , whilst singing "Happy Birthday to twice"! The rationale behind singing Happy Birthday, was to ensure that we spent a longer time washing our hands thoroughly, whilst singing the song.

According to the experts this gives a longer washing time, rather than giving them just a quick rinse. We were advised to repeat this action several times throughout the day. Apparently, the best soap to cut through any germs is Fairy Liquid. We were also told not to touch our own faces with our hands. If we wish to sneeze, ensure that this action is carried out into a tissue paper. Dispose of the tissue paper immediately into a sealed bin. In the event of not having any tissues available, the next best thing to do is to sneeze into our own elbows. This is nothing new, but apparently, we have not been doing it properly across the globe.

The advice from the government is that we need to start deep cleaning all our surfaces, door handles and sanitising not just ourselves, but everywhere around us. This is to avoid the virus multiplying and breeding in places it can easily reach and jump transmission to others tenfold!

We are generally still feeling quite calm as we live each day, expecting someone to say, the virus has gone away, or we have found a cure!! It is all a big mistake or a bad dream if only!........

I started my own quick note taking for this story on Wednesday 11th March 2020. I plan to continue until we reach the other side of this difficult time period. The world feels scary and in essence, people are telling us that this is the "Third World War". Most of the hospitals in the UK are being adapted to become similar to the "Field Hospitals" used during World War 1 and World War 2.

The death rate for the UK in this first wave of COVID-19 in the month of March escalated quickly from 50 on the 19th March to a staggering total of 2,137 deaths by the end of March 2020.

Each day, our lives witnessed profound scenes of death, grief, danger, fear, courage, sorrow, love, hope, all repeated by each hour of our daily lives.

This is a story that that unfolded slowly on the 31st December 2019. Then gained a pace that none of us living through it could have perceived or anticipated.

To my family, good friends, brave heroes and the unsung heroes, who never stopped working tirelessly around the clock 24/7 for all of us.

"Human kindness has never weakened the stamina or softened the fibre of free people.

A nation does not have to be cruel to be tough"

Franklin D Roosevelt

Definition of COVID-19 (Wikipedia)

Coronavirus disease 2019 (**COVID-19**) is an infectious disease caused by severe acute respiratory syndrome coronavirus 2 (SARS-CoV-2). It was first identified in December 2019 in Wuhan, China, and has resulted in an ongoing pandemic. The first confirmed case has been traced back to 17 November 2019.

Traces of the virus have been found in December-2019 wastewater that was collected from Milan and Turin. As of 22 June 2020, more than 9 million cases have been reported across 188 countries and territories, resulting in more than 469,000 deaths. More than 4.46 million people have recovered.

Common symptoms include fever, cough, fatigue, shortness of breath, and loss of smell and taste. While the majority of cases result in mild symptoms, some progress to acute respiratory distress syndrome (ARDS) possibly precipitated by cytokine storm, multi-organ failure, septic shock, and blood clots.

The time from exposure to onset of symptoms is typically around five days but may range from two to fourteen days. The virus is primarily spread between people during close contact, most often via small droplets produced by coughing, sneezing, and talking.

The droplets usually fall to the ground or onto surfaces rather than travelling through air over long distances. However, research as of June 2020 has shown that speech-generated droplets may remain airborne for tens of minutes. Less commonly, people may become infected by touching a contaminated surface and then touching their face. It is most contagious during the first three days after the onset of symptoms, although spread is possible before symptoms appear, and from people who do not show symptoms.

The standard method of diagnosis is by real-time reverse transcription polymerase chain reaction (rRT-PCR) from a nasopharyngeal swab. Chest CT imaging may also be helpful for diagnosis in individuals where there is a high suspicion of infection based on symptoms and risk factors; however, guidelines do not recommend using CT imaging for routine screening.

According to the World Health Organization (WHO),there are no vaccines nor specific antiviral treatments forCOVID-19. Management involves the treatment of symptoms, supportive care, isolation, and experimental measures. The World Health Organization (WHO) declared the COVID-19 outbreak a public health emergency of international concern (PHEIC) on 30 January 2020 and a pandemic on 11 March, 2020. Local transmission of the disease has occurred in most countries across all six WHO regions.

Chapter One
Life turned upside down
Wednesday 11th March 2020

Geoff and I set off on our usual alternate weekly trip to Dalston, Carlisle to look after our granddaughter Autumn who is 4 years old and attends Nursery for 4 days each week, but we share looking after her for one day on a Thursday each week with her other grandad.

For the first 3 years of her life, we looked after her every Thursday and her other grandad looked after her every Wednesday.

The M6 Motorway was closed near where we live due to a multiple car accident caused by a lorry overturning, so on this day of the 11th March 2020 we had to travel on a different route around the outskirts of Manchester. It was miserable rainy day and we stopped at Tebay Services in Cumbria for a toilet break and a coffee.

We normally detour into the lake district en-route and enjoy a walk with Chumley before collecting Autumn from nursery. However, the rain was too heavy, so we decided to go straight to Dalston, unpack and that Geoff would take Chumley out for a walk where our daughter and son-in-law live, whilst I did some shopping in town.

Life was normal, Autumn was overjoyed and excited as always to see us when we arrived at her nursery to pick her up. The smile on her face when we peer through the door just lights up and melts our hearts every time.

We had fun chatting and playing together whilst waiting for Sarah and Paul to arrive home.

After Autumn had gone to bed, we all enjoyed a delicious supper of home cooked Lamb Rogan Josh and Naan Bread.. When the dinner is over, all of us have the opportunity to relax for a while, where we can chat about our daily life.

Thursday 12th March 2020

We played matching pair games with Autumn after breakfast for a while. Then, we all started to get ready to go out in the car for some supermarket shopping. We asked Autumn to choose her own Easter Egg first, then we carried on down the aisles to purchase cleaning products to use in our respective homes. These purchases were essential to comply with the latest government advice.. The advice strongly advocates regular daily cleaning of door handles and all other surfaces in the home.

We prepare a light sandwich lunch together followed by some singing and happy dancing around the kitchen floor, to the local Carlisle Radio station known as CFM.

Geoff took Chumley for another walk in the howling gales and heavy rain. I did some cleaning around the home, ensuring all door handles and surfaces were fully sanitised, as recommended by the government.

Autumn played with her crayons and made lots of pictures for her mummy and daddy, which she put into envelopes with their names on. Her pictures were highly creative and artistic.

During the afternoon, Geoff drew a dragon for Autumn, who used her painting pots to colour in the fire and flames from the dragon's mouth.
The finished creation of the coloured dragon on paper was fabulous. Autumn even signed her own name at the bottom of the picture.

Geoff and Autumn watched a film about witches and dragons together. I completed some more cleaning, cleared the ironing basket and put our bags together, for our journey home later.

We had no idea as we travelled down the M6 that over the next few days our lives would be so drastically changed. I left my writing journal untouched for a few days. Then I began the rest of this story on the morning of Tuesday 17th March, when I decided to write something each day, as a personal record to keep.

Tuesday 17th March 2020

One of our closest friends has a birthday today and is on holiday at their second home in Paphos, Cyprus with his lovely wife Carol, whom I worked with for many years at Danebridge Medical Centre.

Bob and Carol flew out on Monday 9th March 2020. They are due to fly back to the UK on Saturday 4th April 2020. We could have gone with them and seriously considered it a few weeks ago, as EasyJet Flights were reasonably priced. However, we are booked to spend two weeks with them in September when the sea and pool will be warmer, so we decided to wait until then.

We received a message via WhatsApp from Carol and Bob on Saturday 14th March 2020 to say that they may be home earlier as the Coronavirus spreads across the globe and Jet2 are only repatriating passengers up until Saturday 21st March, 2020.

They are hoping that Easy Jet will fly them home on Thursday 26th March, or if this is cancelled, they may have to stay put for a long time once all flights cease to operate. However, they said that there is plenty of food in the supermarkets and as Bob is an author so he can use the extra time to continue writing books.

As the days progressed, Carol messaged us to inform us that their scheduled flight has now been put back until Tuesday 31st March due to many flights being cancelled and airplanes grounded across the globe.

Cyprus has started to shut down all its cafes and bars as tourists begin to disappear. Carol and Bob have

13

sufficient food from the local supermarket. They tell us over a ZOOM meeting that they have done a shop with enough supplies to last a few weeks.

Many flights are cancelled across the globe as every airline brings passengers home and then ceased to operate.

On Wednesday 18th March 2020, the UK is expecting the Prime Minister Boris Johnson to close down all schools in an effort to stem the spread of the virus. We await his briefing broadcast to confirm this action.

However, the Republic of Ireland has closed its schools and other countries are closing schools in a massive effort to reduce the mortality rates and rapid spread of the virus.

The briefing informs us that that cinemas will close across the UK, restaurants and cafes will follow and that all planned events for 2020 are likely to be cancelled.

Shoppers are continuing to panic buy toilet rolls especially and are stripping supermarket shelves of everything in sight whilst they stockpile many essential items of food and cleaning products.

I took our dog Chumley for a walk this afternoon and noticed that car parks were empty, roads were quiet and empty, playgrounds were empty of mums with babies and children were nowhere about. It was eerily quiet in the middle of the afternoon with lots of cars on drives whilst many people were advised to work from home

At the briefing we learn that we have to begin self-isolation, particularly the age group of over 70 years of age.

All social activities must discontinue with immediate effect.

There is concern and anxiety as we listen to this news, but we understand the necessary precautions, along with what we have to do, to stay safe in our own homes and to protect our families.

To continue helping other people around us will require strict adherence to safety measures. For example, it is safe to leave shopping for neighbours on the doorstep. Observation of vulnerable people can be followed through to check people living on their own are not left feeling isolated.

Prices start to rocket for essential medicines Deaths are frightening and increasing. Lockdown of cities across the whole globe

Daily briefings are given to us every day by the Prime Minister Boris Johnson and his team of advisors.

Wednesday 18th March 2020

We cannot undertake our usual trip to Carlisle to look after our granddaughter Autumn as we would be putting ourselves at risk and our family as either of us could be carrying the virus without being aware and it is easily transmittable.

Firm measures are going in place to restrict social behaviour. Self-Quarantine is starting to happen for over 70s. Forefront life looks normal, but it is not.

I took Chumley to Verdin Park this afternoon. As I was walking towards the Park, I spotted Mollie an author friend, from the Vale Royal Writing Group.

We had to keep our distance and talk briefly across 2 metres socially distant from each other, no hugs or touching, like shaking hands with her husband, whom I have never met, it felt bizarre.

Later today we watched the PM Briefing. Decisions were made for schools to close but vulnerable children and those with special needs or with a social worker must still attend school. All teachers to carry on working in schools over the Easter Holidays and set up hubs, to accommodate vulnerable children and to organise risk assessments and online lessons

Thursday 19th March 2020

We walked along the river with Chumley to the Blue Bridge and back. The afternoon was sunny, which helps to cheer us up. On our return back home, a neighbour passed by with her two dogs, where we were standing on the edge of the path, so that she could walk safely past us. Using the open space we were able to speak to our neighbour without touching, hugging, but instead hold an up in the air chat, whilst allowing each of us to continue on our separate walks.

After we arrived home from our walk, we stayed outside to tackle some gardening jobs, in preparation for the summer months.

More details on school closure plans becomes slightly clearer. Key workers have to continue to care for vulnerable children at risk and with special needs.

Teachers are being asked to work over Easter, to set up hubs for vulnerable children. It is anticipated that schools may not re-open until September.

Nursery care businesses may also have to close. To qualify for childcare, a family of two parents, must both be on the Key Worker list, for example all NHS Staff, Teachers, People who are delivering essential services

Friday 20th March 2020

Aldi shelves were empty at 8.00 am. The supermarket car park was full to capacity. People must have been queuing for hours

The aisles were full of shoppers, it was worse than any shopping day at Christmas, totally mind-blowing crazy.

There was no milk on the shelves, still no eggs, margarine, flour, or pasta. Many basic commodities have been taken by the stockpiling greedy public, who have selfishly taken more than they need.

It was the same story at Asda. I managed to collect a few items of shopping from Tesco's on my way home, such as corn flour, wine, Provit margarine to help me to maintain my cholesterol levels, some salad items, garlic relish, herby cream cheese, nachos to accompany a chilli con carne, vegetables for stir frying and sweet potatoes for tea. I pick up currants, pecan nuts and cashew nuts.

The postman delivered a long box of flowers to me from my daughter Sarah, her husband Paul and their daughter Autumn. The flowers were from an online florist called Bloom and Wild. They came with a book of instructions on how to arrange them. The tulips still had their bulbs attached to the stem and apparently, they keep growing. The flowers were wrapped carefully inside green tissue paper. A net surrounded some gorgeous old fashioned pale pink roses and protected their delicate buds and flower heads. There was a lot of foliage too, for arranging them beautifully. Inside the box was a lovely photograph of Sarah and I, which made me smile and feel special, as well as sad, that we are not allowed to see each other because of this dreadful pandemic.

We stay in tonight again, this is over 2 weeks of not going out, and we have distanced ourselves from our family and friends for over one week, whilst we strive to avoid the dangers of catching the virus, then passing it on to our loved ones.

We take Chumley on a walk across the river in the afternoon and carry on to Roker Park, we do not meet people or see anyone other than ourselves.

Part of our walk passes by Waitrose. I pop inside the supermarket, to see if there is any milk on the shelves, as we struggled to buy milk this week. There is not enough left to last us. I am able to buy 4 pints of organic whole milk, which we don't drink, preferring skimmed milk for beverages and semi-skimmed for our breakfast cereals. However, I feel this will be better than no milk at all.

The advice from the government is to stay where we are tomorrow, not travel, not socialise and there are growing concerns about the number of people driving to the coast with their families and children. Beaches and roads are becoming overcrowded with visitors.

The government is against this for our own protection and future generations to come. Masses of people will only spread the disease further across the UK. There will be many infected people who won't even be aware that they are carrying the virus. Some people will have no symptoms, but will be carriers and unknowingly, transmit it to other people to whom they come into close contact with.

We go to bed early and try not to worry too much, but now we are growing quite frightened inside us too.

Lots of kind community acts are occurring with people looking out for each other. Groups being set up to replace socializing, such as Zumba, on-line workshops, on-line meet-up groups for example Vale Royal Writers Group

WhatsApp Groups are sending lots of jokes and support amongst friends, who normally get together. Life is changing by the hour

The Prime Minister's briefing closes down Pubs, Gyms, Restaurants, Cafes, all public events and potential meeting areas with immediate effect tonight. Children leave school today instead of at the end of July

Call for 65,000 retired NHS workers to return. My daughter is a teacher in a deprived area of Carlisle. She is setting up hubs for children to have lessons, preparing online lesson packs, is working flat out to deliver strategic measures and writing up risk assessments for children, staff and parents. Her husband is going into work at 4.00 am every day as he works in a distribution centre ensuring mineral water reaches the public, demand has escalated.

Their 4-year-old daughter doesn't understand that she will be saying goodbye to her friends today and will remain at home until she goes to school at the age of 5 in September, providing we are through this difficult time.

The family were due to go on holiday on the 1st April and have paid for their holiday this week, but cannot travel, they accept it is not safe and anyway planes are grounded too. They were gathering holiday clothes together only last Saturday and now their daughter has to understand that the holiday will not happen, but instead in isolation, they can go for a bike ride or walk.

Children soon adapt and accept. I feel for them and for us as we are no longer able to travel the 135 miles to be with them as it is not safe to do so for them and for us in case one of us gives the other the virus.

Saturday 21st March 2020

Today it was daylight at 6.30 a.m., and we are still blessed and alive with no symptoms. On Sunday it is 'Mothering Sunday', we will speak to our children via phone or Facetime and cannot have a single physical hug.

There are a lot of things to be happy about, trying to ignore the inner voices of fear.

Geoff jet washed the steps at the bottom of the garden and prepared the decking base of his shed for painting.

I decided to drive into Northwich and was just putting my shoes on, when a DPD white van arrived on our drive. A lovely young man came down to the front door with a beautiful white basket full of gorgeous roses and lilies and gerbers in my favourite deep pink colours.

They were a gift for me from my son Anthony and his wife Catherine and made me smile for the pleasure of them. There was a poignant message attached to the flowers from Niamh about Nana. I felt so blessed to have such beautiful floral gifts from my children and fabulous cards too that made me feel incredibly special.

I went to Witton Churchyard to put some flowers on my parents grave and my brother who lies in peace with them. I chose a mixture of cheerful daffodils and some beautiful multi-coloured tulips. I had arranged some of the same flowers for Geoff's mum and dad when we collected the Grave Pot vase with

Mum and Dad lettering on from Davenham churchyard yesterday morning.

Mothering Sunday 22nd March 2020

We are up early and take Chumley out for his first walk of the day, the sky is a deep summer blue, lots of little birds like blue tits, sparrows, thrushes are all singing to us as we walk, the grass is green, and the river is beautifully mirrored back to us in its still waters this morning. On the footbridge that we use to cross the river, some warm-hearted people have chalked messages lighting the way, like "Show me your smile it's a beautiful day" "Stay Happy"

Once breakfast is over, Geoff decides to paint the decking base under his shed, so that it can dry in the warm sunshine today.

I am making some binding for a cushion and prepare the corners with some tacking stitches.

Our son Anthony called us on Facetime, and I enjoy a lovely chat with him and see our 7-month-old baby granddaughter Niamh who is in the background using her walker to navigate around the kitchen.

It is heart-warming to chat to him and to his lovely wife Catherine, they are just getting ready to head out for a walk together this morning and time in the garden this afternoon. The advice is to stay at home, not venture far at all and to remain away from crowded public places.

The National Trust was offering free admission to everyone, but they have had to withdraw this offer and close their premises up. Many High Street shops are also closing their doors, big names such as John Lewis, Marks and Spencer, Next, Debenhams, Joules, White Stuff, H&M, River Island. Cafes, Pubs, and restaurants all closed.

Supermarkets have revised opening times with the first hour of opening in many cases being for the elderly, vulnerable, NHS staff and public sector staff too, I hope this includes teachers, but it is not clear. Shelves continue to empty, and we are informed that £1Billion has been spent on stockpiling food by shoppers who are panicking that food is going to be in short supply, their actions are causing it and we are constantly being reminded that there is enough food to go round if we all only take what is essential and what we need for now.

65,000 NHS retired staff have been asked to return to work voluntarily. The private sector has offered its premises and equipment to help with excessive demands on the NHS.

I chat for a while on the phone to my daughter and she tells me their plans for the day are to go out for some fresh air, but not where it is busy, just to a disused air base from World War 2, where their daughter Autumn can use her scooter.

They were going out for a Sunday Roast Dinner at the Plough Pub, which is closed, however, the pub has arranged to deliver the lunches in sealed containers to their doorstep as the food is in and has been prepared. We had planned a few days with them and would have been participating too, had we been able to travel to Cumbria this week, but could not because of the need for all of them and all of us to stay safe.

I felt ok although a bit sad at not being able to see both our children and grandchildren today, on such a beautiful spring day. I was philosophical though about the reasons and know that it will not be forever. We have hearts full of happy days shared with them both. I just lost it a bit, when Sarah my daughter said, I want to come and stand outside your window mum just to see you. I felt the same with my son Anthony too, knowing that he lives closer to us in Hale and knowing that we cannot even go for a walk with all of them, as Anthony is just shaking off a cold which has lingered for almost

3 weeks, he doesn't know if it is the coronavirus or just a cold. None of us will know as there are too many people now to test and it's an impossible situation.

What we are finding is the difficulty of not seeing family and friends, we miss them so much. Staying put at home is easy to do as we have a lovely garden, can walk outside and work on little projects, can still drive-in isolation if we wish, although we are aware of not heading to crowded places and beaches along with the rest of the senseless people and children doing that today.

It is a hard to cope with the natural pull of a mum on Mother's Day. The sheer longing to see our families for a hug and a proper cuddle, during these extremely difficult days for the whole world.

It is difficult to focus too on any tasks or projects at times, as so many things are buzzing inside our heads. I baked two cakes and then realised, that I had used the rest of our eggs which were nearly out of date and needed using, but there is a shortage of them. Eggs have been missing off the shelves for weeks now. I suspect that some government person has ordered a lot of food for the country to be stockpiled in big warehouses, somewhere like the sugar mountains of a few years ago that reached the ceilings of huge warehouses as part of a plan to feed the world.

Reading the news is just frightening and very grim as the pandemic escalates beyond all our wildest imagination and fear is inside each of us. Today was an extremely difficult draining day emotionally, for Geoff and me as we walked through the hours of fearfulness during the night.

Monday 23rd March 2020

Today, we awoke and thanked our stars and gods above us that we are still alive without contracting the virus and that our family and friends are all safe too.

The weather is dry and mild, no rain for the 4th day in a row. Geoff takes Chumley out for his early morning walk and I enjoy a shower and prepare breakfast, put some washing in the machine. Just another ordinary day in the Leigh household.

We feel stronger today than we did yesterday.

Our plans are to go on an essential shopping expedition for a bottle of milk depending on whether milk is back on the shelves in the supermarkets. We will add to our shopping basket, any other essential requirements we need whilst inside the store. We went to Sainsbury's first and were able to locate our essential shopping needs.

There was nothing we attempted to stockpile from the goods on the shelves. However, we did visit a local farm shop called the Hollies, to see what fresh produce and meat we could buy, to help with meals for the rest of the week.

Our food choices included diced lamb, fresh bread, mushrooms, dark chocolate buttons called Monteszuma Revenge. Geoff and Anthony enjoy this particular brand of chocolate, which is irresistibly dark and indulgent. Naturally, we bought two packets and put one aside in the cupboard for Anthony, as an Easter treat from us. On the way home, we collected 3 bags of potting compost, which were needed for our runner bean and French marigold plants, which we have grown from seed.

We ate lunch outside al-Fresco, with the sun feeling quite warm on our sheltered patio.

After lunch, we took Chumley for his second walk of the day. I took some books to the doorstep of Elizabeth, who is one of my Hartford Girls school friends. She lives just around the corner from us. We were able to chat from a social distance. We were pleased to see each other and air our worries at the same time.

When we returned home, we decided to start cleaning our old greenhouse, to reduce the overgrown moss on all the glass windows. We managed to clean 8 panels and will tackle the rest of the project tomorrow.

Sarah and Autumn Facetimed us. Geoff had great fun making stupid sounds with Autumn, who looked very happy and told us that she had been in Little Bears at Nursery today with five other children.

I noticed that Autumn was wearing the red cardigan I had knitted for her recently. It reminded me that she could do with some summer cardigans for the weeks ahead.

Autumn is very anxious to get outside and play on her new trampoline with her mummy, who is trying to carry on chatting to us. We tell Sarah to go and enjoy some playtime fun with Autumn. I tell Autumn that Nana Banana, is looking forward to jumping on the trampoline with her as soon as we are allowed.

At 8.30 pm tonight, the Prime Minister Boris Johnson announced a complete lockdown of the UK, banning people from leaving their homes or meeting in groups of more than two people as the Government scrambles to enforce social distancing measures to prevent the spread of coronavirus. In a public address to the nation this evening, the Prime Minister said "the public will not be allowed to leave their homes except for a few specific reasons and could be fined £30 for meeting outside in groups of more than two people"

All non-essential shops will close, as will outdoor gyms, kiosks, and places of worship, except for funerals.

The unprecedented measures were prompted by fears in Downing Street that the coronavirus suppression measures have been ignored by the public.

A new modelling of the details has been released, which suggests at least three quarters of people must follow the rules, for the NHS to be kept afloat.

Under the new lockdown, members of the public must not leave their house except to:-

1. **Shop for essentials, as infrequently as possible.**

2. **Exercise outdoors once per day, alone or with household members.**

3. **Receive medical treatment or provide care.**

4. **Travel to and from work if impossible to work from home.**

Boris Johnson announced the greatest restriction in British liberty in the nation's history, closing shops and ordering Britons to stay at home. The number of deaths in the UK rose steeply to over 8,000, with more than 5,498 reported cases this week.

Britain is seriously lagging behind other nations in testing for the virus, with the government nowhere its target of 10,000 tests per day.

Self-employed workers have pleaded with the Chancellor to protect their livelihoods during the lockdown. In Italy, a dip in the number of deaths has fuelled hope that the country's outbreak has peaked.

Tuesday 24th March 2020

Geoff and I did not sleep much when we went to bed after the stark warning in the above address to the Nation and felt fear in our hearts and heads for all of us. We had a cup of tea in bed at 3.00 am in the morning whilst trying to make sense of what is happening to us and everyone around us too.

As daylight filtered through the curtains, we both got dressed. Geoff took our dog Chumley out for his usual walk and that means the exercise that Geoff took is the only one he can do today, outside our home.

I will take Chumley out later this afternoon and that will be my outdoor exercise. In the meantime, we spend time in the garden cleaning our greenhouse.

I do some sewing and find an old bottle of hair root touch up colour that has been in the bathroom cupboard for some time. I apply it to my hair later this morning, then shower and get ready for an appointment at a surgery close to home for an ultrasound on my liver, gall bladder and kidneys. I arrive early for my appointment and see that 3 people ahead of me are queuing 2 metres apart, whilst we wait for our turn to speak to the full face masked (almost like a burka) receptionist on the other side of the window inside the office room she is using in complete isolation.

This process of waiting outside on the car park takes a while as no-one is allowed inside the surgery until it is safe to do so and then only one person is admitted via a masked nurse.

I saw a man with a mask and blood over his face come out of the surgery doors and get in his car. There is a short delay before the locked surgery doors are opened to allow the next patient in.

After a longish wait which almost runs over my allocated appointment time, it is my turn, the door is unlocked and I am told to sit in the empty waiting room, which is normally full of people and children, the normally busy reception desk remains unmanned and eerily quiet, all doors are closed, no phones are ringing.

I feel the long silence and despair in the air, it is strangely unreal to me, who is used to working in busy surgeries for 28 years with the noise of the telephones constantly ringing, whilst the waiting room is also full of lots of patients, queuing up to be seen by the clinical teams. Or waiting to collect their prescriptions, signed certificates for holiday cancellations, sickness notes and death certificates etc.

I use the hand sanitizer as the nurse comes towards me to take me for my scan. She tells me her name is Carolyn, I am questioned by her as to whether I have any symptoms at all or have been in contact with infected people?.

I assure her that I am fit and well and have had no close contact with any other people for over 2 weeks now. I am asked to take my cardigan off, but not my shoes and to lie on the bed, I have to lift my own dress up and tuck paper under my bra and more paper into my underwear to prevent skin contact.

The ultrasound lasts for half an hour during which time the Sonographer who introduced herself to me as Andrea carries on the necessary procedures without taking her full-face mask or gloves off.

At the end of the procedure, I am informed by Carolyn that if I wish to empty my bladder, I can do so in the toilet at the far end of the surgery waiting area.

I decline and try to joke that I have a good bladder from years of doing pelvic floor exercises, but it is not appropriate, my mind is made up. I decide that I will reach home in less than five minutes, as there is very little traffic and also my brain informs me that if I go to the toilet and then wash my hands, I am in effect delaying the wait for the next patient outside, so I leave the surgery for home.

I am half a mile down the road, when I come to a junction with a small mini roundabout located near Slade Street and Pullman Drive. I approach the bridge over the railway, driving slowly over it I am generally not a fast driver at all. I know as I cross the junction to head up over the bridge that there is no car to my right on the roundabout coming from Pullman Drive.

However, a loud bang to the right of my window suddenly hits me like a rocket.

I am alerted to the fact that I now have a white car travelling with me up the bridge road. I stop my car and get out to find my mirror on the road and the driver's door completely scraped with white paint.

I am safe and the driver who hit me is parked further up and gets out of her car too. She is safe thankfully and neither of us are hurt.

As my car is parked just above the foot of the bridge, drivers in Slade Street behind me are shouting that they cannot get out of the road to travel over the bridge as my car is in the way.

I step back inside my car to start the engine and move it; however, a safety feature must have kicked in as my car will not start its engine.

A young man standing on the corner of Slade Street comes to my rescue and offers to help push it down the bridge, then into safety in a parking bay just to the right of Slade Street which is located directly under the bridge which I was crossing.

I get into my car again and he is braced to push me down, luckily my car fires into power once more and with care I am able to reverse and manoeuvre my car to a safe waiting area.

The other lady driver joins me, and we get out of our cars and start to talk and exchange our contact details. The lady who hit my car explained to me that she was travelling fast too catch up with her daughter who was already ahead of her on the bridge. She also told me that she had travelled up from Cornwall earlier that day to start emptying an ex-husband's house who had recently died and was on her way back to Cornwall at that moment, she was using her husband's VW Tiguan and not her own car for the journey as she needed a bigger car.

People going past us in cars or on foot, while we were exchanging paperwork and taking photos of our respective driving licenses on the boot of my car, were shouting down to us, "you are going to catch Coronavirus move away!" We did move apart to ring our respective husbands and the lady had to wait for her daughter to return from Tesco's, where she had gone to ahead of her mum for provisions and fuel for their journey back to Cornwall in two cars.

Throughout this, my brain kept saying why are they out of the county on non-essential business today after the nation's address by Boris last night, but then I thought if someone has died that must be essential business?

In passing conversation, the lady driver who hit me said that she hadn't seen her ex-husband for over 20 years but was now responsible for his funeral and had no money to pay for it. She said her new husband will be angry at the damage to his car.

I looked down at my car and saw the damage and told myself it is just a lump of metal. I am alive, she is too and life as we know it is going to take thousands of lives away in the coming weeks. I didn't feel emotional at all about my car and despite a slight sensation of shakiness in my legs, caused more by the sound of the impact than anything, I felt strangely calm

The lovely young man who had offered to help me was taking photos and reassuring both of us that we were ok. He had taken photos of our cars and offered to email them both to us. He also offered to be a witness to the crash and gave us his phone and address details and then showed me where he lived, should either of us need him. He did tell me that she was going way too fast over the mini-roundabout and that he has seen so many crashes in this particular spot caused by the same problem.

My husband arrived on the scene after a quick call to tell him what had happened. He used to work for an insurance company many years ago and is very good at detail and calmness in these situations. We all talked a bit more at some distance from each other and decided that everything was in order, so that I could safely drive my car home.

Interestingly, during our conversations with the driver who hit me, she also said that as her car is so high and mine was small that she simply didn't see me on the road.

Her car suffered a dent to the front of her passenger side of her car. I made a mental note of her comments for future recording.

As we were about to leave, suddenly three policemen all on separate motorbikes drove into Slade Street as a member of the public had telephoned them to say that there had been an incident and the roads were blocked. The three policemen were very cheerful and positive with us, especially when we told them we were all sorted and just about to leave for home.

My husband asked them where they had come from, they said Knutsford. The policemen checked our vehicles out, commented on what a lovely red car mine was and were satisfied that we could leave for home.

However, before we could leave, they did advise myself and the other driver that they would just need to breathalyse us first as standard procedure in all car driving incidents. The other lady went first, and her test was negative.

When the policeman came to me I cheekily said, well officer, I have just drunk one and half pints about an hour ago, he poised with his pen mid-air and as he was about to say something, I said "it was only water" as I have just been for an ultrasound test!! Interestingly, it took me three attempts to blow hard into the breathalyser and get it to register anything let alone extract a negative reading, possibly due to the fact that I had just been using my lungs and holding my breath a lot in the test I felt, but then I have never been any good at blowing balloons up either.

Wednesday 25th March 2020

We woke up at 4.00 a.m. again and Geoff made us both a mug of hot tea. This is getting to be the normal wake up time for us and we expect other households are just like us too. I cannot go back to sleep, so I leave Geoff in bed whilst I go downstairs and write a story about my car accident yesterday which I have inserted in the paragraphs above with a title called "Oh no my beautiful red shiny Mazda MX5 what did the lady do to you!"

Geoff took Chumley for his usual walk this morning early at 5.00 am and I will take Chumley out after lunch possibly for a swim as the weather is looking good, it is warm and sunny today. Lunch alfresco outside perhaps later.

We have breakfast together and decide that as it is another sunny dry day, that we will spend the day outside in the garden. I want to clean the house thoroughly first though and Geoff must pick his medication up and then wants to check the speed limits where my car accident occurred.

Geoff returned and confirmed that the lady driver who hit me had exceeded the speed limit in Pullman Drive which is 20 mph, and she was travelling at 29 mph and on the roundabout, she was doing 25 mph as detailed in the dash cam footage that her husband had sent to us in an email late last night.

We spend the day pottering in the garden. Geoff finishes the greenhouse which looks really clean and ready for use again, with everything tidied away.

The weather is unusually warm, and we decide to bring some of the outdoor furniture out of the shed and give it a wash down so that we can enjoy using it this afternoon whilst the weather is kind. Lunch was Al-Fresco outside, and it felt good to be in the garden again with blue skies and sunshine looking down on us.

After lunch I got ready to take Chumley with me on my once-a-day exercise regime. It was incredibly hot; I even had my shorts on and a t-shirt. Chumley was excited and happy, especially as he was able to enjoy a swim in the river again after a long wet dark winter.

There were a lot of people out this afternoon, all of us ensuring we kept 2 metres apart from each other, even if this meant going off track into shrubbery. It was amusing trying to talk across 2 metres when I met a friend and her husband down the river and quite easy not to do the usual rushing over and having hugs and kisses on the cheeks as we would have done normally.

I put some washing out when I arrived home as it was still so hot. Geoff had already started to prepare tea, as we had decided to have a Pad Thai tonight and he was busy chopping up the vegetables needed for the meal.

I had arranged a Zoom Meeting practice with my friend Bob who is currently in his holiday villa in Paphos, Cyprus and cannot get flights home until early May if then!

Bob is the Chairman of our writing group, and we are working together with a few other members of the committee to be able to find a solution to interacting with each other and carrying on with our normal monthly meetings and readings etc. We tried Skype on Monday night, but it was a bit cumbersome to use and we were all talking at once as well as fumbling with the software and experimenting with it. We agreed to hold another meeting and try other options in a few days.

I was enthusiastic about Zoom which had been used for my Tuesday Zumba class online and hosted by my dance teacher Sharon Power. Bob and I agreed to try this out tonight to see if this would work better for us as an option. I am pleased to say that it did, it is an amazing piece of interactive software which is easy to use for uploading documents from your own files.

Bob agreed to put a message out to the group for a further meeting to go ahead on Friday afternoon at 3.30 pm for a small group of us from the committee to use Zoom and test it out with each other

Thursday 26th March 2020

It was a stunning beautiful day today with not a cloud in sight! Gorgeous summer blue skies and warm sunshine. A day for wearing shorts and a t-shirt.

We potter in the garden but do not tackle anything really big. A lot of hard work has been achieved this week in our greenhouse project, by deep cleaning the glass and debugging it. The only thing left to do now is some painting along the inside brickwork.

Geoff spent the morning preparing a cottage pie for tea and I made us an egg custard pie for dessert.

As it was a lovely dry day, the 10th one in a row, Geoff spent an hour washing the dirty rainy grime off his car.

My open top red car sat next to his looking sorry for itself with a big dent and lots of white paint on the door following my road traffic collision on Tuesday lunchtime.

We enjoyed eating our lunch outside again, I had a healthy-looking salad and Geoff had a ham salad batch cake.

I took Chumley down the river again after lunch and he thoroughly enjoyed more swimming. What he didn't realise, is that he was due a soapy wash down at home as the river is still a bit muddy on the bottom with lots of sand swirling up following almost a year of rain or at least it feels like a year, the rain started in July 2019 and there haven't been many dry days at all since!!

We both sorted an essential shopping list out for tomorrow morning, when we can join the queue of elderly people being able to visit the supermarket at 8.00 am in the morning. Customers will be allowed in a few at a time.

I washed all Chumley's bedding this afternoon to make it clean and fresh for him and to ensure that we are keeping Chumley safe, and his bedding regularly sanitised too.

I have prepared the last stage of my book cushion for Niamh and looking forward to finishing this little project in a couple of days.

I telephoned Anthony for a chat to see how they all were all coping. Anthony chatted about a few garden projects that were keeping them occupied, he told me all about the spring meadow seeds that they had planted today, whilst entertaining Niamh at the same time.

Anthony sent us a couple of photos of Niamh collecting the newspaper from the front door, trying to read it, the look of shock on her face is just hilarious. Tonight's newly appointed newsreader is Niamh Mary Leigh aged 7 months old.

Sarah telephoned to chat to us at 8.30 pm and it was great to hear that they are all ok.
The things that they are struggling with are as follows:-
Looking after Autumn at home as nursery is closed and we are not allowed to leave the confines of our home to go and help.

Sarah has had to telephone her Head Teacher to say that unfortunately, she cannot go into school as she must look after Autumn. Sarah is working as much as she can from home to help with all the strategic planning needed to house the children who are most at risk (vulnerable children) within their own familiar school.

The education officials have asked schools to create a hub system inside each school to ensure small groups of vulnerable children can still attend school.

Shopping as the shelves empty during their working hours and are shut when they arrive home from work.

Geoff and I spoke to his brother Dave this morning on the telephone to check if he and Linda are both ok where they live in Taunton, Somerset and we asked how his children and granddaughters are too.
Dave's response was that they are all doing ok and that he is working from home every day.

Geoff had a long chat to his sister today on the telephone to see if she and Jim were doing ok and their children too.

Jokes and stories abound still in my various groups Chicks with Sticks, Coffee Buddies, Hartford Girls (school friends from over 50 years ago) Laughter is truly the best medicine and the sharing of family life with strong friendship to support each other through these difficult and strange times.

The Sandiway walking group were scheduled to meet on Sunday for a walk and pub lunch organized by Geoff and me but as with everything else, this has had to be cancelled and especially since "Lock Down" now prevents us going on any journey unless it is to collect medication, essential foods, travel to work.

My phone pinged and a lovely video of Autumn singing, appeared instantly on my screen "See you on the Wing" was the song Autumn was singing to us, which was Great Grandad's all-time favourite saying for goodbye to each of us.

Then I received some lovely funny photos of Niamh as a news reader, on my phone. Apparently, she had reached the front door in her baby walker just as the newspapers were pushed through.

Geoff and I participated in the NHS round of applause at 8 pm by everyone coming out of the front door to clap and send our heartfelt thanks to all of the doctors and staff working around the clock. A lot of our neighbours were outside clapping, it was a moving experience.

Friday 27th March 2020

Geoff and I were up early and off to the supermarket by 8.00 am as all supermarkets in our area are allowing workers from the NHS, Social Care, elderly and vulnerable people to shop without the supermarket being crowded and to allow this group of people to be able to select the items they require safely.

A young couple who live across the road from us, shouted across to Geoff earlier this week, that as they were working from home, if there is anything, we need such as shopping or anything else they would help us, we only have to ask. It made us feel blessed to have such good neighbours, it also made us feel older than we feel inside our heads and bodies.

Geoff and I are lucky that we are not frail and don't have serious health problems at all. In fact, we feel frustrated at not being allowed to leave our homes and do something for other people. We have been labelled into the 'older generation' who must stay inside and not catch the virus as we are so vulnerable due to our age. We know that we are quite physical fit as we have always remained active.

Our lives are full of walking, as well as undertaking various jobs around the home, such as gardening, baking, cooking, reading, writing. We take our dog out for walks over 3 miles long twice a day.

These walks are done independently of each other as each person is only allowed one outdoor activity each day. Previously, before "Lock Down" we would walk an average of 3 miles together, 2 or 3 times a day and longer walks when we could go out in the car.

In the afternoon, after I had taken Chumley on his usual walk, using my once-a-day exercise. I logged onto my laptop as I have agreed to participate in another

ZOOM test with my writing group colleagues. Our mission is to test the feasibility of the software, as a potential solution, for the group to be able to hold 'online writing group meetings'.

Saturday 28th March 2020

We were awake just after 4.30 a.m. this morning with the sound of the Police Helicopter hovering over the resident's homes where we live in Riverside Park, Castle. The whirring noises and huge spotlights are disturbing and worrying for us to hear and see. We realise that something like an accident or incident must have occurred within the area where we live.

At 6.00 a.m. Geoff is up and dressed ready to take Chumley for his early morning walk down the river. When he returns, he tells me that there is a huge police activity going on in the area, with police vehicles parked by the Weir, more police cars parked in Northwich, the Fire Brigade are there and the ambulances along with a paramedic team.

We found out later during the day, that the incident involved a young couple, the lady was 20 years old, and the man was 21 years old, they were out walking at 4.00 am along the river near the Weir which is fast flowing and their dog fell into the water, they both jumped in after the dog, the lady managed to reach the edge of the riverbank, unfortunately though her partner drowned, his body was eventually found and pulled out later this afternoon by the police divers.

Today, it is our daughter's birthday and thank goodness we posted a card and present up to her a couple of weeks ago. We had also arranged a delivery of Letterbox flowers for today, along with one of her favourite candles from Mills and Boo who have introduced a new range called Rhubarb and Ginger Tonic.

We have arranged to link up at 3.30 pm this afternoon on ZOOM as a video conference and we are so looking forward to being able to interact with our children and grandchildren once more. It has been one of the hardest things, during this pandemic not to be able to spend time with our family, whom we love dearly.

Ever since Autumn was born on the 12th September 2015 we have travelled from Northwich to where they live in Cumbria, every two weeks initially, whilst Sarah was on maternity leave.

When Sarah returned to work. Geoff and I were overjoyed to be asked if we would like to look after Autumn every week on a Thursday, with an overnight stay in their home on the Wednesday.

It has been one of the happiest times of our lives since our own children were born in 1978 and 1979. We absolutely loved collecting Autumn from nursery and taking her to nursery whilst Sarah worked full time initially. Our lives have been so blessed to have the opportunity to be fun loving grandparents and to build a special bond with the granddaughters and with the spouses of our children too.

We look forward to our weekly drive to Cumbria and often deviate around the Lake District for a walk and of course coffee and cake in many of the Lake District towns and villages.

To us it is just like having a drive out every week in our retirement years and we embrace the trips as a total joy every week. The bonus for us, is the sheer pleasure of being with our first grandchild every single week. We simply love it so much, that the 300-mile round trip never phases us at all.

Geoff decides to tackle some fence painting this morning as we have a total of 39 fences that need the annual repainting task.

I decide that our home needs another deep clean from me this morning. We are becoming paranoid about staying at home, whilst checking that no nasty bugs can land on our surfaces. I clean everything in sight with products where the label states, designed to kill 99.9% of germs including influenza, etc.

We noticed when shopping yesterday that the packs of anti-bacterial wipes have escalated in price not just double but treble and beyond! 0.80 pence for a large packet of 120 wipes just 2 weeks ago. £4.00 now for a smaller packet of 60 wipes. Under normal circumstances, we spend a total of approximately £30 in Aldi each week for our grocery shopping, £28 in Asda and £30 in the local butchers shop in Hartford.

However, today our supermarket shopping was a total of £109 and our butchers bill was £39 giving us an extra £60 onto our normal weekly shop of £88 in total. We are not surprised, as it is obvious that prices will rise for food on a supply and demand basis following a severe over-reaction by masses of people who have bought excessive quantities of food causing a wave of panic buying to set in.

The government and the supermarkets have now introduced special opening hours for people working in the NHS and those in services where people are vulnerable and the elderly. Geoff and I join a queue outside Asda at 8.00 am this morning.

The queues around Aldi and Sainsbury's were far too long to wait outside in the cold. The staff were only allowing a few in at a time and most shops are only allowing either one person or two people into their shops. It has reduced panic buying significantly. We were able to buy the essentials on our shopping list and have always chosen not to stockpile and to think of others instead.

I tell my friends in the Hartford School Girls group that we have organized a family ZOOM session later today. I send them some useful links to install this piece of software onto their own systems i.e., mobile phones, iPad, laptop, desktop computers, so that we can continue to share coffee and cake together from our own homes using this technology. If we all use ZOOM, then at least we would be able to see and support each other as lifelong friends.

My sister-in-law Jean rang from Southport this morning. We had a lovely time chatting about their recent holiday to Paphos in Cyprus at the end of February and into Mid-March, before the lockdown and cancelled flights arrived on all our doorsteps. We exchanged family news and how we were all coping with the lock down and the fears for our children and grandchildren that we carry with us 24/7.

The highlight of our day, however, was linking up live with our children and 2 granddaughters Autumn and Niamh. We were all able to chat and see each other on the screen.

We enjoyed some family fun and laughter along the way, especially our rubbish singing of Happy Birthday to Sarah. Our time together lasted for over one hour. Geoff and I found that the experience was the best gift of all just to see them again. We listened to their stories of life in the workplace with this dreadful pandemic.

We told them how frustrating it is for us as we feel so fit, active and healthy. However, we cannot see or help them in any small way. Their overriding concern is for our wellbeing, for us to stay virus free and safe. This is why they are continuing to work in stressful, often difficult jobs, whilst protecting us too. However, we feel that it is us that should be protecting them and safeguarding their future lives. Geoff and I enjoy a delicious chicken and Jasmine rice meal for tea. The chicken was cooked in a lemongrass and Thai fragrant sauce.

We watched some of the series called Hannah and then tried to watch the film The Professor and the Mad Man about writing the English Dictionary at Oxford. It didn't light our fires, in the end we turned it off.

We changed the clock time forward by one hour and went to bed at 9.30 p.m., although really it was only 8.30 pm, Needless to say we were wide awake at 2.30 a.m. and having cups of tea in bed and both telling each other that we had been awake worrying about our two children and their families.

They are both working flat out in their respective jobs, Paul who is Sarah's husband has been working 14 hour shifts and setting off for work early every day. Sarah has been at home some parts of the week, but likewise is very busy setting up the new hubs in a purpose-built building that can house several schools together with their own head teachers and teaching staff for the foreseeable future.

Each Hub will probably house about 20 vulnerable children and children at risk, complete with their own teaching staff. Each school will have separate toilets and entry/exit points. We both felt that Sarah and Paul looked totally exhausted during our family conference on Zoom. For us as parents, we still want to put a protective arm around each of our children and their families. We are totally frustrated at not being able to travel to Cumbria, to help and support them both through these tough difficult days.

Sunday 29th March 2020

Having gone to bed last night far too early, we are more tired this morning than usual and try to go back to sleep for a few more hours, but unfortunately our heads are full of our families and the rest of the world as we watch and wait for the Coronavirus to spread to its expected peak by Easter in two weeks. A startling news item brought the message loud and clear to us when we heard that large buildings were being turned into makeshift mortuaries to house the dead with a capacity at least of 12,000 dead bodies. Staggering and frightening!!

Whilst Geoff is out on the first walk of the day with Chumley. I prepare the vegetables for our Sunday Roast Dinner later today, we are having a piece of beef accompanied by roast potatoes and vegetables, served with gravy. The desert will be Jam Roly-Poly pudding, complete with homemade custard.

We both feel tired, but agree that after breakfast this morning, we will relax today. There is no rush for us to complete lots of tasks and jobs just to stay busy.

Decision made for today to sit and read our books.

After we have finished reading. I decide to hand sew the binding onto my completed quilted book cushion cover. This task takes me most of the morning, however, we enjoy being in the warm sunshine in our conservatory today. Geoff is enjoying reading a book and we enjoy a hot chocolate drink mid-morning.

After lunch, we both take Chumley for his afternoon walk towards Verdin Park and Furey Woods. We forgot just how steep the steps are today for the climb up. It is a lot colder now than the earlier days of the week. However, we remain cheerful and optimistic for our futures.

Between us, we finalise the preparations for our Roast Beef Dinner later. I set the table in the dining room for a change from the kitchen.

We enjoyed our roast dinner; it seems so long ago that we cooked a normal roast. When Geoff's dad was alive, we would bring him to ours every Thursday and Sunday for his meals and to spend time with him.

Throughout our life, a Sunday Roast dinner has been a much-loved favourite by us and our family.

However, we stopped cooking a full roast after Geoff's dad died 3 years ago. Instead, we have cooked various other meals that we enjoy, but you simply cannot beat a roast dinner, especially when it is followed by jam roly-poly and homemade custard, then washed down by a good glass of Malbec wine from Argentina!

The amount of email traffic and messages we receive each day has escalated. There is an abundance of jokes flying around in the form of cartoons or videos capturing the funny side of life as always.

It amazes me how much effort people go to in providing us with instant humour to keep us laughing, until tears roll down our faces and we are doubled up in laughter. It is definitely one of life's best tonics when in crisis mode across the globe, to be able to release something other than grim news, like reading a good book or watching a great film and losing yourself in the imagination and fantasy of the authors and producers.

Geoff and I were able to enjoy another family connection after tea with Sarah, Paul and Autumn using an app called 'House Party.' It was just brilliant to chat to them again and watch Autumn helping to prepare and cook tea with them. They were all making a home-made pizza. Autumn had been making cheesy straws on her own, grating cheese and then making a rocky road tray bake with marshmallows and chocolate of course!!

We stayed up a bit later tonight rather than going to bed too early even though we were both tired.

I had just got into bed when Sarah texted me to say that Paul's colleague had been tested positive for Coronavirus and that Paul had worked in the same office with him last Wednesday. The hospital had sent the man home as he wasn't in need of a ventilator. Sarah said that she is worried about Paul who has been working 14 hours shifts and has a reduced manpower in the factory due to sending people home with the symptoms.

Sarah also mentioned that she had heard from a friend whose Grandad died today from Coronavirus in Leftwich, near where we live and an old school friend who has died today, but she is not sure what from. Geoff and I discussed the possibility of the fact that Sarah, Paul and Autumn could all contract the virus and become ill or need self-isolation within their home and therefore, we wondered if this meant that we could go and look after them if this scenario happens.

We go to sleep knowing that this virus has its long fingers and toes that are coming closer now, reaching for our front doorsteps like the black plague.

Monday 30th March 2020

It is another dry day when we wake up, but a very cold one after the warm days of last week. Geoff took Chumley out for his early morning walk and I have a shower and prepare breakfast as well as empty the dishwasher.

After breakfast, I spend some time researching for tutorials on a piece of software called Scrivener which I am not familiar with. I manage to import my book project completed in Microsoft Word into the software, but I am not sure how to organise it through Scrivener.

I spend most of the morning learning my way around the various screens and looking at a couple of YouTube tutorials as well as downloading the user's guide manual for Scrivener.

Our lawn care treatment company arrive to scarify our lawns and to put the first feed of the year down. We are surprised that they arrive to complete this work, as we thought all non-essential work is not being completed.

However, the man assures us that he will work independently on our lawns and has also sanitized his hands in the van before knocking on our front door.

The chap doing the work assured me that he will sanitise them again when he leaves.

Geoff and I feel that we are both living in a bubble where life on the surface is continuing normally, but the stark reality is like seeing bombed out streets in every town and deserted cities, whilst we look on powerless watching horrific scenes unfold before our eyes that make us feel humble and helpless at the same time.

Our daily thoughts are there for the doctors and nurses in the NHS working around the clock dealing with the pandemic at the coalface. We remain humble at teachers continuing to teach and care for the "vulnerable" and "at risk" children, along with thousands of other unsung heroes who are all out there working on our behalf to ensure we have food and warmth in our own homes.

We feel helpless, as we are only both just 66 years of age and feel perfectly fit and healthy.

Our wish is to help others, who are so totally restricted at home for this "lock down" 750,000 people have already volunteered to help in any way that they can for the country and the NHS, even if it is just telephoning the people who are isolated and lonely.

I have applied and submitted the relevant form, but the government is overwhelmed by the massive response and have closed the recruitment process down until further notice.

Geoff is busy preparing a Chilli Con Carne for our tea later, before heading outside to sort our Begonia bulbs into individual pots in the greenhouse. Geoff plans to paint some of the fences again this afternoon, whilst I take Chumley out for my daily exercise of the day.

We enjoy a light lunch of sandwiches together, before I leave home for the afternoon walk.

I take Chumley down the river at the back of where we live. I follow a new fisherman's path underneath the Blue Bridge which no-one is using. I enjoy a long walk with Chumley in total isolation.

Tuesday 31st March 2020

Geoff and I enjoy our breakfast together after Geoff returned from Chumley's first walk of the day. We each discuss our plans for the day. Geoff is going to complete some more fence painting on the right-hand side of the garden. I am going to tackle the steep learning curve for Scrivener and my book project.

I was one hour into my tutorial when a sharp knock on the window alerted me to Geoff standing there asking me to come and help him.

Normally, it is a mug of tea that he wants me to make, but there was a hurried anxious look on his face. I went to the front door and met Geoff who told me that the bucket of fence paint he was using had been accidentally knocked off its resting place on a high bar stool all over the lawn, patio and some of the garden furniture.

We had only bought 2 buckets of the fence paint for our 39 fences, so this would leave us short, but not to worry, no-one was injured and despite my exclamations of what on earth were you balancing a bucket of paint on a high stool for?!! We managed to swill the paint away with copious amounts of water and some hard labour brushing it away. I expect we will find tell-tale signs of it everywhere in the coming months as paint finds its own pathways which we cannot always eliminate in that first flush of cleaning the spillage up!!

After, returning to my tutorial and several attempts at trying to understand it, I finally give up and anyway it is now lunch time. However, before lunch, I pop to the supermarket for some essential food.

I have not been to the supermarket since last Friday and found big differences in how the supermarkets have responded to the risk of infection to its customers. Firstly, I queued up outside Waitrose, standing 2 metres apart from other shoppers, we were allowed in one at a time, there were four male staff ensuring we followed the rules and they stood 2 metres apart from us as well, no one is speaking and every face shows fear for each other, the worries and anxieties are all written there and the silence hovers over us sending a clear message of this is going to get worse, so stand clear.

We don't shop in Waitrose often, but we do like the occasional treat from there in the same way we once shopped in Marks and Spencer until the Northwich branch closed its doors last summer. It was quiet inside the supermarket, and everyone kept their social distance, some shelves were quite empty notably biscuits and chocolate, presumably now that so many people including children are all camped at home, demand is greater for those people who would have eaten at work, or gone out for lunch, or enjoyed school dinners.

I didn't feel comfortable shopping, but managed to make a few purchases before checking out, my trolley was immediately taken off me for sanitizing before the next customer would use it.

I went to Sainsbury's and Aldi after Waitrose to obtain some soda crystals, which I use for cleaning my washing machine after washing Chumley's dog towels or bedding.

The same experience was in place in Sainsbury's and the same shelves were empty of biscuits, crisps and chocolate, along with depleted wine and beer stocks. I write about this not because I am an alcoholic or a chocaholic, but merely want to share my observations of what is going off the shelves faster this week.

For the last 2 weeks it has been packets of pasta and rice that has emptied shelves. Long before the lock down was announced, toilet rolls went off the shelves in their millions. Aldi have installed plastic shields from the conveyor belt to above the cashier's heads, they reminded me of bullet shields, effective use for the workforce which I found impressive.

At the pet shop, I was asked to wait outside 2 metres, then I would be invited in to sanitise my hands and asked to read the government regulations about essential shopping.

The manager asked me not to touch anything that I was not going to purchase, I told him that I had entered the shop for one item only, which is dry shampoo for dogs, was essential to maintain Chumley's healthy coat.

When I reached the till, the cashier asked me to stand two metres away and stretch my arm out with the item held in my hand to be put through the till. I had to pay in the same way in isolation from her via the card machine under a protective barrier.

I felt a little bit shaky in my legs after my very brief shopping trip, realizing just how unsafe the world is out there and felt fearful for all the people who are risking their lives for us to be able to continue our lives, not as we would do normally, but still in better circumstances than they face every day that they go to work.

I feel humble as well as guilty and shaky. I drive home and have a big hug with Geoff for the sadness and despair of this global death reaper!!

We enjoy some toasted teacakes together for lunch, before I start to get ready for an on-line ZOOM tutorial with our writing group to test out what it looks like ahead of our normal monthly meeting on Monday 6th April, 2020 which will take place online, after we have tested the video conferencing this afternoon.

My mobile is constantly pinging as more jokes and chats come through from my Hartford School Girls, my Chicks with Sticks, my Zumba Gold Group, my Walking Group, my family and my close friends.

Many of the jokes are so funny, I have tears rolling down my face, some of the jokes are so rude that they make me blush!!

Some of the chats are so heartfelt and supportive as well as sharing reflections on life outside our homes, that they do bring a tear to the eyes too. I think it is absolutely fantastic that everyone wherever they live are all supporting friends and family through these difficult days.

I also think it is amazing how very quickly humour has increased at a rapid speed to keep abreast of the latest news items and be able to turn our fears into laughter at times. The abundance of material being produced by individuals, then shared across the networks by young and old alike, is probably far greater than the number of Coronavirus cases being published daily!!

Geoff uses my afternoon exercise to take Chumley along the river this afternoon, whilst I am in the video conference call with the Vale Royal Writing Group.

Our evening meal is one of our favourites and is a South African Mango Chicken Chutney dish served with homemade potato wedges. It was absolutely scrummy delicious.

By 7.30 pm I am back online at my Zumba Gold Dance Exercise class. Tonight, there are eight of us participating and it is good to see everyone and interact briefly, before the class starts. We all have a good workout, our dog Chumley looks on in amazement from behind the closed lounge doors, wondering what on earth I am doing in there and why he can't join me if I am having fun bouncing around!! His quizzical expression makes me laugh. After the class is over, Geoff and I give Chumley a cardboard roll with a treat inside, he has to work out how to get the stuffed kitchen paper out of each end of the roll, before being able to reach his treat, eventually, he does manage to retrieve his treat, with a little help from us, but it was a good ten minutes of him using his brain. We have noticed that he is finding being inside, a bit boring, which we are aware of and make time for play with him as well as walks too.

Geoff drives over to the churchyard to collect the grave pot from his mum and dad's grave, so that I can put some roses and daffodils in for what would have been Geoff's dad's 100th Birthday tomorrow. We miss him so much.

Chapter Two

This is no April Fool
Wednesday 1st April 2020

Geoff took Chumley out for his early morning walk, whilst I arrange the flowers for the churchyard.

After breakfast, we drive to the churchyard and place the flowers onto the gravestone, which looks beautiful now, hard to believe it is 3 years ago since Harold died on his 97th Birthday. He would have been 100 years old today and we miss him so much still for all his gentleness, his wisdom, his humorous ways, his unconditional love.

We hope that we can pass his teachings on not only to ourselves daily, but to our children and grandchildren.

I am typing again after we return home and still trying to understand Scrivener. The telephone rings and it is my 4-year-old granddaughter Autumn who tells me that she is wearing mummy's knickers, I ask her why and my daughter says she is not wearing my knickers at all listen again, so I do listen and can decipher the word slippers!!!

Our granddaughter has a Cumbrian accent, I can generally understand her clearly when with her, but over a phone line it was a bit more pronounced than usual. Autumn tells me that she has drawn a rainbow for Granddad Geoff and wants to send it to him and speak to him, she is going to photograph it and send it over WhatsApp for him.

I go and find Geoff and pass the telephone to him and he enjoys a long conversation with Sarah our daughter and Autumn.

Geoff tells me afterwards, that whilst he was talking to Autumn that she said to him as in a questionable voice "Grandad" "yes Autumn he replied" and Autumn said "nothing" It is something that Geoff says quite a lot to our children, to Autumn in the past, other friends' children and it always brings a laugh. For Autumn to remember this saying and play it on Geoff just cracked him up today.

Thursday 2nd April 2020

Geoff took Chumley out before breakfast, he won't let me do the early morning walk, as he is concerned about me being around the river or quiet places when it is very early in the morning still.

The weather looked dry today and I decided to tackle a pile of washing that was in the basket and hang it out to dry. We also turned our new heavy mattress over again which is what you have to do with new mattresses.

Once the washing was on the line and I had helped Geoff to move the front garden bench onto the lawn for a jet wash. I decided to teach myself how to use scrivener for my book project and at last I managed to make some sense of it and put my word document into some semblance of order within scrivener.

I am undecided whether to continue with the trial version or bite the bullet and pay £43 for a full licence, which may give me more stability within the software.

I work hard until lunchtime on my project when a particular chapter would not save and after several attempts I gave up. It did me good to have a break. I shared a sandwich lunch with Geoff and then took Chumley for a long walk over to Verdin Park (my once-a-day exercise) and across the railway bridge into another park.

I didn't meet anyone on my walk or see anyone on either of the two parks, all very eerily quiet.

Geoff had decided to go and buy some fresh milk and a few other essentials for us, as we can only shop singly now and not as a couple which makes sense and is added protection not only for us, but for the staff working inside the supermarkets.

On return from my walk with Chumley, I receive a message from Boots Pharmacy to collect my medication which they were short of yesterday.

I head off to collect this from Boots and post a parcel to a friend who will be 70 next week and I cannot take it to her personally, because of COVID-19.

Geoff and I sit and talk about what our plans are for the next few days. Geoff has drawn a list of little and big jobs in the garden to keep us busy over the weekend which is supposed to be warm and sunny. The washing is dry and ready for ironing.

Tea tonight was a delicious lemon and pepper tagliatelle, just like we enjoyed 12 months ago when holidaying on the Amalfi Coast.

My group of friends continue to send supportive messages, banter and jokes all day long. Laughter is truly a great medicine as is lifelong friendship that spans over most of our entire lives from being at school and work together.

Many of my friends have been in my life from the age of 5 sharing friendship spanning over 62 years.

We know how to share love, laughter, happiness, joy, fears, tears, and heartache between us all. True friendship does not come with a price tag, it is something that stays strong and supportive at all times day and night.

Likewise, it is the strong bond of our family which keeps us safely joined in unbreakable bonds, as we face these dangerous times together. Geoff and I miss our family very much, especially our children and 2 granddaughters, who whenever we see them are like a breath of fresh air blowing through and around us in their presence.

We miss hugs with all of them the most, the way their smiles and cheerful banter are like sunlight and rainbows in our lives. It is the young that keep us going. We are the parents who watch from the side-lines as each of them build their own family lives. We know that they will learn, as we once did. In fact, we never stop learning any of us!! We hope with all our hearts, that our children and their children live long and happy lives together.

Friday 3rd April 2020

For the past few days, Chumley has been disturbing our sleep by needing a couple of toilet breaks during the early hours of the morning. We resolve to feed him earlier in the afternoon. He is restless at night and perhaps not getting the exercise he used to get or our attention, as we sit avidly watching the Coronavirus latest news and TV most nights.

We do have playtime and cuddle times with him too, but like children, dogs pick up tensions in us just the same and he knows that his routine of regular walks with the two of us is now a lot different, where only one of us can go in a morning and one in the afternoon because of government guidelines.

We certainly don't enjoy the walks as much now that we are not walking together. Geoff and I find we are paranoid about meeting other people and other people are just like us too.

We cross over the road or move to one side into shrubbery to avoid all potential contact of someone touching us or even worse sneezing those lethal droplets onto our bodies or clothing.

We have even become scared of visiting the supermarket and even two metres apart sometimes fails in cases where other people may not comply, not necessarily on purpose but just because we are all caught up in the moment of getting inside to collect the basics and getting the hell out of there again.

All the people that we see in passing whether on foot or in the cars going past wear the same grim face, nobody smiles, the silence is unbearable.

Life feels like we are all waiting in the wings, for Coronavirus to come and take one of us like the grim reaper of death.

Much worse is a parent's nightmare of losing their children and grandchildren, close family members and lifelong friends.

It is our natural desire to want to help others so much. Instead, we are limited to elderly neighbours whom we keep an eye on and supporting the constant friendship groups, where humour reigns. However, beneath the exterior surface like the faces of a clown, there are wobbles and fears amongst each and every one of us as we face the most difficult time in our entire lives.

All that we can do is stay safe as advised by the government, follow the advice given to us 24/7. by them.

We worry and listen to our children who are not only working at the coalface but trying to save us in the process!! When naturally as a parent, it is us who want to save them. we have lived a good life so far and their lives are more precious to us than life itself is for us at 66 and 67. Our children and grandchildren are the future, we are not!!

Last night it was not Chumley who kept us awake, but Geoff who was having vivid dreams that woke him up in the early hours of the morning.

As always, he can never go back to sleep again, so he must get up and make a cup of tea no matter what time of the night it is.

We enjoy our brews in bed at 4.00 am this morning and try to snuggle down again for at least another hour or two, however, it is a lighter sleep with both of us wanting daylight and the morning to arrive, to relieve us of our disturbed dreams and inability to sleep.

Geoff took Chumley out at 6.15 a.m. I get up to prepare breakfast and type a few lines of this COVID-19 story and purchase a Scrivener licence for my book project detailing the life of my birth mother.

After breakfast, we discuss our plans for the day ahead. The weather outside is dry and cold still, so we both deal with computer administration. Geoff checks our account and reads the local news and weather forecasts. I check in with my groups on WhatsApp and circulate the first jokes or quotes of the day to keep us all motivated and share what plans we all have for the day ahead.

Geoff is going to sand the bench down and paint the decking underneath the Arbor, then cut the back lawn, so I suggest that perhaps I could tackle the fence painting on the left-hand side of the garden which Geoff agrees with and helps me to prepare the area with dust sheets, brushes and paint.

We only have one tub of paint left and about another 20 fences to paint, we do need at least another tub and half of fence paint, but we agree for me to do as much as I can and then the rest will wait. I make us both a mug of tea before we start and I gather soapy water and a sponge for any drips that might fall onto the path, despite covering up. I enjoy fence painting and being outside in the garden.

By lunchtime at 1.00 pm, I have managed to paint 9 fences, including the 3 tall ones on top of the decking area. I am quite pleased with the result and probably have enough fence paint left to start on the fences behind the greenhouse.

However, there is only enough paint really for one fence panel, so we decide to leave the rest of the fences, until we can obtain fence paint again from B&Q sometime in the distant future. Alternatively, we can investigate what can be ordered on-line? We are not too bothered, as we have managed to paint 28 fence panels out of the 39 fences we have in our garden.

Geoff makes us a sandwich lunch, mine is salmon and cucumber and his is ham. We have another drink and then I take Chumley out for his afternoon walk and my once-a-day exercise. I take him to Verdin Park and see no-one on the park or anyone in passing until I am returning home down Queensway and there is a man with his dog picking the dog's poo up and so I cross over to avoid being too close, but I do say hello from the other side of the road.

When I arrive home, Geoff has finished tidying everything up in the garden, he has also cut the grass on the front of our property and our front lawn.

He was just getting ready to have a shower, whilst I quickly hoover the house up and then I too have a shower and get changed. We sit outside for a while in the warmish sunshine and contemplate what a lovely garden we have that enables us to sit out this stormy time. We both comment how lucky we are.

We notice that it is getting later in the afternoon and that we need to prepare tea. Geoff and I agreed this morning that we would eat something quick and simple. So we have fish fingers and homemade spicy wedges accompanied with the last of the tenderstem broccoli with bread and butter, which was delicious, especially as we could eat it outside for the first time this year and enjoy a glass of beer and a glass of leftover chardonnay from the small bottles of wine we buy to cook with.

After tea, we watch the latest news and I respond to items coming in from my group about the death of David Simpkins who is the husband of our dentist Angela Simpkins at Beach Road, Greenbank, he died from a Myocardial Infarction (heart attack) this morning and was only in his early fifties.

Another friend texted to say a local Northwich close friend, has been rushed to Leighton Hospital with severe breathing difficulties. We are surrounded by sadness and fear as death creeps its icy silent fingers over the whole globe and drags itself nearer to us now every nano second, we breathe.

It is hard to switch off from all this gloom, so we decide instead of watching the TV to enjoy an evening inside our conservatory, read a book and eat chocolate. Chumley fetches his toys to us for playtime and we both give him some attention. Neither of us can concentrate properly.

Geoff is annoyed that my phone keeps pinging, it is my Hartford School Girls one of whom wanted to know how to tie a scarf on her head like Hilda Ogden used to do in Coronation Street.

One of my close friends in the group Barbara who was also my chief bridesmaid explains how to do it. I join in with a reminder to Barbara that when we were at school, we produced a sketch on stage from our drama group about Coronation Street, she was Ena Sharples, and I was Hilda Ogden. I remember it as clearly as yesterday and inform the group about this snippet of our past school history.

Unfortunately, Barbara cannot remember it at all and marvels at my amazing memory.

The conversation plays back and forth a bit much to my husband's annoyance and he disappears off into the lounge muttering about how I cannot leave my phone alone and that we were supposed to be having a night together in the conservatory in companionable silence reading.

I remind him that we were doing just that, I bought him some of his favourite dark chocolate in from the fridge to enjoy. We both sat reading, occasionally, one of us would look up and glance outside, then comment on how beautiful the garden looks tonight. I cannot see the harm answering my phone after it had pinged a few times, I had ignored it for as long as I could, until curiosity got the better of me.

Our group have all agreed a cut off time for messages at night and we comply with that very seriously. In the end it resulted in us being distant with each other for the rest of the night. Then my phone pinged, and Geoff's did too at the same time, but he ignored it. The messages were from the family group app with photos of our two granddaughters looking so happy and lovely, that I am suddenly reduced to a tear falling down my face, I miss them both and our children so very much, at this exact moment right now! I wish that I could just give them a hug.

Even tears do not change Geoff he remains angry and hurt with me. I finish some ironing and write these notes up.

Geoff took Chumley out for his last wee of the day and we end up in silence between us on his return, which is not how it should be, but sometimes you just need space between you, as well as honesty to put the paths we are all on straight again, to help each other.

The two of us are all we have right now, which could end at any given moment in a nano second!

We will sort it out with a cuddle and our arms around us in bed, I will have to resort to reduced time on my phone and in secret!! We try to nod off, but neither of us can quite catch sleep. I came to bed just after Geoff and whilst shaking the dog's bed outside to rid it of any detritus.

I notice that an ambulance is across the road at Keven and Claire's home. Kevin has had a significant number of health problems and operations in the last 3 years but has made a remarkable recovery and I so hope that he is ok and not caught COVID-19 from anyone.

I let Geoff know and we both keep checking to see if they are ok. The Paramedics are there long after midnight has passed and eventually leave just before 2.00 am in the morning.

Geoff falls into a deep sleep, whereas I toss and turn around and just can't catch my sleep tonight as my head is so full of worries for the whole world around us.

A friend texts our craft group in response to a message from another friend who is having trouble sleeping, I text back to say that I am in their non-sleep club too and we pass a few minutes trying to reassure each other through this long night where 3 of us are wide awake.

I go downstairs to pour myself some water into a glass and sit on the sofa drinking it, as I have a very dry mouth and keep wondering is this the Coronavirus come to get me or is it just the result of central heating causing my dry mouth.

Geoff woke up before I heard the slight ping on my phone and seemed to be in some sort of wild dream as he was thrashing about and suddenly, I was whacked by the duvet, I said hey "stop that what's the matter with you?" He didn't answer just sat in a trance on the side of the bed, then got back into bed and went straight to sleep again.

It was not long before we were having another cup of tea in bed at the same hour of 4.00 am with Geoff denying any wild dreams and throwing the bedding over me.

Saturday 4th April 2020

We are still here, and nothing changes, only the death toll that keeps rising.

Geoff took Chumley out and I bake some fruit scones for us, it is only 6.30 am in the morning! It is quite cold outside with a chilly wind blowing.

After breakfast, we decide what each of us is doing this morning. Geoff is going to oil the front bench; I am going to email my friend Bob with a few questions about the Scrivener software for writing my stories. I have been working through a couple of tutorials this week, which gave me the help I needed to learn about the software by trial and error. Bob telephoned me and we have a ZOOM conference where he can show me the answers to my questions along with more tips to help me. We have a good chat and I spend a few minutes talking to Carol on ZOOM. I enjoyed the chance to catch up with two of our dearest friends who are on holiday at their second home in Paphos and cannot get a return flight for a few months possibly. Apparently, their scheduled 2nd May flight may be cancelled due to air traffic disruption. Carol tells me that they are ok and that the supermarkets have plenty of food and other products in stock. All the tourists have left for their homes in the UK and elsewhere.

Cyprus locked the island down long before the UK and already they cannot leave their property or go to the beach. They have to produce a document stating where they are going, and it has to comply with the valid reasons that the government have authorized, otherwise they will be fined 150 Euros on the spot. They are not allowed out after 9.00 pm and before 6.00 am as a strict curfew is in place.

Bob and Carol are happy to stay in their home until such time as they can get a flight out whenever that might be!! After all, they have the warm sunshine and if they did come home then they would still be in the same situation and have to social distance themselves from family and friends.

They are keeping busy with their home and Bob is busy writing his next novel as well as releasing his latest novel this weekend.

After our ZOOM conference. I decide to spend the rest of the morning outside and complete the jet-washing and bleaching of our patio to help remove the spilt fence paint by Geoff earlier this week.

The telephone rings and it is Sarah, Paul and Autumn having a 'house party' chat to us which is done through an app that lets you talk and see what each other is doing. It was great fun chatting to them all and interacting with Autumn again.

Autumn is just so funny and has been busy learning her phonics this week. We long to see them and hope that we can do so very soon, although we know in our hearts that it could be months off that day arriving.

We feel it will take all the rest of summer possibly!! In September, Autumn will go to school, which means we won't see her every week, perhaps only once a month. Geoff and I are going to produce a video of us reading her bedtime stories and hope to complete this later today or tomorrow if possible.

It is now lunchtime and I make us some toast and we enjoy one of my scones. After lunch I take Chumley out and feel a bit uncomfortable, as there seem to be lots of families and people out cycling, walking, or just sitting on benches.

I steer clear of all people coming and going near to me and keep walking through to Roker Park and home on one of our circular routes. I decide to take Chumley out a little later in the afternoon in future. I feel that after lunchtime is always going to be a popular time slot, for mums and dads who want their children to burn some energy off outside whilst they are allowed.

We do not have any green vegetables or fruit left. I go to the nearest safest shop which is Waitrose who are only allowing one customer in at a time.
However, once inside, I quickly select the fruit and veg that I need along with an easter egg for Geoff and I and

two fluffy toy lambs for our grandchildren and 2 bottles of a very expensive Malbec which has just been reduced from £10.99 to £6.99

I cook tea for us tonight and we enjoy salmon cooked with red peppers and chillies and lemons in the oven with some homemade vegetable potatoes and runner beans followed by another delicious scone.

After tea, we chat to our lifelong friends Steve and Sue on a WhatsApp video call. It was Sue's birthday yesterday. Simply great to be able to see them, catch up on the exciting building project on their home.

Sunday 5th April 2020

Today, we are expecting a hot sunny day with temperatures reaching 20 degrees outside. We manage to sleep better last night but only until 4.00 am. We both read books last night and kept away from the news reports about the rising number of deaths as we head towards the peak median.

The weather is not as hot as predicted, so not a shorts and t-shirt day at all as there is a cool wind blowing.

Geoff took Chumley out for his early morning walk at 6.00 am, whilst I prepare breakfast for us on his return and enjoy a long shower whilst waiting. I am looking forward to my bran flakes this morning with blueberries, strawberries, and a banana on them as a change from my daily porridge and honey.

After breakfast, I make a Christmas Cake, fully intending to store it until it matures after a period of time from now until end of June, when hopefully, we may be out of this dreadful situation and lockdown. I am using dried fruit left over from the festive season and often use it to make scones which I did yesterday, but still found that I had a large quantity of sultanas, raisins, and currants going spare in the cupboard.

Geoff is most anxious that I don't store the cake as he feels it is best to eat it now and enjoy it, part of me agrees, but the other part thinks well this will feed us for at least a few weeks, if we only take a small piece at a time or it could keep for a big family celebration when all of this Coronavirus is over, if indeed it ever does become over!!

Whilst out walking Chumley this afternoon, I decide that Geoff is right and what is the point of storing cake that we may not live to enjoy and that would be a great loss especially for Geoff who absolutely loves fruit cake. It just means that I cannot give the cake its weekly feed of brandy (and me too) or that I cannot add any marzipan or icing to the cake. I know how quickly the cake will be consumed too, but what the heck!! Let food be the pleasure of today and if tomorrow is snatched away, then we have had our fill beforehand!!

Geoff and I compile a story-time video for each of our grandchildren Autumn and Niamh. Geoff reads one section and then I read the next section of our chosen stories.

The story for Autumn is called the 'Bravest Ever Bear', the story for Niamh is called 'Love is a Handful of Honey' Geoff is very good at narrating and speaks clearly, I am not as confident, which is hardly surprising because, behind me Geoff is pulling funny faces at the camera and doing invisible things with his hands over my hair to amuse Autumn and it is a bit off putting to say the least!!

We do fall about laughing when we replay the video though. We have to split the video in two parts to be able to email them to the children and write a message in the email to say we will endeavour to improve and will do a few story telling videos depicting us telling the stories over the coming weeks, as our way of staying in touch with Autumn and Niamh in addition to our Facetime, ZOOM and House Party chats.

Sarah finds the video clips funny with Geoff acting daft and loves his voice telling the stories. However, she feels that I am speaking as if I am in a business style meeting and that my facial expressions need to be more child friendly, great!! I actually thought I was ok Hmmm!!

Niamh pricked her ears up at the storytelling clip and Anthony told us that she did look as if she knew who was speaking. It was the 23rd February, when we last saw Niamh and now, we are in the month of April.

As the promised heat has not arrived, it is too cold to sit outside. Instead we spend some time relaxing in our conservatory with good books to read and a mug of tea. We move the arbour onto the lawn and Geoff sands it down and oils the roof and bench seat, but he does feel that it needs to be painted in a colour as the wood is quite old now and oiling it has not given a good finish at all.

We both agree to paint the arbour in cream next week as we have some in stock that can be used towards painting the whole arbour and if we don't like it, then we can change the colour to blue or sage as we do have a lot of these colours on various items of wood such as the balustrades around our decking and the wooden flower tubs in the garden.

I make us some scrambled egg on toast for lunch, we sit outside for a while, but it is not very hot and is quite windy still. At 2.00 pm I take Chumley out for his afternoon walk and my daily exercise. It is quite pleasant and warm, so I choose the river route and walk as far as the Blue Bridge over the River Weaver and back down the other side of the river, where Chumley enjoys swimming.

The people that I pass are all respectful and keeping a good social distance, there are not as many people out today as yesterday and there is an atmosphere of charged emotion and respect for each other although we are all strangers, our faces show the same stories on each of us and that gives a sense of sharing what is happening around all of us collectively, we are in this global pandemic situation together and we will come through it together too somehow.

I catch up with all my family and friends group news after returning from our walk and this takes a while as so many messages and jokes have come through whilst I have been out. There are more emotions surfacing as the lockdown continues and people cannot be with their families and friends.

By staying home each of us can save at least 366 lives, which for Geoff and I is a total of 732 lives, and we have to comply, in fact we don't even think about it or not complying we simply do it without question and without judgement or confrontation.

We want to survive, and we want everyone else to survive too and come through this together, so life is simple, do as we are asked and focus on the human race continuing for the future generations which include our children and grandchildren.

To think otherwise is unthinkable to us and therefore we don't even consider lockdown being a nuisance, more a necessity and the most selfless act we can do for all those we love and all those who have made the same sacrifices for us in their lives, our parents and grandparents.

Geoff has cooked us a delicious chicken dinner with roast potatoes, carrots, and cabbage with wine gravy and of course a glass of red wine.

We will watch the Queen's speech to the Nation at 8.00 pm tonight this is an unprecedented occasion where we understand the Queen will be asking us to comply with the government regulations and help our country to come through this pandemic together as in war time.

As we journey through these difficult days and nights, I often reflect on the religious upbringing I was given as a child, attending Sunday school, learning about religion at primary school and at my comprehensive secondary school too.

I was taught to go to church and to respect Christian worship and the Bible, I was also taught to say my prayers every single night, to say thank you for my meals, to stand up when the National Anthem was played in cinemas and other events such as sporting or celebrations like New Year. I was taught the 10 commandments. This upbringing stood me in good stead, and I still have an inner belief in some of the lessons I was taught. These lessons will continue to help guide me in my life today, by following the moral beliefs given to me by my parents and teachers at that time.

The generation of our children does not always feel that it needs to conform to religion as we once did with christenings, weddings and burials or even attending Sunday services and Sunday school. We accept their beliefs and move with the times as each generation finds new ideas and their own beliefs, quite rightly too. The rules that applied to our generation have been replaced with new ones which is how it should be. There is much more freedom to express what you believe is right for you and your family compared to our own personal upbringing.

At the end of the day my belief is mine personally to me, my inner soul is unique to me.

Today's generation have moved away from living at home close to family units. People move and live all over the globe, often quite far from the family nest. We would probably locate elsewhere, if we had been born into this generation. We have been privileged to enjoy a happier and peaceful time upbringing, than our parents and grandparents did.

We have not been to war, but it feels like it right now and it is an invisible war, a deadly serious one that will take a long time to recover and heal from.

In quiet moments, I often think of some of the bible stories I learnt as a child, for instance, the story in Matthew 21, 12 where Jesus overthrew a table in the temple where money changers were trading goods in a house of prayer, they were corrupt and uncaring towards the poorer people and Jesus was angry with them for turning the inside of a temple into a den of thieves.

I also remember the stories in the Old Moores Almanac about how at some point in the future, man himself will destroy the earth and it will no longer exist. It feels like that time has come now and I am fearful of the prophecy.

Mankind has indeed sought more wealth and opportunities beyond my wildest dreams, salaries paid for some jobs are more than I have earned in my entire lifetime, with a lot of people enjoying comfortable lives, which to be fair a lot of them, they have worked hard to achieve.

Our generation did not go off to war, like our parents and grandparents did, nor did we all have the opportunities, that we have given to our children such as attending University and seeing the world at much younger ages, when travel is so much more affordable, and the world of University and found their own friends and partners to go on holiday with.

Since our first flight, we have been able to see the world too and have enjoyed the most amazing holidays and adventures beyond our dreams which we never thought possible. Richness and wealth exist everywhere and, in most countries, but so does abject poverty. We have seen for ourselves that the new class system is Rich or Poor with nothing in-between for many countries in the world.

Some humans living on this beautiful earth, continue to throw their trash into the rivers, countryside, the oceans and everywhere we walk.

There is endless litter where people just throw it down and think someone else will pick it up, takeaways, cups, fly tipping, plastic bottles, tin cans, dog poo, some people are responsible, and some people are irresponsible!!

The natural structure of the planet is not sustainable for us to keep polluting it every single day we live and walk on our earth.

When the skies above us cleared, following a drastic decline in pollution during this pandemic, we all noticed a huge difference in the air quality and the vivid colours displayed by nature. It was a 'wow' factor moment, especially the cities across the globe with high pollution levels.

We used to holiday in caravans at Rhyl or just have days out at Blackpool. It was 1995 before Geoff and I flew abroad with our two children, this was also the last family holiday together before they went off to university

Monday 6ᵗʰ April 2020

The Rainbow Children *

The history books will talk of now,
That time the world stood still.
When every family stayed at home,
Waved out from windowsills-
At those they loved but could not hold,
Because they loved them so.
Yet, whilst they did they noticed all the flowers start to grow.

The sun came out, they can recall,
And windows, rainbows filled.
They kicked a football in their yards,
Until the night drew in.
They walked each day but not too close,
That time the world stood still.
When people walked straight down the roads, which once the cars did fill.

They saw that people became ill,
They knew the world was scared.
But whilst the world stood still they saw, how much the whole world cared.

They clapped on Thursdays from their doors, they cheered for the brave.
For people who would risk their lives,
So, others could be saved.

The schools closed, they missed their friends, and they missed their teachers so.
Their Mum's and Dad's helped with their work; they helped their minds to grow.

The parents used to worry that,
As schools were put on hold,
Their children would not have the tools,
They would need as they grew old.

But history books will talk of them,
Now adults, fully grown.
Those little boys and girls back then,
The ones who stayed at home.
They will tell you that they fixed this world,
Of all they would fulfil.
The RAINBOW children building dreams,
They had dreamed whilst time stood still

*Poem reproduced by kind permission of the author Gemma Peacock

The Queen's speech which was broadcast to the Nation last night at 8.00 pm made Geoff and I feel quite humble as detailed below:-

The Queen has said the UK "will succeed" in its fight against the coronavirus pandemic, in a rallying message to the nation.

In a rare speech, the monarch thanked people for following government rules to stay at home and praised those "coming together to help others".
She also thanked key workers, saying "every hour" of work "brings us closer to a return to more normal times". It comes as the number of people to die with the virus in the UK reached 4,934.

Speaking from Windsor Castle, the Queen said: "While we have faced challenges before, this one is different. This time we join with all nations across the globe in a common endeavour, using the great advances of science and our instinctive compassion to heal. We will succeed - and that success will belong to every one of us. We should take comfort that while we may have more still to endure, better days will return, we will be with our friends again; we will be with our families again; we will meet again."

The Queen, 93, also said the "painful sense of separation from their loved ones that social distancing was causing for people reminded her of the experience child evacuees had during the Second World War."

"Now, as then, we know, deep down, that it is the right thing to do," she said.

In her address, the Queen said everyone who was following guidance to stay at home was "helping to protect the vulnerable and sparing many families, the pain already felt by those who have lost loved ones".

"Together we are tackling this disease, and I want to reassure you that if we remain united and resolute, then we will overcome it," she added.

She also stressed the value of self-discipline and resolve, she hopes that in the future, everyone would "be able to take pride in how they responded to this challenge".

An hour after the Queen's broadcast, Downing Street announced that Prime Minister Boris Johnson had been taken to hospital following his Coronavirus diagnosis. Mr Johnson has been self-isolating since he tested positive for the virus on 27 March.

Lying in bed this morning, I spent a few minutes reading the latest headline news from the BBC and came across the story below: -

Disability effect*

'Coronavirus':

'I know my life will not be saved in this pandemic' Lucy Watts MBE is 26 years old and preparing to die if she contracts Coronavirus.

The disability advocate has a life-limiting condition which includes multiple organ failure and restrictive lung disease requiring 24-hour care.

As the British Medical Association (BMA) releases guidance preparing doctors to make 'brutal' decisions and prioritise treatment for those most likely to recover, Lucy fears that if she contracts Covid-19 she will not be saved.

"My life is devalued on the basis of my disabilities and needs, rather than my life and the difference I have made to the world," she says.

This is an edited version of a blog that Lucy wrote over several days trying to make sense of her personal situation with her dog Molly at her side.

"I know full well in this Covid-19 pandemic that my life is not one that will be saved. This is part-writing therapy, part-rant. It's full of anger and hurt and fear. It's trying to make peace; it's wanting to fight back. And it's true, every last word.

I will be isolating for a minimum of 12 weeks, possibly longer. I have 24-hour care needs and am usually cared for by intensive care nurses for 16 hours per day, but my nurses could be recalled to the NHS at any time. My mum can manage the nursing role, but she cannot do my care 24/7.

We are practising strict infection control. I have made the difficult step to say that if I get Covid-19, I will not be going to hospital. I will be considered too frail, too unlikely to survive and too difficult to be weaned off ventilation on the other side. I have respiratory muscle weakness and therefore I'm unlikely to return to a meaningful quality of life - and that's only IF I survived. This situation is about who has the greatest chance of survival.

I have had to accept this over the last few days. It does not sit comfortably with me. I rage and cry that my life is devalued based on my disabilities and needs, rather than my life and the difference I have made to the world.

I am the 9th most influential disabled person in Britain, I have an MBE for services to young people with disabilities and in 2019 I became a fellow of the Royal Society of Arts for my commitment to disability rights.

I have more than proved my worthiness of being alive, but it counts for nothing in this pandemic. I have changed hearts and minds through work, passion, determination, skills, and experience.

But my life will not be deemed worth saving where cut-throat (metaphorically) decisions must be made due to limited resources and the large numbers infected with Covid - we are struggling now, and we are not yet near the peak.

Whilst the decision not to go to hospital is mine, the decision about treatment is not within my control. I must accept my life is not a priority and will not be saved. But as much as it makes me livid and distraught, I am a level-headed person who knows this is about saving those who have the highest chance of survival. My body is on its last legs.

I have so much going on - a nameless syndrome that stops cells making enough energy for my organs and muscles to work. I have multiple organ failure, restrictive lung disease and respiratory muscle weakness, a bowel that is always in and out of obstruction, chronic pancreatitis that keeps flaring up, an immune system that doesn't fight infection well and a new issue causing joint pain and fever 80% of the time.

And yet, I have managed to survive sepsis 14 times is that not a great track record? Doesn't that show, despite how weak and fragile my body is, I have got a 100% success rate in surviving life-threatening events?

But do I have a high enough chance of surviving this virus - potentially at the expense of someone else's life? It is a funny head space to be in feeling like I want to live at all costs but knowing efforts to prolong my life could cost someone else's. I have gone through the stages of grief - denial, anger, bargaining, depression - but the end of this cycle for me does not end in 'acceptance'. I do not accept this. I do not accept that my life is less worthy to be saved".

*Article written by Lucy Watts and reproduced with her kind permission

The rest of today went amazingly fast whilst I spent the morning writing in this book project. I am also in the middle of writing a short Easter story to send to our two granddaughters.

In the afternoon, I took Chumley on a 5 mile walk along both sides of the River Weaver at the back of where we live. The river was bathed in that crystal clear light which happens sometimes, especially when the sun and water, clearly reflect the images before your eyes like a mirror. The effects of this phenomenon had me rooted to the spot lost in wonder, using my eyes to photograph the scene before me to store in the memory bank of outstanding vistas.

Geoff has been removing some old grout out of the patio near the decking.

In the evening I took part in a ZOOM conference with my writing group and enjoyed a lively interactive meeting with 23 of my writing group friends, where we completed a writing exercise for the first 10 minutes, then caught up with each other's news. A few of us read some of our work out to the group. After my meeting ends, Geoff and I settle down to watch the last episode of the TV drama Liar.

Just as we are waiting my phone pings with an urgent announcement that the Prime Minister Boris Johnson has been admitted to the Intensive Care Unit at St Thomas's Hospital in London with breathing difficulties

Boris was diagnosed with COVID-19 over one week ago and has been self-isolating inside a flat above number 10 Downing Street, London. However, he started to develop a very high fever which would not go away on Sunday and doctors admitted him then for further test investigations on his organs, since early this afternoon, his condition has deteriorated significantly and although he is conscious, it may be necessary at some stage to put him on to a ventilator.

The news is not good at all for the nation. He is being looked after by the best possible care that can be given, but it is now a race and fight for his life. If he does recover, he will remain weak for a long time ahead.

In the meantime, his deputy will be in charge of carrying out the Prime Ministers day to day work and all other cabinet ministers regardless of which party they belong to have pledged to work collaboratively together to keep the country running smoothly.

Tuesday 7th April 2020

We were awake early again and drinking our mugs of tea in bed at 5.00 am this morning. Geoff took Chumley out at 6.00 am and I got up to do some writing work. The day looks as if it is going to be a warm one with clear blue skies. I decide that today, I am going to stay outside and enjoy being in the sunshine and our garden.

The windows need a good clean after months of rain, so I tackle them first.

Geoff is busy trying to solve a problem with our fence posts that have moved due to the ground moving beneath them on a steep bank at the bottom of our garden. He is happy mixing cement and fixing the problem this fence has caused. He needed my help to put the fence back inside the concrete panel and concrete fence post.

We enjoy lunch outside in the garden. It is so lovely to be in the warm sunshine, however, Chumley keeps looking at me as it is time for his afternoon walk and my once-a-day exercise.

I reluctantly leave the comfy chair I am sitting on outside and take Chumley on his afternoon walk. I steer clear of the river as he just likes to swim in it every day and then needs washing down. I take Chumley along part of the river and then through Roker Park. Not many people are out walking, and it is very quiet.

I was almost home after our 2 mile walk when my phone rang and it was my granddaughter Autumn on the other end of it, I could hear her mummy Sarah too, but could not quite see them.

I spoke to Sarah and said I am nearly home, ring me back in five minutes, she said why not turn your screen on mum and keep walking we will keep talking to you, so I did, and it was just lovely to see them and feel that they were actually walking home with me and Chumley.

Sarah and Autumn both had their sweater jumpers on, I was in my shorts and summer t-shirt. They commented on how lovely the sunshine and blue skies looked. They were outside in the garden too, but they said it was a bit cooler today and not much sun around.

When I arrived home, both Geoff and I were able to continue a long chat with them both and see the things Autumn has been occupied with, like sowing some coriander seeds with her daddy, baking hobnob biscuits, she showed us her trampoline and the lessons she has been enjoying with mummy learning her phonics and writing all her letters down too. Autumn looked well and as always full of fun and chatter to us.

It was good to chat to Sarah too and find out how the school hubs are working out for the vulnerable children. Geoff and I felt happy showing Autumn what we had been doing too in our garden and around the home.

We wander into our kitchen to show Autumn that she is the star person on our April calendar picture this month. The photo we chose for April is one of Autumn underneath a large glass dome, she is surrounded by lots of yellow ducks at the ice-cream farm this time last year, when her mummy and daddy were on honeymoon in
Sri-Lanka and Autumn stayed with us for 10 days.

It was a massive boost for us being able to chat to them this afternoon and more importantly see them. Autumn used several different masks on Sarah's phone app as we ended the call, such as a dinosaur, skeleton, lion, dog, alien, whale, shark with big teeth. It looked as if the mask was being worn by Autumn, but it is just the way it works. She showed us how high she can jump inside her trampoline too. Such fun and happy times shared over the phone this afternoon.

Geoff made a delicious chicken and chorizo pasta tonight for tea, whilst I cleared some ironing.

Then I took part in my online Zumba group class and Geoff watched Car SOS on the TV about old classic cars being renovated

It was a strawberry moon tonight and we were able to see it, although it was quite high in the sky by the time we saw it after 8.30 pm still beautiful though, albeit smaller than if we had been able to travel to the coast to see it rise as a large full moon.

My brother Chris Hope telephoned just as I was about to start my Zumba class as he is hoping to host weekly ZOOM meetings with as many family members as possible. We all live in different parts of the country, and he would like to connect up with each of us regularly during these difficult times. He is going to arrange a family ZOOM for Easter Monday with the extended family across the UK. Watch this space.

My phone is constantly clogged with so many messages and jokes daily, I can't keep up with the pace and quantity at times, however, they show a kindred spirit between all of us as close friends, where each of us is playing a supporting role for each other and our families to keep our spirits up. We use laughter to ease the pain and strength with our deeply caring words of advice for those wobbly times too. Most of all we look out for each other and use whatever it takes to help each and every one of us. I will download a few of them and insert them in these pages.

Wednesday 8ᵗʰ April 2020

Another early morning start with a brew in bed at 5.00 am, although we slept a little better than other nights.

Geoff is soon up and out with Chumley by 5.45 am and I stay in bed catching up on the latest news and deleting over 1,000 messages in one of my WhatsApp groups. How fast so many messages arrive containing lots of jokes, videos and supportive messages from all my Hartford School girl friends. It has only been 3 weeks and to have that many messages is incredible, the same will be true for my family and other groups such as Chicks with sticks (craft group of knitting and sewing friends).

We all learn the innovative technology quickly during Lockdown. Especially, how to socialise more closely on the Internet.

The overall result is that we give ourselves a bigger headache with storage of data in the cloud, on the phone, plus the time it takes to forward really funny messages to all our other friends, so it goes on, all good fun, but time consuming too!!

We are locked into our own personal world of peace and quiet, but it is where we stand still, praying with hope that everyone we love comes through to the other side, knowing that there are many who have already lost their lives to COVID-19.

After breakfast, which I prepare for us both, Geoff took our conservatory blinds down for me, so that I can clean the inside windows properly and the blinds themselves. The task turns into a much bigger job than anticipated, the morning just disappears into lunchtime very quickly.

We eat a couple of crumpets for lunch, I have some herb and garlic cream cheese on mine and Geoff has butter melting on his, which I love but my cholesterol does not!!

After lunch, I drive to the supermarket for our essentials like milk, tea, cereals, butter, potatoes, and a few bits of cleaning stuff that we have run out of in the last few days.

Geoff took Chumley for his afternoon walk instead of me, whilst I do the supermarket shopping, as only one person is allowed in at a time.

Asda and Sainsbury's have customers queuing around the supermarket but at safe distances of 2 metres apart, they allow one customer in and one customer out. I always stand 4 metres or more away from the customers waiting outside and with my mask on. I quickly complete my shopping and head home. Browsing for items not on the list and lingering around are not what shoppers do in these difficult days

Once home, I discover that Geoff has arrived back at the same time, so we make a drink after helping each other to put the shopping away and then head outside in our garden with a brew of tea for Geoff and a glass of orange for me, it is lovely at last to relax and chill outside in the garden with our shorts and a t-shirt on. The afternoon beverages soon become a glass of beer and a glass of wine, but we only had the one, yes honestly!!

There is a knock on our front door and a postman is standing there, he asks me my name and address. I ask him for his name and we both make sure that we are standing 2 metres apart whilst talking. He then tells me that one of his neighbours had received a special delivery parcel from me, for someone called Mrs Sandbach and that she doesn't know who this lady is, so she sought the help of Mr Casey the postman standing in front of me now.

I tell him that this is a very close friend of mine who is celebrating her 70th Birthday on Easter Sunday and that I posted it an over a week ago and according to the post office tracking it had been signed for by Mrs Sandbach. He tells me that the address on the parcel is 8 Rayleigh Avenue, Davenham where his neighbour lives and she is not called Mrs Sandbach, Mr Casey doesn't know anyone of that name either, but then he only moved into Rayleigh Avenue just before Christmas and so doesn't know everyone yet.

I am puzzled and check my address book and telephone my friend Liz Sandbach to check with her, however, she must be in the garden as she does not answer the phone.

I tell Mr Casey that I will try later, I take his phone number so that I can confirm the address. It is so very kind of him and his neighbour to be so honest and try and track me down as the sender of the gift inside the parcel which is a special bracelet as a gift for Liz's birthday this weekend, when she should have been wining and dining at the Swettenham Arms with her family and then in July at the Ritz and travelling to the Italian Lakes at the end of May on her own first solo trip. All her plans and bookings have been cancelled.

Teatime arrives and we use food from the freezer that we have cooked previously and saved. Geoff enjoys a steak pie and I have coq-u-vin dish. We ate al fresco whilst it was still warm. There is something different about eating out in the fresh air, which is infinitely more pleasurable.

We spend the night catching up with the news and I complete some more work on my writing project.

Thursday 9th April 2020

We are both up early again and with little sleep, 5 hours better than none. Geoff took Chumley out and I finish the shopping list for the butchers and fruit and vegetables.

By 9.00 am I am standing in the queue outside our local butchers shop in Hartford called Littlers. Geoff waits in the car as only 2 people are allowed in the shop at any one time. There is only one person before me and 2 in the shop already.

I choose quite a lot of meat as I don't want to be visiting any food shops or supermarkets in the next two weeks due to the peak in COVID-19 being predicted for the UK and the number of deaths are rising scarily every day, 2 deaths per minute was reported on the news tonight.

The cashier tills my order of chicken breasts, a turkey crown for Sunday, 2 fillet steaks, some mince for a chilli or moussaka and some bacon, then tells me the cost is £120 which I find unbelievable!! She double checks and assures me it is correct and shows me the electronic view of the items purchased, I notice that there is a luxury cheese on the list for £47 and some of Mrs Darlington's jam preserves.

We agree that there must be an error and that the customer before me has paid their bill, but the till has not cleared it off, so we agree to add up my bill with a calculator which gives a figure of £68.68 an improvement but is still a lot to pay for my meat bill this week, however, I have doubled up this week, so that I don't need to come out shopping next week or the week after, so over a fortnight this amount is probably the correct expenditure for our weekly meat bill.

I feel in general, that we are spending more money on food than ever before but then we are reducing spending elsewhere and besides whilst we are all confined to staying in the confines of our own homes, then let food be the pleasure of life along with wine and chocolate, because we are not going anywhere else for the foreseeable future!!

We go to the Hollies to purchase fresh fruit and veg after we have finished at the butchers, but as we drive into the car park, we notice the queue is right round past the shop to the closed café and they are only letting one person in at a time.

The Hollies is a specialised farm food shop and one that is so well stocked with delicious products and samples of cheeses, that it does take a long time to shop inside and make the necessary purchases. We abandon the idea of obtaining fresh fruit and vegetables from here, so we head home, and I suggest to Geoff that if he puts the meat away, I will nip into Waitrose and obtain our fruit and vegetables from there. We no longer have a market in Northwich due to a fire and although we buy lots of fruit and vegetables from Aldi, the shelf life is not as long as obtaining fresh food from the suppliers direct.

I arrive at Waitrose and find a long queue outside, with everyone positioning themselves 2 metres away and I resign myself to waiting for at least 45 minutes or more before I will be allowed in on the same basis as the Hollies, one in one out.

I am patient and wait along with the other customers, some of whom are wearing face masks and the atmosphere is quite grim. Once, I am allowed inside the store, I make my purchases quickly and decisively.

Fruit and vegetables first, followed by fresh fish for Good Friday from the in-store fishmonger, I chose a filleted piece of fresh cod for a recipe that I have at home. Normally, I am a salmon and sea bass fish lover, but we have had salmon this week already and seabass is not available.

I buy some cheese, a San Francisco sour dough loaf for lunch, a bottle of red wine and a bottle of white wine, some Moretti Beer for Geoff and some Mexican lime juice which is very refreshing with lemonade in the predicted hot weather for Easter.

I head home and put the shopping away. We have sufficient food in the fridge, freezer and cupboards to keep us away from danger for the next two weeks and I suspect it will be just milk that we will run out of.

After a delicious lunch of ham and cheese salad with the freshly baked sour dough bread, I head out for my once-a-day exercise with Chumley down the river. It is a hot day, so I decide to let him have a few swims in the river to cool down, he enjoys swimming, and it is so funny to see how he launches himself into the water after his ball doing a complete belly dive.

There are only a few people out and the people that I meet are adhering to the social distance guidelines with great respect.

Geoff is cooking a Pad Thai for tea tonight which I know will be delicious.

We enjoy sitting outside to eat our tea and it makes such a difference to the pleasure of the meal when you can eat it on a bistro table in the sunshine.

Tonight at 8.00 pm we go outside to cheer and clap the NHS workers, doctors, staff, nurses, everyone who is working around the clock trying to save lives including that of our Prime Minister Boris Johnson who is still poorly in ITU on oxygen but is pulling through and not on a ventilator. The clapping gets louder and more emotional every week, we hear hooters sounding and bells being rung out, we find our brass bell that belonged to Geoff's mum and dad and give it one almighty ring for a few minutes to join in the well-deserved applause for the whole NHS.

After Chumley's last toilet break we go to bed and manage to sleep for a good 6 hours which makes us feel better.

Friday 10th April 2020

After Chumley's first early morning walk and breakfast. Geoff and I make a small video recording to send to Autumn and Niamh for Easter, we also take a new photograph of us outside on the patio.

Geoff emails the video and I send the photograph, along with a story about A Tale of Two Fluffy Baby Lambs for Easter, which I have written for Autumn and Niamh as I bought them a fluffy white lamb each for Easter, along with their chocolate easter eggs.

Whilst I am sending the emails, my mobile rings and it is Autumn who tells me that she has her own phone now, which is mummy's old one and she chats for ages, showing me her outfit. Jo Wicks exercise class on a Friday is a dressing up day, her mummy is Minnie Mouse, her daddy has a yellow dress on, and Autumn is dressed as a princess with bunny ears.

They look like they are having a ball and have even been outside this morning playing hopscotch together. I wander around the house talking to Autumn, Sarah and Paul, then show Geoff so that he can join in too. Autumn stayed up last night and went outside to clap the NHS too, bless her cotton socks.   Sarah tells me that they are going to do some baking later and I ask Autumn what she is planning to bake, perhaps a chocolate cake as this is normally her favourite. However, today she is going to make a lemon drizzle cake for tea which I also love too. It was good fun chatting, but I lost signal and so hung up and said goodbye.

For the last 3 years, Autumn has stayed with us over Easter, whilst her mummy and daddy have been away for a week to Prague, then New York City where Paul proposed and last year on their honeymoon to Sri Lanka.

They were all due to go on holiday together this year to Cape Verde and had planned to stay with us, after their week away, until Easter Sunday this week. We find it hard not to feel sad, but at least we are all safe so far and hopefully, it will not be too long before we meet up again soon for a big group hug.

I get changed into my shorts, make us both a brew and help Geoff with some of the fence painting which he is doing where the fences are extremely high on top of a big brick wall. He needs my help to steady the ladders.

Once he is safe doing the bottom fences, I decide to clear the debris off the decking and wash down our garden furniture.

I cook the fish for tea today, it is a recipe using fillet of cod baked underneath a lemon and chive crust made with wholemeal breadcrumbs. I am happy with the result, and it tasted delicious. We enjoyed a Hot Cross bun each for dessert.

During the evening we each had a glass of red wine and some Galaxy caramel chocolate to eat, whilst we watched the incredible Cirque du Soleil perform Alegria and Kooza which was brilliant.

Below is my Easter story for Autumn and Niamh. Geoff's imagination is far superior to mine when it comes to making up stories for the little ones.

A Tale of Two Fluffy Baby Lambs

By Linda Leigh

Nana Banana was feeling a bit sad today because she is missing all of her family and friends whom she enjoys being with throughout the days of her life. Today, especially she is missing her two little granddaughters Autumn and Niamh very much.

It will soon be Easter she thought this morning. Thank goodness that Autumn chose a Dinosaur chocolate egg when we stayed with her mummy and daddy on the 12th March and took Autumn with us to buy lots of cleaning stuff for their home. Autumn's home is not in the least bit dirty, however, there is a nasty germ on its way to us and it is important to make sure we eliminate all germs around us now, by protecting every surface, so that it cannot take a hold and grow more germs in our homes.

However, the most important part of our shopping was to buy an Egg for the Easter Bunny to keep safely for Autumn. We almost brought it home with us for the Easter Bunny who lives in Northwich.

Geoff and I decided that it was probably better if the Dalston Easter Bunny kept the egg safely for another few weeks. Grandad Geoff would only eat the egg if it stayed in Northwich, as he just loves chocolate so much.

We have been "locked down" inside all our own homes now since Tuesday 17th March, 2020.
Spring has finally arrived bringing warm sunshine. I expect that there will be lots of lambs being born now too. Every morning we wake up to the little birds singing to us.

Nana Banana feels both happy and sad about this as we love going up the M6 motorway every alternate week in our car with Chumley.

We look forward to seeing all the new-born baby lambs skipping happily in the fields at springtime. It is now 29 whole days since our last visit to stay with Sarah, Paul, and Autumn. We must stay safe for a long time yet and remain at home, whilst this dirty germ keeps feasting on everyone around us.

It is 47 days since we last saw Anthony and Catherine with our baby granddaughter Niamh, who is growing and changing so much, as each developmental stage arrives.

We are lucky to have two gorgeous little girls in our lives and cannot wait to see them both again for the longest and biggest bear hug ever! In the meantime, we gaze affectionately at photos and catch up on facetime or house party apps that allow us to interact with them on the screen.

Nana Banana has a good plan for Eastertime. Nana and Granddad Geoff cannot travel to see the two little girls and the baby lambs. But she does have two fluffy white baby lamb toys that Nana Banana has named Daisy and Maisy. It seemed a good idea at the time to buy each granddaughter a toy lamb for Easter along with some chocolate and the book cushion that Nana has made for baby Niamh.

However, what we did not expect to happen was that the whole planet known as Earth would become invaded by an invisible enemy who had come to cause havoc and sickness to many thousands of people and children. This unknown enemy is a fast-spreading germ which is infecting people's lungs with nasty bugs that caused them to become poorly very quickly.

Somehow, like a witches spell or a magician's curse, these germs had started in a country called China where in the marketplace, some unusual animals had become very sick and somehow that sickness had been passed by the animals to lots of mummies and daddies and children.

Then every day, each of these people went to see another person in their family or jobs and the sickness bug just got passed around by everyone, without knowing that they had somehow carried it on to the next person they met.

Instead, what Nana Banana is going to do now, is to incorporate Daisy and Maisy into this little story which can then be read out to the two girls by their mummies and daddies over Easter.

So, say hello to Autumn and Niamh, by giving them a very quick bleat please Daisy and Maisy.

The children will be your new friends to play with one day soon. I know that each of you will enjoy playing with them, as they are just lovely, adorable little girls whose smiles light up their faces and our hearts every time we see them. Autumn is 4 and half years old and Niamh is 8 months old. They are cousins to each other and try to meet up as much as they can, but it's just a bit difficult now, with these horrible germs everywhere, but hopefully, we will all be safe soon.

You both look incredibly happy today Daisy and Maisy. I heard you playing in the bedroom, where Autumn sometimes sleeps when she stays with us.
I hope you have tidied the bedroom up and put everything away properly, not just used your newfound legs to kick everything out of sight!

On the bed is a lovely book cushion that Nana Banana has made for Niamh. Inside is a book with a story called 'Love is a Handful of Honey' for Niamh to keep in her home. Next to this is Autumn's book cushion, which has a book inside with a story about 'Giraffes who can't dance', but I think that the story also reminds me of Granddad Geoff, who can't dance too or can he?

Now then, what did you do with the chocolate treats for Autumn and Niamh are they still in the hiding place, for when they come down to see you Daisy and

Maisy? I hope so as the shops are running out of chocolates.

I noticed the empty shelves where chocolate would normally be piled high. More people and children are buying lots of chocolate whilst they are stuck inside their own home, due to the 'Lockdown' Easter arrives next weekend and everyone needs an Easter egg from the Easter bunny, including you two fluffy lambs as well. Although, most days you drink milk from your mummy Herdy Sheep, which in fact is made into chocolate too.

Herdy is still busy grazing near your pen in Cumbria, so that you can still enjoy lots of milk as well as grass. I have brought some down for you from Herdy and it is stored in our fridge.

There is enough milk to last for the next 5 days. When we run out, I can soon obtain some more milk and have it delivered to our home for you both. Your dad whose name is Lambswool, sheepishly said he was missing you both, even though you do dance around his feet a lot, especially when he is busy herding the rest of the sheep into the pens, who are too old to travel now.

Lambswool stays at the back of all the sheep so that they all get safely home. He lets the big black and white sheep dog round them all up at mealtimes and bedtimes.

In the meantime, down here at our home, we do have plenty of grass for you to graze on the front and back lawns of our home. The sunshine is just lovely today, so off you go Daisy and Maisy to play outside. Chumley will enjoy chasing you both round the garden and you can always kick his ball to him with your back legs.

See you on the wing soon, Autumn and Niamh! Love and hugs from Nana, Granddad, Chumley, Maisy and Daisy too. xxxx

Saturday 11ᵗʰ April 2020

After a quick breakfast of the usual cereals, cornflakes with hot milk for Geoff, Bran flakes with lots of fresh fruit for me today, as a change from eating porridge oats with honey. We prepare the vegetables for tea in the slow cooker. Lamb shanks cooked in red wine, with juniper berries, orange peel, cinnamon, and lots of fresh vegetables to accompany the dish.

We head outside in our shorts as it is already quite warm outside. Geoff is going to jet wash the decking and I am pottering around helping in the garden to tidy up and sort lunch out for us. We do enjoy sitting and reading whilst it is warm too and so after the jet washing is finished, we spend some time just enjoying the weather.

I have a bit of problem with my knee this morning. I think it's because I have been walking Chumley out in my Birkenstock Sandals. We don't have any ibuprofen in the cupboard. So I walk to our nearest shop, to see if I can buy some stronger painkillers. The paracetamol I took yesterday, is not touching the inflammatory pain that I am experiencing today. Ibuprofen is not good for using for COVID-19. The reasons we are given, is that this pain-relief can make the breathing symptoms far worse. However, I have not got the virus yet and hope to avoid it if I can. We just don't know who will fall under its lethal clutches and who will not catch it?

After lunch, I take Chumley for his usual walk down to the river and he enjoys some more swimming. He does a belly flop into the water every time which just makes me laugh and he would stay there all-day swimming if I let him.

Geoff is cutting the front lawn at home whilst I am out, and I will help him to tidy up as soon as I get back. It is strangely quiet everywhere and there are not many people around, a family with young children, a couple of cyclists and another dog walker, we all stay far apart and more than the recommended 2 metres, in fact all of us in passing go out of our way to stay in areas off the pathways, like jumping into clearings!!

We find ourselves getting more paranoid every day as time goes on and the UK death tolls rises by 917 deaths today bringing the UK total to 9,000 these figures include children of all ages, young adults and older vulnerable people, no one is safe from it. The good news is that our Prime Minister Boris Johnson is doing well and out of ICU and on the ward now.

I drop a plant off for one of my school friends Elizabeth, who lives around the corner. I leave it on her path by leaning over the gate so that we are not in close contact at all. Her family are all outside in the garden tidying up and it was good to see them from a distance looking well, keeping busy and staying safe too. Elizabeth often leaves us books on our front drive. Last week, there was a box of Lindt chocolates in the bag of books, for us to enjoy over Easter, she is extremely kind and thoughtful, always thinking of others first.

Geoff and I sit reading for the rest of the afternoon. We both enjoy the chance to read a book from beginning to end, it's just like being on holiday, we say to each other. However, we feel so guilty and helpless that outside our bubble of safe living, people around us are battling for their lives on this sunny warm day of Easter Saturday on the 10th April 2020.

There are thousands of frontline workers out there in the NHS and at other key worker industries, such as the distribution of food to the supermarket, the workers inside the supermarkets, the delivery men, the postmen.

We talk about the many unsung heroes out there whilst we sit in quietness reading. Geoff is enjoying a beer; I sip my Gin and Tonic with pleasure. Our tea is cooking slowly, and all seems surreal and peaceful, no cars, no planes, just the sky, the trees and the birds singing along to us.

We tried to watch the Andrew Lloyd Webber production of Jesus Christ Superstar tonight which was being streamed live. However, after half an hour we turned it off. Neither of us was enjoying this show as much as all his other musicals. Instead, we watched a film called the Aeronaut with Eddie Redmayne about a hot air balloon in 1862, it was a fabulous film and made us think about the scientists and adventurers that first travelled up in the sky this way, reaching a height of 28,000 miles which we take for granted now in airplanes. However, in 1862 this was a battle against nature and the elements showing danger in every mile that they climbed up in the first hot air balloon.

Easter Sunday 12th April 2020

Today, is a tough day for Geoff and I. We are safe in our bubble called home, we are fit and well.

However, we cannot help but feel a bit sad as it is one whole month ago today since we saw our daughter Sarah, son-in-law Paul and Autumn. We know that we will speak to them later and that it may be on facetime or via WhatsApp or house-party, so we resign ourselves to feeling blessed that all of us are safe for now.

Outside our little bubble, we know that a battle of life and death is happening across the country, where lives are lost to this dreadful COVID-19.

We also miss our son Anthony, daughter-in-law Catherine and baby Niamh who was just 6 months old when we saw her on the 23rd February. We decide to fill the day with busy things to keep active which will help us to stay focused on how lucky we are, instead of feeling sorry for ourselves.

So, whilst Geoff is out with Chumley this morning, I put some eggs with smiley faces onto our bistro table outside. I arrange some of the chocolate mini eggs onto a plate for Geoff, which he loves. I am usually the butt of family jokes each year for hiding them out of sight as often they are eaten long before Easter.

Geoff is busy painting the balustrades on our decking and I spend the morning putting some washing out and then writing about what we did yesterday in this book of daily life for us in 'Lockdown' It soon reaches lunchtime, I make us a little picnic to eat outside consisting of a bowl of salt and pepper crisps, some fruit cake with the mini eggs and a hot drink each. The weather is much cooler today, then yesterday. I have peeled the potatoes for tea and yesterday we prepared the vegetables, so it is only the turkey roll that needs to be cooked later this afternoon, after I have taken Chumley out.

Anthony telephones first and shows Niamh to us and we wave and smile at her, she doesn't show any sign of recognising who we are? Although we don't say anything, we feel a bit sad inside for the fact that it is now over 2 months, since we last saw Niamh when she was just 6 months old. Suddenly she is now 8 months old.

We chat to Anthony and say Happy Easter to him and Catherine. Anthony tells us that he has been busy at work and is looking forward to a walk later with Niamh. They will be spending more time in the garden again, like yesterday. Niamh enjoys being outside and they have a paddling pool, which they will fill with plastic balls to make a ball pond for Niamh to play in Geoff and I chat about life, what we are all doing today, for Easter, then say our goodbyes. Anthony sent us a video first thing this morning of Niamh, enjoying her first Easter with some new toys and a book.

Sarah also sent some lovely photos of their Easter breakfast of croissants and chocolate. They all looked incredibly happy and well. Sarah telephoned us back at lunchtime, just as I was getting ready to go out with Chumley and it was a Facetime call. So we enjoyed a lovely long chat with them. Autumn told us all about the Easter Bunny arriving in the middle of the night. Then she showed us her chocolates and the pretty dress she was wearing today, with unicorns and flowers on.

We enjoyed a delicious Roast Turkey Dinner at 4.00 pm with home-made sage and onion stuffing balls, cauliflower, carrots, and roasted potatoes in goose fat, red wine gravy. Geoff had a bottle of Norton Malbec Red Wine; I had a bottle of Maree White Wine. We resisted drinking a bottle each, but instead settled for two glasses of wine, to toast our family and friends with over WhatsApp.

After tea, we cracked open our easter eggs to each other, Geoff had a handmade dark chocolate and orange one. I had a raspberry and white chocolate one. I save half of mine for tomorrow, but Geoff ate all his which is just typical as he is a chocoholic. I like to leave some for the next day, rather than eat it all at once.. However, it is Easter and if we can't enjoy chocolate whilst living on our own, through what would normally have been a lovely family day together, either over a meal or at the seaside. Then today's strangeness, has to have some degree of normality in it to keep us smiling.

Often we remember all the Easter Holidays that we spent taking walls down, building fireplaces, replacing windows, or just simply decorating over the long bank holiday weekends. In general, a lot of busy parents would often catch up on those house jobs, over a long Bank Holiday weekend.

However, I always baked lots of yummy Easter treats for us, but somehow Geoff and the children would discover other chocolate mini eggs that I hid in secret places, convinced they would never find them, wrong! The number of Easter Eggs that both children received were usually 7 each, from different relatives and our friends

We would normally have a roast dinner on Easter Sunday, often with one set of grandparents joining us. If the weather forecast was good, we would invariably head out to the beaches of Anglesey with our Labrador dog Amber, or explore different castles in Wales, like Conway Castle, or go off with the grandparents for the day. Uncle Dave and Auntie Linda would often join us with their children, who were cousins to our two children.

Easter wasn't all about working on the house and garden, especially when our children were young. That time period with them were truly the best part of our lives. I was a stay-at-home mum, until after the children went to school. And I loved every minute of each day with them.

We had dinner early tonight so that we can sit and watch the live streaming of Andrea Bocelli performing solo at the Duomo Cathedral in Milan 'Music for Hope' It didn't disappoint and we sat entranced as his music sent goosebumps down us and touched our hearts and soul with profound love. Seeing the pictures all around the globe of empty cities was heart-breaking. Listening to Amazing Grace by Andrea Bocelli uplifted our spirits.

We then trawled through previous concerts by Andrea Bocelli on YouTube and watched him sing a duo with Ed Sheeran to the song 'Perfect' which also showed how this recording was made. It took us back to when Autumn was a baby and I would hold her in my arms and dance around Sarah and Paul's kitchen singing to Autumn, her mummy and daddy did just the same with her too. Autumn has always loved music and dancing as I do too. Then one day, Autumn asked Alexa for the song to be played herself on the Sonos, soon after this happened, Autumn could not only ask Alexa to play this song, but she could also sing it word perfect herself. Hearing it again on the YouTube video made me remember the happy times spent with Autumn singing and dancing every week with her in the kitchen.

I always enjoyed taking Autumn to Music Makers every Thursday afternoon to dance and sing with all the other toddlers in the class. These happy memories are etched permanently in my heart, which also caused a few tears of pure joy and happiness to fall last night for the magic of those special times. We also cried watching Andrea Bocelli sing 'Time to say goodbye' with Sarah Brightman.

Just as we were getting ready for bed, two new videos arrived onto our phones from Sarah and Paul who were using **TikTok** to create funny actions and singing from them, Paul was outside their home trying to work out how to get past the line holding us all in by singing the song 'Whoo I can't go any further than this and I want to so badly' and Sarah was using a saw to play and sing music on the hosepipe of their Dyson Hoover a song that sounded like ooohooo. Crazy pair both of them but they sent us to bed laughing and smiling that they were happy and enjoying making funny memories together, apparently, all 40+ years old have discovered the fun of playing with TikTok, wonder if 60+ years old can work it out too and join in, will have to try tomorrow!!

Easter Monday 13th April 2020

Another beautiful day as we wake up and peek through the curtains to see what the weather is doing outside. It looks a bit cold though and the sun is not quite out yet at 5.00 am. Whilst Geoff took Chumley out for the first walk of the day. I strip our bedding off and put it in the washer.

This morning we allowed Chumley a luxury cuddle on top of the bed with us. We have not let him come upstairs, or on our bed for months, since his last leg operation. Having a dog in the bedroom is something that we both actively discourage. We learnt a few tough lessons the hard way with a very wild bouncy Red Setter, that we had when we were first married and who was total spoilt by us at the time by being treated like a baby.

I do quite like Chumley on the bed occasionally, as he is very tactile and enjoys the cuddles and relaxes with us, he makes us laugh when he gives a long sight of contentment. Chumley almost talks to us with his eyes and body language, he lets us know when he just wants to be cuddled or stroked, we know the difference in his eyes when he wants a drink or a walk or just simply some play time with us.

Often, when we are with anyone who is not a dog lover, we notice his body language and sad eyes acutely, as he will try to be lovable with whoever it is, but often that person may ignore him or be frightened of dogs. We say nothing and just stroke Chumley ourselves to reassure him that everything is fine.

Unless you are a dog owner or own any type of pet, we often find that it's hard to explain to others that animals have feelings too and want the same as we do, simply to be loved, fed, watered, played with and talked to. Dogs and all other pets understand more than we give them credit for!! In fact, I would go as far as to say, that animals are more sensitive to feelings that we have no conception about. Their senses are far more finely tuned and homed, than human ones are.

We have a quick breakfast together and get ready for a Skype call to my cousin Alan and his wife Joyce in NZ this morning at 8.30 am which will be 7.30 pm for them. Geoff sets my iPad up in the conservatory and we log on and chat until 9.00 am as we then have a ZOOM conference to log onto with my brother and extended genetic family the Hopes in Bury St Edmunds.

Alan and Joyce look very well, and they tell us that their country was locked down very quickly, with borders closed and all tourists sent home. They have only had 4 deaths to date which is an amazing achievement. They tell us that their Prime Minister is Jacinda Arden who is an excellent leader. Alan and Joyce both have health problems, they cannot leave their home to shop or exercise, but they can sit in the garden and their family are dropping shopping off on the doorstep for them. There is no panic buying and plenty of food to go round.

The police are monitoring the roads and using drones too. We chat about what we each of us think the world will look like after this difficult time for everyone. We all conclude that it will take a few years to return to where we were before COVID-19.

We feel travel will be much reduced, probably too expensive for us. In general, most people will not want to travel in planes, or on cruise ships for a long time, even if they can afford to.

None of us can predict the future and just must keep smiling through each day. We chat about being at home on 'lockdown' how each of us feels that we are inside a bubble, unable to help anyone ourselves that is out there saving lives.

There is an overwhelming sadness around us of people battling for lives and dying. It is beyond our comprehension of how and why this virus came about to destroy the world, in one foul swoop across the entire globe.

Alan and Joyce tell us that they firmly believe it has been caused by the amount of unusual animals and insects that people in the Far East and China in particular are using which are not part of the normal type of food we should be eating like bats, snakes, dogs, etc

We agree, having travelled to some of these countries ourselves and being totally unable to understand what the attraction is for eating animals that are not part of the normal food chain for humans to consume. However, we also have a niggling feeling that this virus may have been generated in a laboratory where something went wrong in the science of the work being carried out with devastating results, we will never know!!

Finally, it is time to say goodbye to Alan and Joyce after explaining about ZOOM being one of the best pieces of software to use for social chatting and interaction. We explained that if they set it up, they could potentially speak to their family and us at the same time in the UK with my friend Elizabeth, who is also their niece. We promise to send them some easy instructions on how to set it all up.

I log onto ZOOM following the invitation from Chris my brother in Bury St Edmunds, he has purchased the full version of ZOOM and is bringing the HOPE family together this morning between 9.00 am and 11.00 am to wish Rebecca Hope a very happy birthday from all of us.

Whilst on ZOOM, other family members log on and we start to interact with each other and to wish Rebecca an incredibly Happy Birthday too, she is 50 years old today and works as a Community Matron attached to a GP surgery. I was a Practice Manager for 28 years in total for two large GP surgeries, so I am interested to hear from Becky what it is like working at the coalface. Becky explains that the lack of PPE is a worry, and she is wearing her medical face mask much longer than she should be doing and it is risky.

It is quite exciting meeting all the Hope Family online with ZOOM and chatting to each other and seeing all the children too with their mummies and daddies. My Auntie Shelagh and her husband Cyril join in the meeting, it is only 5.00 am in the morning there, so a very early start to their day, but they were interesting to talk to and looked well too.

Shelagh said she will be 80 in September this year, so we arranged to meet up on ZOOM again to wish her a happy birthday and agreed to do this at 2.00 pm on the day of her birthday which is a more civilized time slot for them both as they live in Ohio, USA. It was really good fun listening to everyone's stories of how COVID-19 is affecting them personally and in general. Geoff joined in from the garden for a few minutes, he is on a mission to sand our decking balustrades down today and then repaint them, the trouble is we don't have any paint and cannot buy it either.

Message below from my iPhone that I sent to Sarah and Anthony who were unable to join in this morning.

ZOOM was good with the Hope clan and their children this morning. Sarah Hope who lives in Manchester had her girls Libby and Niamh there too. Some of them work in the NHS as District Nurses and told it how it is with the lack of PPE! I helped Chris with ZOOM familiarisation this morning. Shelagh and Cyril were interesting talking about Ohio and Malaysia/India. Rhys has just secured an English teaching job in Kent as a complete job change from restaurants like Carluccio's. Rhys thinks it is more of a 9 to 5 job, told him it is 24/7 Sarah and he laughed as heard that too from other friends.

We have agreed to meet up on ZOOM at 7pm on my birthday Wed 6th May and on Tues 2nd Sep at 2pm for Shelagh's 80 Birthday. If you get chance can you email your addresses to Chris, to include in the group for my birthday, as lockdown will still be here, we think next month! Love mum xxxx

In the afternoon after a lunch of teacakes outside, we enjoy the rest of our Easter Monday pottering in the garden and taking Chumley out.

I did sneak out for a short drive to take our hanging baskets as arranged with a local nursery less than one mile away, who is desperately trying to keep her business going for her regular customers. I felt incredibly guilty but did collect some essential food enroute, saw no-one and there was just the plant owner and me who kept our distances from each other including paying by card.

We think this will be the normal stance for everyone long after we come through this period of time as people will avoid crowds and everyone is so used to giving each other a wide berth now and we have learnt how to do this very quickly and will not go back to being in each other's personal space.

For dinner tonight we enjoyed the leftover turkey along with some tender stem broccoli and another glass of wine each. My fruit cake is almost all gone now, and we enjoyed a piece each during the evening whilst watching the new Quiz drama about a cheat who stole £1 million pounds whilst participating in the game show Who wants to be a Millionaire some years ago.

Watching the drama was like looking back at our own history as we all grew up in this era and in fact used to tune into this show. It looked so dated seeing the family homes and what they were wearing!! We thought we were modern at that time!!

Tuesday 14th April 2020

Well, that is Easter 2020 all over done and dusted now!! It truly was the strangest quietest Easter ever, yet we were privileged and blessed to be able to enjoy good weather with lots of sunshine, enjoy delicious food and online chats with family and friends, eat Easter egg chocolate, drink wine and live our lives as normally as possible, albeit confined to our own homes.

We were determined to push all feelings of sadness to the back of our minds over Easter as just knowing that for now all our family and friends are safe was the best Easter present we could have in 2020.

We know we will meet up again and for now we content ourselves by being busy and enjoying our Facetime and ZOOM catchups with everyone. We see the news every day out there where death is taking so many lives and the daily tally of deaths reminds us all of the grimness of the people who cannot even hold their loved one or say a final goodbye to them.

We have nothing at all to moan about in these 'Lockdown' days of our life at this time period when the whole world is suffering and standing still in silent grief and tears.

We busied ourselves with garden tasks and I washed all our outdoor furniture down today, ready for using in the predicted sunny weather tomorrow. I also booked into my on-line Zumba Class for 6.00 pm today.

I ordered a pattern for a sundress and shorts to make for my two gorgeous granddaughters, starting with Autumn first. However, I will also need to purchase some fabric, cotton and a zip from an on-line shop. I will wait until the pattern arrives first, as it might take a long time to deliver.

After lunch, I take Chumley out for his usual walk across the locks, through Roker park, then through the deserted ghost town of Northwich.

I carry on along the pavement and onto Verdin Park, as I was crossing a path on the way back home, I saw my friend Elizabeth and Charlie coming towards us, which is just lovely as I enjoy being able to have a face-to-face chat with them albeit we are standing 2 metres apart from each other. We long for the day when we can hug again, but for now content ourselves with just being able to see each other.

I thoroughly enjoyed my Zumba class tonight it was the full version class and not our usual Zumba Gold Class, I thought it might be too difficult and fast for me, however, I managed to keep pace and only lost a bit of my co-ordination in a couple of the dances that I hadn't done before.

After Zumba we ate tea which was chicken Fajitas full of peppers and spices. Then we watched part 2 of the drama QUIZ which is a true-life story of a cheat on the game show from the seventies called 'Who wants to be a Millionaire'

I chatted to a close friend Liz Sandbach on the telephone who rang to thank me for her birthday gift. Liz was 70 years old on Easter Sunday 12th April, lots of exciting plans for her special celebration had been put in place by Liz and her family and friends, including afternoon tea at the Ritz in London, a family meal together at the Swettenham Arms and a solo trip for Liz to Italy. However, everything had to be cancelled long before 'lockdown' when we all realised this virus pandemic was going to be here for the long haul, not the short haul. It was just lovely to put the world to rights between us whilst chatting on the telephone together.

I watched the 10.00 pm news whilst Geoff took Chumley out for his bedtime toilet needs. I found it so sad listening to the stories about the city of Birmingham having the highest death toll, due to its central location and high-density population of people living there.

I watched with great sadness the makeshift marquee style mortuaries being built on wasteland, being equipped with several refrigeration units to house the dead bodies of the people arriving from hospital in their van loads with existing mortuaries already being full to capacity.

I was staggered to see shelf after shelf being erected like you see in the big warehouses like B&Q and the stark realisation that these are to store the dead bodies inside their coffins on!

The next news item was about the last patient to leave the new hastily built hospital unit in Wuhan that we watched being built in the early part of January 2020. One of the nurses had worked there tirelessly, without a break not even for a day off during the last 3 months. This nurse was finally leaving the hospital at the same time as her patient. The nurse told us that she will return back home now, to be with her husband and daughter, whom she is going to show just how much she loves.

The nurse told us that the UK is just about at the same stage now where she was 2 months ago. She was confident that we will come through, but not without huge losses of lives.

I went to bed tired, but unable to sleep. I processed the news inside my head and how our lives and deaths, are determined by where and how we live our lives.

We are so fortunate to live in a suburban area with the countryside and coast within easy reach of less than one hour, in any direction.

Our town ,Northwich, is not a big city. We do not have an overcrowded population living in high rise flats or in poverty to the extent that the area is deemed high deprivation. In fact we are blessed to the extent that we are living in a peaceful and well served location with amenities and riches way beyond the lives of the people living in Birmingham who are at a much higher risk of catching and dying from this virus than we are. Not that COVID-19 is discriminatory, it isn't, but the numbers of people living in Birmingham, as opposed to Northwich are massively different and that gives us a better fighting chance, than they have.

I have never felt so fearful of this enemy than anything I have ever experienced in the whole of my 66 years of life on this earth.

Chapter Three

Easter Eggs are long gone

Wednesday 15th April 2020

This morning I woke up feeling a bit tearful and wobbly, I think it is lack of sleep and the news items last night that touched me deeply for the suffering and pain going on out there, whilst we live relatively comfortably in our bubble being safe at home and by being safe we are saved.

However, we are unable to reach out and save others or help others in the way we would do in other normal situations of life, such as accidents, illness, loss of jobs, health issues, family crisis etc

This is alien to us being kept away from danger, whilst others face danger every day and night of their lives, particularly the NHS staff, teachers, social carers, cleaners, shop workers, distribution workers, delivery drivers, transport workers, post office staff and post people who just keep working, despite the closeness of working with colleagues and handling packages or dealing with surfaces that might be contaminated with the virus.

I have not heard from our friends Carol and Bob in Paphos, Cyprus, for a few days, so I text Carol to see if they and all their family in the UK are doing ok. Carol replies and tells me that she has felt a bit wobbly, as despite being safe over there at their holiday home, they do miss their close family and grandchildren very much. Particularly, when their grandson asked them on Facetime, why they aren't catching a plane home? As he misses them so much.

I reply back to Carol to give her reassurance and that I am having the same wobble, as despite being in regular contact with our family and grandchildren, using facetime or ZOOM, it is not quite the same as that real hug and bond we have with them under normal circumstances.

My friends are all active in the WhatsApp groups. We support each other from morning until bedtime, we can contact anyone of us separately, just to chat and share our feelings and help each other.

There is much banter happening in these groups, with jokes and funny stories to tell and hilarious videos flying around all day long. I do not know how people think them up so fast and put them out there on social media or to individuals.

A lot of messages and stories/videos are quite poignant and moving too with profound messages and music that literally gives you goosebumps and tears falling from your eyes.

Geoff and I retrieved all our stored cushions for the outdoor furniture from out of our loft today. We spent the morning assembling all the furniture together in the garden. We enjoyed seeing the garden look great.

All our hard work on the fences and tidying up projects has made everywhere look so lovely. We decide that today, we are going to eat lunch and tea outside and just enjoy the weather and relax a bit more than we have done lately. It was a perfect day, not too hot and not cold at all.

Lunch was delicious, salmon salad sandwiches for me and some roast ham with black garlic sauce for Geoff.

I took Chumley out for a long walk in the afternoon and headed along my usual route of the Locks, Roker Park and Verdin Park.

On the way home I saw a couple coming towards me in the middle of the road in an area known as Queensgate on Castle. I thought that they were about to turn into a driveway that I was just passing as I presumed it was their home.

I quickened my pace and went by the driveway quite fast and after I had passed the couple, the lady shouted out "Linda is that you?" I turned round and discovered it was one of my old friends Susan with her husband Ian. I was totally amazed, as today on our Hartford Girls Group, another school friend had just been chatting about Susan, whose mum was our dinner lady at school.. Susan had thick hair which was always in plaits, and she still has a mop of thick hair today and always looks very glamorous. It was fabulous to stand 2 metres apart and chat to Susan and Ian. I read out the messages written this morning about Susan and her mum.

I gave them the telephone number for Elizabeth who has organised our Hartford Girls group.
I suggested that she should join us as we are a supportive group who share stories, messages and funny jokes and banter all day long to keep our friendship strong during these difficult days for the world.

Susan told me that she did not own an iPhone only a very basic phone that cannot connect to the Internet and that once the shops open again, she is going to buy one. I asked her husband Ian if he had an iPhone and he confirmed that yes he has one, which I would have expected him to say, as he owns a hairdressing shop locally in London Road, Northwich. I suggested to Susan, that she uses her husband's phone to join our group and he said, "that's a good idea, but then I will never see my phone again", to which I replied, "well at least you will have some peace and quiet!!" I said my goodbyes to them both and wished them well and to stay safe.

Later that afternoon, I noticed that Elizabeth had included Susan into our group, and we were all able to send her messages saying what a mad lot we are!! I find it totally fascinating, how fate plays a big part in how our paths can just suddenly cross out of the blue

111

and the co-incidence of meeting my old school friend from both primary and secondary school just like that out of the blue whom we have all just been reminiscing about today.

Dinner was fillet steak, accompanied by tender stem broccoli, with chips and giant mushrooms and of course half a bottle of Argentine Malbec wine to accompany the meal. This was quickly followed by one of the last two pieces of my fruit cake made 2 weeks ago. This fruit cake has not had the additional benefit of being soaked weekly with brandy for at least 2 months before being consumed!!

Interestingly, the result of my fruit cake was that it is one of the best ones I have made. For some strange reason, my fruit cakes at Christmas this year were a bit dry and crumbly, however, this one is on a par with the wedding cake I made two years ago for my son Anthony and daughter-in-law Catherine. That too turned out just perfect!!

We watched the end of the QUIZ drama tonight which concluded with the couple being found guilty as charged.

Thursday 16th April 2020

Today, promises to be another hot sunny day, we are going to make the most of being outside again all day until the NHS clapping at 8.00 pm tonight which gets louder and stronger every week!! The dedication of the doctors, nurses, cleaning staff and everyone involved is phenomenal. We hope that by staying at home we are helping to save lives too.

There are so many battles taking place in the world around us. Lots of people are still having to go to work like our daughter Sarah and Paul, whose jobs are on the front line every day. Sarah as a teacher and Paul her husband, who has to be at his factory which is producing greater quantities of mineral water due to increased demand. 14-hour long days are their normal lives at the moment. In addition, they have to make alternative arrangements to look after their daughter Autumn, who is unable to attend nursery or have us stay with them, to lend a hand with childcare.

We feel so frustrated as Geoff and I are physically fit and well, but the risks are too great, so we dismiss the mad ideas of driving up to help them both out. We know already that today; the government will announce an extended further lockdown of another 3 weeks. This will take us up to the day after my birthday on the 7th May

We have come this far with the rest of the country and now it is just a short hop to May for all of us. I am going to contact our local Castle and Winnington Community Group today, who are making scrub bags for the NHS today, using old duvets and pillowcases, to see if I can make some to help too

Today was very warm in the garden this morning. Geoff decided to try and remove some ivy from the trees in the woods behind us and some of the young saplings that were already growing tall

I decided to sort all my baking tins out and change some of the equipment in one of the corner units in our kitchen where the shelf keeps falling off the brackets due to the weight of the rice cooker and slow cooker stored in there along with a plethora of other kitchen stuff. We have a tall old cupboard in the garage that would be better suited to housings some of the equipment in the kitchen.

I undertake a good clearance and improved utilisation of the kitchen equipment, including moving some of my baking tins to different areas of the tall cupboard in the garage which gives me improved storage space for these items.

Whilst I am just finishing off the task, the telephone rings. I answer the phone, feeling a rush of excitement to hear the voice of our granddaughter Autumn on the other end, she is chatting to me about the fact that she is outside eating a snack of cheese, humous and cucumber.

Autumn tells me that her mummy has painted her nails for her. Also, they have been making hoops and threading beads through.

Today, she has been playing on her own a bit, whilst Sarah dealt with some telephone calls to staff and families of the children at school.

We have a good long chat together on the telephone and Autumn and Sarah tell me about the walks that they have been finding near where they live. I can hear Autumn in the background telling me that she knows Chumley would like them too. I pass the telephone to Geoff who has just come into the garage, so that he can have a chat with Sarah and Autumn too.

After we finish on the telephone, Geoff fixes the shelf in the kitchen cupboard for me, which takes a while as it is a bit awkward. Then we have some lunch together before I head off to take Chumley on a five mile walk up the river to Vale Royal Locks, where I stop and admire the Bluebells that are flowering profusely in the warm sunshine today. Chumley enjoys lots of swimming in the river.

We head home and enjoy the rest of the afternoon in the garden and have a salmon risotto for tea along with a glass of wine and the last two pieces of my fruit cake.

Geoff's sister is undergoing a cystoscopy test this afternoon and we wait to hear from her that all is well. Becky her daughter is recovering slowly, from contracting COVID-19 but she has not turned all the corners yet.

At 8.00 pm we head outside for the NHS clapping with all our neighbours, we shout, clap and ring bells, making as much noise as possible to send our heartfelt thanks and prayers to everyone working in the NHS, not just saving lives, but giving love and care to each and every patient that they look after. The work is endless and repeats through every minute of each 24-hour day.

Friday 17th April 2020

This morning I felt a bit sad and down, for no reason. I think just sometimes the emotions of the mind just overcome our bodies as we go through each day wearing our positive hats and staying strong along with our family, friends, and the whole country, in fact the whole world. To be able to save the lives of our family and friends, likewise for them to be able to save our lives by not visiting each other. I know that we are doing exactly what the government has requested us to do by remaining inside our homes every day, during this 'Lockdown' period, not to go out, unless for the following four conditions:

- To purchase essential food, using the social distancing guideline standing at least 2 metres away from the person before and after you.
- To obtain medicines
- To exercise once daily for each person
- To travel to work

I used the rule for essential food shopping today, to obtain fresh fruit and vegetables for us. I avoided the big supermarkets and stood outside a local Farm Food shop for 30 minutes this morning with more than 2 metres between the other customers.

Only one person was allowed in as one person came out. Everything is being totally sanitised and I feel perfectly safe, but as always, no-one lingers or browses, it is a case of purchasing exactly what you need and leaving to allow other customers the same consideration.

We spent the morning cleaning the house from top to bottom giving it one of those good deep cleans, although we are far more paranoid now than ever before and I often find myself constantly cleaning the surfaces regularly throughout the day, even though I know from years spent working with doctors and my own common sense, that actually, a little bit of dirt and bacteria is more healthier for your immune system to build up its natural defences, rather than put our bodies in clinical sterile homes and gardens!!

Lunch was delicious Olive bread for me with a delicious cheese and onion pastry roll, Tiger bread for Geoff with a roast hog filled sausage roll,. followed by homemade scones.

I sent Becky a WhatsApp message today to see how she is doing with the Covid virus? This was passed on to her from her boss Becky thinks at Leighton Hospital. She says she has had some rubbish days and been poorly but is getting better now. It takes weeks to recover from and at any point in time, this virus can go from being a mild dose to a severe terminal dose of it. I remain worried about Becky..

Geoff chatted to his sister Christine in the afternoon who is also undergoing a few tests for blood in her urine recently. Jim her husband, also has an illness that has not been diagnosed with a full explanation of what his illness is being caused by? The illness has left his arm muscles feeling weak like stroke effects.

Christine has had a cystoscopy which has come back clear and tomorrow she will have a CAT scan as a final check of her organs too.

Christine told us that Becky is not well at all, but is still considering returning to work next week, against all advice from her and the doctors. Geoff said to tell Becky not to return to work. However, if she does go back then her Uncle Geoff and Auntie Linda will be severely cross with her! We do not stand a chance as all our children are just the same when it comes down to their commitments to work and are no different than we were when working too.

Chumley seemed very tired today and a bit lethargic in the warm weather, I decided not to walk as far with him today. Also, to limit his swimming exercise which was vigorous yesterday. We walked to Verdin Park instead and it was totally empty.

Tea was a quick meal of a Weetwood Steak and Ale Pie with frites and runner beans for Geoff. I had roast turkey with frites and runner beans. We both enjoyed a delicious chocolate twist pastry for desert and a glass of red wine.

Promised ourselves to eat less carbohydrates tomorrow, but today we just needed the treat at this halfway point of 'Lockdown'

Andrew Lloyd Webber has given the world the opportunity to watch all his musicals through 'YouTube' every Friday evening at 7.00 pm and the choice this week is Phantom of the Opera. We are excited to be able to see this show again, as we watched the performance live over 20 years ago at the Manchester Opera House. The show tonight is the 25th Anniversary of the Opera which was performed at the Royal Albert Hall in London. It was brilliant, especially as we turned our Sonos system up to its full capacity!! The sound was just outstanding, as was the whole performance!!

At the end of the show, Andrew Lloyd Webber brought the original cast onto the stage including Michael Crawford and Sarah Brightman who performed the songs again.

The show was brilliant, it truly was a totally exhilarating evening for Geoff and me to be able to see this fantastic musical again. Not sure that our neighbours would agree though, as the noise from our home was blasting out all over the cul-de-sac Geoff noticed, when he took Chumley out for a toilet break.!! As we started to get ready for bed, we continued playing the music, through our bedroom speaker system.

Geoff wrote a short story for Autumn and Niamh today and I am so proud of him for using his imagination and skills! His story is below, and I feel he should continue writing and create a book of short stories for children during this COVID-19 Lockdown period of our lives. Geoff is totally brilliant at using his natural imagination and had started telling Autumn this story straight out of his head when we were last up in Carlisle on the 12th March, 2020 as Autumn was fascinated by Dragon Stories and he just made part of this one up and has now completed the full story.

<u>Gorgan the Dragon & Zola the Mouse</u>

By Geoff Leigh

Once upon a time in a land far away, a long time ago, there was a little village in the countryside where all the people who lived there were very frightened.

They were frightened because in the hills above the village lived an enormous dragon that, when he was hungry, he would come to the village, and spitting great big balls of fire, would burn things down and eat anything or anybody he could.

The dragons name was Gorgan, and he wasn't bothered if he ate a cow or a sheep or a horse or sometimes even a little boy or a little girl.as long as he had something to satisfy his hunger. Gorgan was not afraid of anything at all.

One day when a little boy called Peter was in the fields looking after his dad's herd of cows, he heard a great big roar and just knew that Gorgan the dragon was coming closer. In Peters pocket was his pet mouse called Zola. Now Zola was very small and went everywhere with Peter, even to bed at night.

Peter started to get frightened and wanted to run away, but he knew that if he did run away Gorgan would eat all of his dad's cows and he would get into big trouble, so, he decided to try and hide, but the trouble was Gorgan was so big he could see everything.

Peter crouched down behind a fallen tree and poor little Zola fell out of Peters' pocket. Suddenly a very loud voice boomed out

"I CAN SEE YOU LITTLE BOY HIDING BEHIND THAT TREE AND I AM NOT FRIGHTENED OF ANYTHING AND I AM GOING TO SPIT FIRE AND COOK YOU AND EAT YOU ALL UP".

Poor Peter was terrified and was unable to move. Little Zola thought "I'm not going to stay here and be cooked and eaten" so he ran to try and hide in the long grass.

Zola was only small, but he could run extremely fast and when Gorgan saw this tiny little mouse running he thought to himself, "I'll have that for my afternoon snack. The trouble was that Zola was running so fast, Gorgan lost sight of him and could not find him. "Whoa" screamed Gorgan, "where did that little mouse go?" and Gorgan could not find him at all.

Gorgan became very confused and sat down in the field trying to think. Just then Zola ran like a streak of lightning straight past the big scary dragon and made him jump.

"Hey" Screeched Gorgan "what was that? I don't think I like things that move so fast, I can't keep up with them, I'm not sticking around here anymore, I'm off home"

So Gorgan spread his mighty wings and with his tail between his legs flew back home to his cave in the mountains.

Peter, who had been hiding behind the fallen tree had seen all of this and he called over to Zola. He said "Zola, how clever you are, you have frightened the big scary dragon away, wait until I tell all of the people in the village that all they need to do from now on is have a little pet mouse and the dragon will never come back and eat any of us again" And as a reward for saving everybody Peter gave Zola some of his favourite cheese. Can you guess what type of cheese it was?

The End.

Saturday 18th April 2020

A bit of a non-day really, it rained today, the weather was cold after all the lovely warm sunshine of the last few days. The rain is much needed for the garden, and it is a welcome treat for all the spring plants and flowers pushing up now from their long hibernation over the winter months. Truly a joy to behold in these long days of being locked down. Interestingly, the spring flowers and trees seem to be more vibrant and prettier than usual.

Everything in the garden is bathed in crystal clear light each day and it is breath-taking to see and enjoy. It is like seeing an artist at work, painting the garden in glorious technicolour oils to be preserved forever in this particularly difficult time period of 2020 for the whole world.

Many of us wonder if the colours are more vibrant this year because of the reduced pollution levels in the atmosphere. Or is it mother nature showing us that she is always there and that we need to look after her and take more care than this generation of ours has done in the 21st Century?

Mid-morning is coffee time with a delicious pan-au-chocolate for a treat. After our coffee break, I telephone Carlisle Bookends. I noticed on Instagram that they have a good selection of books and jigsaws to buy for children to read and use during this time of being at home. They will deliver them with free postage for customers.

After chatting to the lovely Jane on the phone,, I order a 100-piece jigsaw to be sent to Autumn our granddaughter that has a picture of lots of unicorns dancing under rainbows. It will be posted out on Monday to reach Autumn's home by Wednesday. I ask Jane to put a message inside that tells Autumn it is with love from Nana Linda and Granddad Geoff.

The whole world is covered in rainbow paintings in windows, walls, pavements as a message of hope from all the children of the world. Autumn coloured one for us and we received it by WhatsApp which we printed out and put on our bedroom window to remind us, that after the storms and rain, rainbows will appear in the sunshine giving us all hope once more.

I used to love dancing with Autumn at Music Makers every Thursday afternoon to the song "I can sing a rainbow" and we would both dance with floaty coloured scarves and sing our hearts out together. A magic memory that is etched like a rainbow inside my heart.

Lunch is liver pate with chillies and some delicious olive bread for me and tiger bread for Geoff.

For the first time in weeks, Geoff and I take Chumley out together for a wet rainy walk through our deserted parks and town travelling first across the river behind us where normally at this time of year it is alive with all the canal boats passing through the locks.

Today, it is totally deserted and everywhere we look on our walk, we are reminded not to walk closely together or go on narrow paths and to avoid socialising with others at all costs. The afternoon is spent reading books and catching up on social media and the latest news.

We Facetime Anthony, Catherine, and Niamh. They all look well; Niamh is busy playing happily.

Anthony put a tower of cups out of her reach, and she took one look at where they were and just crawled straight to them!! Such a joy to see her do that and we really can't wait to be able to have cuddles again soon with both Niamh and Autumn

Geoff decides to cook tea early for us, we are having a Chicken Thai Lemongrass stir fry with Jasmine rice. It was delicious and full of lots of vegetables, including spinach, spring onions, chillies, ginger, red peppers, mange tout and sweet corn. We ate at 4.30 pm which was good at the time but made the night feel a lot longer and although we watched an episode of Outlander and another Cirque de Soleil performance called ZED the night stretched on interminably for us both. In the end we called it a day and went to bed with our books at 9.30 pm. The night was a restless one though with Chumley disturbing us for a toilet break and us both awake a lot during the night.

I read the latest news feeds that would fill the papers tomorrow and our local community group news on social media. I have included a few items of interest, that were available to read on the latest news feeds from last night. The words are thought provoking, with regards to the government's delay in not ensuring we were locked down much sooner. No effort was made to cease all travel to and from the UK. People are still going on holiday and returning from abroad, without being quarantined.

Extract from the Times today: - *

Coronavirus: 38 days when Britain sleepwalked into disaster.

Boris Johnson skipped five Cobra meetings on the virus, calls to order protective gear were ignored and scientists' warnings fell on deaf ears. Failings in February may have cost thousands of lives

On the third Friday of January a silent and stealthy killer was creeping across the world. Passing from person to person and borne on ships and planes, the coronavirus was already leaving a trail of bodies.

The virus had spread from China to six countries and was almost certainly in many others. Sensing the coming danger, the British government briefly went into wartime mode that day, holding a meeting of Cobra, its national crisis committee.

But it took just an hour that January 24 lunchtime to brush aside the coronavirus threat. Matt Hancock, the health secretary, bounced out of Whitehall after chairing the meeting and breezily told reporters the risk to the UK public was "low".

This was despite the publication that day of an alarming study by Chinese doctors in the medical journal, The Lancet. It assessed the lethal potential of the virus, for the first time suggesting it was comparable to the 1918 Spanish flu pandemic, which killed up to 50 million people.

Unusually, Boris Johnson had been absent from Cobra. The committee, which includes ministers, intelligence chiefs and military generals, gathers at moments of great peril such as terrorist attacks, natural disasters and other threats to the nation and is normally chaired by the prime minister.

Johnson had found time that day, however, to join in a lunar new year dragon eyes ritual, as part of Downing Street's reception for the Chinese community, led by the country's ambassador.

It was a big day for Johnson and there was a triumphal mood in Downing Street, because the withdrawal treaty from the European Union was being signed in the late afternoon. It could have been the defining moment of his premiership — but that was before the world changed.

That afternoon, his spokesman played down the looming threat from the east and reassured the nation that we were "well prepared for any new diseases". The confident, almost nonchalant, attitude displayed that day in January would continue for more than a month.

Boris Johnson went on to miss four further Cobra meetings on the virus. This was because Britain was hit by unprecedented flooding. Boris completed the EU withdrawal, reshuffled his cabinet, and then went away to the grace-and-favour country retreat at Chevening where he spent most of the two weeks over half-term with his pregnant fiancée, Carrie Symonds. It would not be until March 2 another five weeks that Johnson would attend a Cobra meeting about the coronavirus. But by then it was almost certainly too late. The virus had sneaked into our airports, our trains, our workplaces, and our homes. Britain was on course for one of the worst infections of the deadliest virus to have hit the world in more than a century.

Last week, a senior adviser to Downing Street broke ranks and blamed the weeks of complacency on a failure of leadership in cabinet. In particular, the prime minister was singled out. "There's no way you're at war if your PM isn't there," the adviser said. And what you learn about Boris was he didn't chair any meetings. He liked his country breaks. He didn't work weekends. It was like working for an old-fashioned chief executive in a local authority 20 years ago. There was a real sense that he didn't do urgent crisis planning. It was exactly like people feared he would be.

One day there will inevitably be an inquiry into the lack of preparations during those "lost" five weeks from January 24. There will be questions about when politicians understood the severity of the threat, what the scientists told them and why so little was done to equip the National Health Service for the coming crisis.

It will be the politicians who will face the most intense scrutiny.

Among the key points likely to be explored, will be why it took so long to recognise an urgent need for a massive boost in supplies of personal protective equipment (PPE) for health workers; ventilators to treat acute respiratory symptoms; and tests to detect the infection.

Any inquiry may also ask whether the government's failure to get to grips with the scale of the crisis in those early days, had the knock-on effect of the national lockdown being introduced days or even weeks too late, causing many thousands more unnecessary deaths.

An investigation has talked to scientists, academics, doctors, emergency planners, public officials and politicians about the root of the crisis and whether the government should have known sooner and acted more swiftly to kick-start the Whitehall machine and put the NHS onto a war footing.

They told us that, contrary to the official line, Britain was in a poor state of readiness for a pandemic. Emergency stockpiles of PPE had severely dwindled and gone out of date after becoming a low priority in the years of austerity cuts. The training to prepare key workers for a pandemic had been put on hold for two years, while contingency planning was diverted to deal with a possible no-deal Brexit.

This made it doubly important that the government hit the ground running in late January and early February. Scientists said the threat from the coming storm was clear. Indeed, one of the government's key advisory committees was given a dire warning a month earlier than has previously been admitted about the prospect of having to deal with mass casualties.

It was a message repeated throughout February, but the warnings appear to have fallen on deaf ears. The need, for example, to boost emergency supplies of protective masks and gowns for health workers was pressing, but little progress was made in obtaining the items from the manufacturers, mainly in China.

Instead, the government sent supplies the other way shipping 279,000 items of its depleted stockpile of protective equipment to China during this period, following a request for help from the authorities there.

The prime minister had been sunning himself with his girlfriend in the millionaires' Caribbean resort of Mustique when China first alerted the World Health Organisation (WHO) on December 31 that several cases of an unusual pneumonia had been recorded in Wuhan, a city of 11 million people in Hubei province.

In the days that followed China initially claimed the virus could not be transmitted from human to human, which should have been reassuring. But this did not ring true to Britain's public health academics and epidemiologists who were texting each other, eager for more information, in early January.

Devi Sridhar, professor of global public health at Edinburgh University, had predicted in a talk two years earlier that a virus might jump species from an animal in China and spread quickly to become a human pandemic. So, the news from Wuhan set her on high alert.

"In early January, a lot of my global health colleagues and I were kind of discussing 'What's going on?'" she recalled. "China still hadn't confirmed the virus was human-to-human. A lot of us were suspecting it was because it was a respiratory pathogen, and you wouldn't see the numbers of cases that we were seeing out of China if it was not human-to-human. So that was disturbing."

By as early as January 16 the professor was on Twitter calling for swift action to prepare for the virus. "Been asked by journalists how serious the Wuhan Pneumonia outbreak is," she wrote. "My answer: take it seriously because of cross-border spread (planes means bugs travel far & fast), likely human-to-human transmission and previous outbreaks have taught over responding is better than delaying action."

Events were now moving fast. Four hundred miles away in London, from its campus next to the Royal Albert Hall, a team at Imperial College's School of Public Health led by Professor Neil Ferguson produced its first modelling assessment of the likely impact of the virus. On Friday, January 17, its report noted the "worrying" news that three cases of the virus had been discovered outside China two in Thailand and one in Japan. While acknowledging many unknowns, researchers calculated that there could already be as many as 4,000 cases. The report warned: "The magnitude of these numbers suggests substantial human-to-human transmission cannot be ruled out. Heightened surveillance, prompt information-sharing and enhanced preparedness are recommended."

By now, the mystery bug had been identified as a type of coronavirus, a large family of viruses that can cause infections ranging from the common cold to severe acute respiratory syndrome (Sars). There had been two reported deaths from the virus and 41 patients had been taken ill.

The following Wednesday, January 22, the government convened its first meeting of its scientific advisory group for emergencies (Sage) to discuss the virus. The membership is secret, but it is usually chaired by the government's chief scientific adviser, Sir Patrick Vallance, and chief medical adviser, Professor Chris Whitty. Downing Street advisers are also present.

There were new findings that day with Chinese scientists warning that the virus had an unusually high infective rate of up to 3.0, which meant each person with the virus would typically infect up to three more people.

One of those present was Imperial's Ferguson, who was already working on his own estimate, putting infectivity at 2.6 and possibly as high as 3.5, which he sent to ministers and officials in a report on the day of the Cobra meeting on January 24. The Spanish flu had an estimated infectivity rate of between 2.0 and 3.0, so Ferguson's finding was shocking.

The professor's other bombshell in the same report was that there needed to be a 60% cut in the transmission rate, which meant stopping contact between people. In layman's terms it meant a lockdown, a move that would paralyse an economy already facing a battering from Brexit. At the time such a suggestion was unthinkable in the government and belonged to the world of post-apocalypse movies.

The growing alarm among scientists appears not to have been heard or heeded by policymakers. After the January 25 Cobra meeting, the chorus of reassurance was not just from Hancock and the prime minister's spokesman: Whitty was confident too. "Cobra met today to discuss the situation in Wuhan, China," said Whitty. "We have global experts monitoring the situation around the clock and have a strong track record of managing new forms of infectious disease, there are no confirmed cases in the UK to date."

However, by then there had been 1,000 cases worldwide and 41 deaths, mostly in Wuhan. A Lancet report that day presented a study of 41 coronavirus patients admitted to hospital in Wuhan which found that more than half had severe breathing problems, a third required intensive care and six had died.

And there was now little doubt that the UK would be hit by the virus. A study by Southampton University has shown that 190,000 people flew into the UK from Wuhan and other high-risk Chinese cities between January and March. The researchers estimated that up to 1,900 of these passengers would have been infected with the Coronavirus, almost guaranteeing the UK would become a centre of the subsequent pandemic.

Sure enough, five days later on Wednesday, January 29, the first coronavirus cases on British soil were found when two Chinese nationals from the same family fell ill at a hotel in York. The next day, the government raised the threat level from low to moderate.

On January 31 or Brexit day as it had become known — there was a rousing 11pm speech by the prime minister promising that the withdrawal from the European Union would be the dawn of a new era unleashing the British people who would "grow in confidence" month by month.

By this time, there was good reason for the government's top scientific advisers to feel creeping unease about the virus. The WHO had declared the coronavirus a global emergency just the day before and scientists at the London School of Hygiene and Tropical Medicine had confirmed to Whitty in a private meeting of the Nervtag advisory committee on respiratory illness that the virus's infectivity could be as bad as Ferguson's worst estimate several days earlier.

The official scientific advisers were willing to concede in public that there might be several cases of the coronavirus in the UK. But they had faith that the country's plans for a pandemic would prove robust. This was probably a big mistake. An adviser to Downing Street, speaking off the record, says their confidence in "the plan" was misplaced.

While a possible pandemic had been listed as the No 1 threat to the nation for many years, the source says that it had long since stopped being treated as such.

Several emergency planners and scientists said that the plans to protect the UK in a pandemic had once been a top priority and had been well-funded for a decade following the 9/11 terrorist attacks in 2001. But then austerity cuts struck. "We were the envy of the world," the source said, "but pandemic planning became a casualty of the austerity years when there were more pressing needs."

The last rehearsal for a pandemic was a 2016 exercise codenamed Cygnus which predicted the health service would collapse and highlighted a long list of shortcomings including, presciently, a lack of PPE and intensive care ventilators. But an equally lengthy list of recommendations to address the deficiencies was never implemented. The source said preparations for a no-deal Brexit "sucked all the blood out of pandemic planning" in the following years.

In the year leading up to the coronavirus outbreak key government committee meetings on pandemic planning were repeatedly "bumped" off the diary to make way for discussions about more pressing issues such as the beds crisis in the NHS. Training for NHS staff with protective equipment and respirators was also neglected, the source alleges.

Members of the government advisory group on pandemics are said to have felt powerless. "They would joke between themselves, 'Ha-ha let's hope we don't get a pandemic,' because there wasn't a single area of practice that was being nurtured in order for us to meet basic requirements for pandemic, never mind do it well," said the source. "If you were with senior NHS managers at all during the last two years, you were aware that their biggest fear, their sweatiest nightmare, was a pandemic because they weren't prepared for it."

It meant that the government had much catching up to do when it was becoming clear that this "nightmare" was becoming a distinct possibility in February. But the source says there was little urgency. "Almost every plan we had was not activated in February. Almost every government department has failed to properly implement their own pandemic plans," the source said.

One deviation from the plan, for example, was a failure to give an early warning to firms that there might be a lockdown, so they could start contingency planning. "There was a duty to get them to start thinking about their cash-flow and their business continuity arrangements," the source said.

A central part of any pandemic plan is to identify anyone who becomes ill, vigorously pursue all their recent contacts and put them into quarantine. That involves testing and the UK initially seemed to be ahead of the game. In early February Hancock proudly told the Commons the UK was one of the first countries to develop a new test for the coronavirus. "Testing worldwide is being done on equipment designed in Oxford," he said.

So, when Steve Walsh, a 53-year-old businessman from Hove, East Sussex, was identified as the source of the second UK outbreak on February 6 all his contacts were followed up with tests. Walsh's case was a warning of the rampant infectivity of the virus as he is believed to have passed it to five people in the UK after returning from a conference in Singapore as well as six overseas.

But Public Health England failed to take advantage of our early breakthroughs with tests and lost early opportunities to step up production to the levels that would later be needed.

This was in part because the government was planning for the virus using its blueprint for fighting the flu. Once a flu pandemic has found its way into the population and there is no vaccine, then the virus can take its course until "herd immunity" is acquired. Such a plan does not require mass testing.

A senior politician told this newspaper: "I had conversations with Chris Whitty at the end of January and they were absolutely focused on herd immunity. The reason is that with flu, herd immunity is the right response if you have not got a vaccine.

"All of our planning was for pandemic flu. There has basically been a divide between scientists in Asia who saw this as a horrible, deadly disease on the lines of Sars, which requires immediate lockdown, and those in the West, particularly in the US and UK, who saw this as flu."

The prime minister's special adviser Dominic Cummings is said to have had initial enthusiasm for the herd immunity concept, which may have played a part in the government's early approach to managing the virus. The Department of Health firmly denies that "herd immunity" was ever its aim and rejects suggestions that Whitty supported it. Cummings also denies backing the concept.

The failure to obtain large amounts of testing equipment was another big error of judgment, according to the Downing Street source. It would later be one of the big scandals of the coronavirus crisis that the considerable capacity of Britain's private laboratories to mass-produce tests was not harnessed during those crucial weeks of February.

"We should have communicated with every commercial testing laboratory that might volunteer to become part of the government's testing regime but that didn't happen," said the source.

The lack of action was confirmed by Doris-Ann Williams, chief executive of the British In Vitro Diagnostics Association, which represents 110 companies that make up most of the UK's testing sector. Amazingly, she says her organisation did not receive a meaningful approach from the government asking for help until April 1 — the night before Hancock bowed to pressure and announced a belated and ambitious target of 100,000 tests a day by the end of this month.

There was also a failure to replenish supplies of gowns and masks for health and care workers in the early weeks of February despite NHS England declaring the virus its first "level four critical incident" at the end of January.

It was a key part of the pandemic plan the NHS's Operating Framework for Managing the Response to Pandemic Influenza dated December 2017 — that the NHS would be able to draw on "just in case" stockpiles of PPE. But many of the "just in case" stockpiles had dwindled, and equipment was out of date. As not enough money was being spent on replenishing stockpiles, this shortfall was supposed to be filled by activating "just in time" contracts which had been arranged with equipment suppliers in recent years to deal with an emergency. The first order for equipment under the "just in time" protocol was made on January 30.

However, the source said that attempts to call in these "just in time" contracts immediately ran into difficulties in February because they were mostly with Chinese manufacturers who were facing unprecedented demand from the country's own health service and elsewhere.

This was another nail in the coffin for the pandemic plan. "It was a massive spider's web of failing, every domino has fallen," said the source.

The NHS could have contacted UK-based suppliers. The British Healthcare Trades Association (BHTA) was ready to help supply PPE in February and throughout March, but it was only on April 1 that its offer of help was accepted. Dr Simon Festing, the organisation's chief executive, said: "Orders undoubtedly went overseas instead of to the NHS because of the missed opportunities in the procurement process."

Downing Street admitted on February 24 just five days before NHS chiefs warned a lack of PPE left the health service facing a 'nightmare' that the UK government had supplied 1,800 pairs of goggles and 43,000 disposable gloves, 194,000 sanitising wipes, 37,500 medical gowns and 2,500 face masks to China.

A senior department of health insider described the sense of drift witnessed during those crucial weeks in February: "We missed the boat on testing and PPE. I remember being called into some of the meetings about this in February and thinking, 'Well it's a good thing this isn't the big one.'

I had watched Wuhan, but I assumed we must have not been worried because we did nothing.

We just watched. A pandemic was always at the top of our national risk register always, but when it came, we just slowly watched. We could have been Germany but instead we were doomed by our incompetence, our hubris and our austerity."

In the Far East, the threat was being treated more seriously in the early weeks of February. Martin Hibberd, a professor of emerging infectious diseases at the London School of Hygiene and Tropical Medicine, was in a unique position to compare the UK's response with Singapore, where he had advised in the past. "Singapore realised, as soon as Wuhan reported it, that cases were going to turn up in Singapore. And so, they prepared for that. I looked at the UK and I can see a different strategy and approach.

"The interesting thing for me is, I've worked with Singapore in 2003 and 2009 and basically they copied the UK pandemic preparedness plan. But the difference is they actually implemented it."

Towards the end of the second week of February, the prime minister was demob happy. After sacking five cabinet ministers and saying everyone "should be confident and calm" about Britain's response to the virus, Johnson vacated Downing Street after the half-term recess began on February 13.

He headed to the country for a "working" holiday at Chevening with Symonds and would be out of the public eye for 12 days. His aides were thankful for the rest, as they had been working flat out since the summer as the Brexit power struggle had played out.

The Sunday newspapers that weekend would not have made comfortable reading. The Sunday Times reported on a briefing from a risk specialist which said that Public Health England would be overrun during a pandemic as it could test only 1,000 people a day.

Johnson may well have been distracted by matters in his personal life during his stay in the countryside. Aides were told to keep their briefing papers short and cut the number of memos in his red box if they wanted them to be read. His family needed to be prepared for the announcement that Symonds, who turned 32 in March, was pregnant and that they had been secretly engaged for some time. Relations with his children had been fraught since his separation from his estranged wife Marina Wheeler and the rift deepened when she had been diagnosed with cancer last year.

The divorce also had to be finalised. Midway through the break it was announced in the High Court that the couple had reached a settlement, leaving Wheeler free to apply for divorce.

There were murmurings of frustration from some ministers and their aides at the time that Johnson was not taking more of a lead. But Johnson's aides are understood to have felt relaxed: he was getting updates and they claim the scientists were saying everything was under control. By the time Johnson departed for the countryside, however, there was mounting unease among scientists about the exceptional nature of the threat. Sir Jeremy Farrar, an infectious disease specialist who is a key government adviser, made this clear in a recent BBC interview. "I think from the early days in February, if not in late January, it was obvious this infection was going to be very serious and it was going to affect more than just the region of Asia ," he said. "I think it was very clear that this was going to be an unprecedented event."

By February 21, the virus had already infected 76,000 people, had caused 2,300 deaths in China, and was taking a foothold in Europe with Italy recording 51 cases and two deaths the following day. Nonetheless Nervtag, one of the key government advisory committees, decided to keep the threat level at "moderate".

Its members may well regret that decision with hindsight, and it was certainly not unanimous. John Edmunds, one of the country's top infectious disease modellers from the London School of Hygiene and Tropical Medicine, was participating in the meeting by video link but his technology failed him at the crucial moment.

Edmunds wanted the threat level to be increased to high but could not make his view known as the link was glitchy. He sent an email later making his view clear. "JE believes that the risk to the UK population [in the PHE risk assessment] should be high, as there is evidence of ongoing transmission in Korea, Japan and Singapore, as well as in China," the meeting's minutes state. But the decision had already been taken.

Peter Openshaw, professor of experimental medicine at Imperial College, was in America at the time of the meeting but would also have recommended increasing the threat to high. Three days earlier he had given an address to a seminar in which he estimated that 60% of the world's population would probably become infected if no action was taken and 400,000 people would die in the UK.

By February 26, there were 13 known cases in the UK. That day, almost four weeks before a full lockdown would be announced, ministers were warned through another advisory committee that the country was facing a catastrophic loss of life unless drastic action was taken. Having been thwarted from sounding the alarm, Edmunds and his team presented their latest "worst scenario" predictions to the scientific pandemic influenza group on modelling

(SPI-M) which directly advises the country's scientific decision-makers on Sage.

It warned that 27 million people could be infected, and 220,000 intensive care beds would be needed if no action were taken to reduce infection rates. The predicted death toll was 380,000. Edmund's colleague Nick Davies, who led the research, says the report emphasised the urgent need for a lockdown almost four weeks before it was imposed.

The team modelled the effects of a 12-week lockdown involving school and work closures, shielding the elderly, social distancing, and self-isolation. It estimated this would delay the impact of the pandemic but there still might be 280,000 deaths over the year.

The previous night Johnson had returned to London for the Conservatives' big fundraising ball, the Winter Party, at which one donor pledged £60,000 for the privilege of playing a game of tennis with him.

By this time, the prime minister had missed five Cobra meetings on the preparations to combat the looming pandemic, which he left to be chaired by Hancock. Johnson was an easy target for the opposition when he returned to the Commons the following day with the Labour leader, Jeremy Corbyn, labelling him a "part-time" prime minister for his failure to lead on the virus crisis or visit the areas of the UK badly hit by floods.

By Friday, February 28, the virus had taken root in the UK with reported cases rising to 19 and the stock markets were plunging. It was finally time for Johnson to act. He summoned a TV reporter into Downing Street to say he was on top of the coronavirus crisis.

"The issue of Coronavirus is something that is now the government's top priority," he said. "I have just had a meeting with the chief medical officer and secretary of state for health talking about the preparations that we need to make."

It was finally announced that he would be attending a meeting of Cobra, after a weekend at Chequers with Symonds where the couple would publicly release news of the engagement and their baby.

On the Sunday, there was a meeting between Sage committee members and officials from the Department of Health and NHS which was a game changer, according to a Whitehall source. The meeting was shown fresh modelling based on figures from Italy suggesting that 8% of infected people might need hospital treatment in a worst-case scenario. The previous estimate had been 4%-5%.

"The risk to the NHS had effectively doubled in an instant. It set alarm bells ringing across government," said the Whitehall source. "I think that meeting focused minds. You realise it's time to pull the trigger on the starting gun."

At the Cobra meeting the next day with Johnson in the chair a full "battle plan" was finally signed off to contain, delay and mitigate the spread of the virus. This was on March 2nd, five weeks after the first Cobra meeting on the virus.

The new push would have some positive benefits such as the creation of new Nightingale hospitals, which greatly increased the number of intensive care beds. But there was a further delay that month of nine days in introducing the lockdown as Johnson and his senior advisers debated what measures were required. Later the government would be left rudderless again after Johnson himself contracted the virus.

As the number of infections grew daily, some things were impossible to retrieve. There was a worldwide shortage of PPE, and the prime minister would have to personally ring manufacturers of ventilators and testing kits in a desperate effort to boost supplies.

The result was that the NHS and care home workers would be left without proper protection and insufficient numbers of tests to find out whether they had been infected. To date 50 doctors, nurses and NHS workers have died. More than 100,000 people have been confirmed as infected in Britain and 15,000 have died.

A Downing Street spokesman said: "Our response has ensured that the NHS has been given all the support it needs to ensure everyone requiring treatment has received it, as well as providing protection to businesses and reassurance to workers.

The prime minister has been at the helm of the response to this, providing leadership during this hugely challenging period for the whole nation."

Article reproduced under licence from the Times Newspaper Group

A harrowing local story from our Castle and Winnington Community Group:-

"A Harsh Reality"*

Imagine, you are at home with your partner and two young children. You're all young and healthy with decent jobs, a loving home and you both drive a nice car. You've mostly been socially isolating, apart from going to the supermarkets. The queues are still long, and you hear someone coughing in front of you, but you only think about it for a minute but dismiss it as a bit of the old "Covid paranoia".

However, you see that same person a couple of times in the supermarket and think to yourself "they look a bit sweaty" but again you don't really register it. As you pass, you smile nicely at each other, being careful to observe the social distancing guidelines.

You go and pick up your essentials, which includes the pack of pasta that the previous person picked up... but then decided against as they already have enough... so they put it back on the shelf.

You go back to your car, unload the shopping and drive home, briefly thinking how nice that traffic is calm. When you get home, you put the shopping away, read a text and then wash your hands afterwards.

A few days pass and all is going well... but you suddenly notice everyone in the house feeling achy with sore throats. Overnight, your partner takes a turn for the worse, so they go and sleep in the spare room.

All the while, you can hear continuous dry coughing throughout the house.

In the morning, your children are rough and snuggled on the sofa, but your partner hasn't come downstairs, so you head up to see if they want a cup of tea. As you reach the door you feel a strange sense of foreboding, and, as you open it you're met with a horrible rasping noise - your partner - shallow breathing, pale, sweaty and trying to mouth words at you but clearly struggling...

You panic. You're somewhere between not wanting to disturb the Emergency Services as they're so busy and almost feeling embarrassed to call them - but you have no choice and dial 999 for the first time in your life. The call taker is calm and advises you that help is being arranged, but they are extremely busy so someone will be there as soon as they can. They tell you that in the meantime, if anything changes, ring them back - and then they're gone.

After almost two hours you're even more worried and not knowing what else to do, you call back, only to be given the same reassurance. Almost twenty minutes later, a huge wave of relief floods over you as the crew pull up outside, but after minutes go by, you wonder where they are, and what they're possibly doing? You look out the window to see that the ambulance is still outside, and the crew are putting on PPE which takes several vital minutes to do... and then only one crew member walks in. This seems odd but you take the first crew member upstairs.

Thankfully, they're calm and friendly - but once they walk into the bedroom, they see your partner and radio the second crew member straight away requesting their assistance.

They carry out some basic checks, and the atmosphere has changed from friendly and relaxed to a sense of urgency; professionalism has kicked in and everything is done quickly and precisely. They explain that your partner is going to hospital - urgently so they begin getting ready for the extrication to the truck. Whilst they do that you organise your older child to look after the younger child. You get your shoes, jacket and phone and wait by the door as the crew bring your partner of eighteen years - your high school love - down the stairs. The crew pause, briefly, by the door and give you a pained look. They explain that they are sadly unable to take relatives with them as you wouldn't be allowed into the hospital.

You're confused, overwhelmed and struck with a feeling of grief and helplessness. As you see you partner loaded into the back of an ambulance, you feel yourself start to shake, and try as you might, you're suddenly overcome with long, racking sobs. You do not know it, but this is the last time you see your partner. This is goodbye. The funeral is held just over a week later, but as your remaining family still have symptoms, you are not allowed to attend. This is the incredibly sad and harsh reality of what is currently happening in the UK and around the world. There is no excuse. We are still on an upwards curve. Please stay at home, or this could be your story.

Article reproduced by kind permission of the group administrator

- **Stay at Home**
- **Protect The NHS**
- **Save Lives**

Sunday 19th April 2020

Woke up this morning to beautiful deep blue skies and sunshine. It is a bit cold outside yet, but it does promise to be a lovely day and hopefully, on our patio the sunshine will be warm as it is a sheltered area.

Today would have been the 61st birthday of my brother Derek who died 4 years ago from lung cancer. I will visit his grave later today when I take Chumley out on his afternoon walk.

Later today, we are going to enjoy a roast lamb lunch with plenty of vegetables and potatoes sprinkled with fresh rosemary from the garden herbs.

I have some home-made sticky toffee pudding in the freezer too for desert with Cornish ice-cream and raspberries.

I place an order for a small wooden Grimm's rainbow arch from a company called Natural Baby Shower and arrange delivery of this by Royal Mail, direct to Niamh our granddaughter.

This gift is something she can play with now and will be able to keep as a reminder of this time in her life and ours, where rainbows appeared in all windows coloured and produced by all the children of this world as a message of love and hope. Autumn made us one and it is in our front bedroom window. I have always loved rainbows and the song about a rainbow too. I often use it to help others going through stormy difficult times as there is always a rainbow in the sky after heavy rain and whenever I see one, they simply take my breath away.

I remember taking Autumn to music makers in Carlisle every Thursday afternoon and we used to dance and sing to the song " I can sing a Rainbow" waving floaty coloured scarves around in time to the music and words. Happy rainbow days.

We enjoy pottering around outside and checking on the seedlings in our greenhouse. Geoff is busy preparing the ground for his runner beans to be planted.

I chat on WhatsApp to Geoff's sister Chris and see how they are all doing and especially Becky who is poorly with the coronavirus and just waiting for confirmation from the swab results. Becky is recovering slowly, and we have all our fingers and toes crossed for her.

Today goes very quickly and the afternoon did become much warmer. It was just lovely to eat our evening meal outside with a glass of wine too. It made the night a lot shorter by the time we had washed up and put everything away.

We watched the programme screened live on Saturday night called 'One world together at home' Many musical artists had recorded songs and messages for all the NHS staff from their own homes. Some of the recordings were good and others were poorly recorded making the songs difficult to listen to without all the usual background instruments, but it was an amazing tear-jerking experience to watch.

The programme also showed us lots of heroes working out there and sacrificing their lives for others on a daily basis. One family needed the 9-year-old daughter to look after her dad who is on kidney dialysis due to the mum being a full-time nurse, it was a very poignant story, and the programme presenters organised a meet up with her family and some actors popped into the online chat too.

It was very emotional watching the scenes played out all round the country of everyone working tirelessly with good humour and such amazing positive attitudes.

A lot of the celebrities showed us what they were doing in lockdown with their families. At the end of the programme a lot of young children asked questions of a medical doctor, and some were very sensible questions about the corona virus. One little girl of 5 years old asked if it was safe for children to still hug their mummies and daddies bless her cotton socks.

9.00 pm arrived and time to watch the family saga Belgravia which finishes tonight, then bedtime once more.

A few WhatsApp messages from school friends

Hi all, back home again! So sorry Eileen & Jude, that you had a bad night. I think we can all empathise as well as sympathise. The only compensation is that you will hopefully have a wonderful deep sleep tonight as your body catches up. Look after yourselves today. There is nothing that needs doing that will not wait a bit. We only do a couple of miles Norma, so we are only going around and through the village at the moment, building up our strength for longer rides in the coming weeks. It was lovely to greet and chat to complete strangers. Long may that continue! Take it easy dear friends. Thinking of you all ♥xxxx

It was lovely to see you and Charlie this afternoon on my walk Elizabeth. Meeting you both made me feel human again, to be able to see someone in passing that is real and so lovely too!!

That explains the Police presence then down the river this afternoon and across Roker park where I walked before Verdin Park! I do hope they find the lady who has gone missing.

Walked through ghost town Northwich too, which was totally empty of human life, bizarre and unreal.

Please forward the name of your plumber too as I want a tap like that with wine pouring out!!

Morning ladies just spent a couple of hours reading The Daily Mail the columnists are having a right go at the Government for reacting so slowly to Covid 19, the lack of PPE and the lack of care for staff and residents in care homes. I have just caught up with all yours messages and jokes. Thanks so much cheered me up no end friends xxx

Loving the funnies ladies! I'll have to have some sewing lessons off you crafty lot when we're back to normal. I have bought some patterns and material to make the girls some dresses etc. but do not want to risk starting them without the girls being able to try them for size. PS just put the heating back on! xx

Hi Sue! Great to see you again! Would recognise you anywhere. Looking fab my friend! This is not just a friendship group, but a great support group too! Welcome home xx

Morning everyone! Just stopped sobbing over Mr Tom and seeing all the messages that the elderly in care homes were holding up for their families to see. It broke my heart. Still, we all need to focus on being positive so enjoy a beautiful day my friends, whatever your planning to do. Much love. xxx

Morning Jude and everyone. It looks like it is going to be a lovely sunshiny day outside. We are hoping to prick a few plants out that we are growing from seed.

Geoff just read that garden centres might open soon in a 'one in one out system' like the supermarkets.

Monday 20th April 2020

We enjoyed opening the curtains this morning and seeing the start of another sunny day outside and gave our thanks for being alive and safe still at home and for all our family and friends too. We enjoyed another leisurely breakfast of cereals, cornflakes and hot milk for Geoff, a dish of bran flakes topped with raspberries, blueberries, grapes and banana, hmm delicious. Geoff tells me that my breakfast looks very fruity today. I tend to vary between enjoying a bowl of porridge with honey, most days, to help my cholesterol problem, but if there is lots of fresh fruit in the fridge, I do enjoy my bran flakes.

After breakfast Geoff decided to work outside and asked me to help him to empty all our pots and troughs of the daffodils and tulips that have finished flowering now and need to be stored for Autumn, once the leaves have died back leaving just the bulbs.

Before I head outside though I do some research for buying on-line dress fabric to make Autumn a summer dress. If it is successful, I will make Niamh one too. I find an on-line fabric shop in Neston called Calico Laine who have some gorgeous children's fabrics and I order 3 metres of a Disney design with lots of Princesses and words like dreamer, friends, voice, spirit on which appeals to me, and I just know that Autumn will love it too. I add some interfacing and cotton to my order and the final bill is £35 which is a lot of money.

However, I feel it is worth it to create something different rather than the usual shop bought dresses that are much cheaper, but then everyone has the same dresses, especially if bought from all the major supermarkets, Asda, Sainsbury's, Morison's, Primark, Joules, Next, Matalan. These stores provide mass produced cheap dresses that are gorgeous, but not as special as a one-off dress created by Nana. Having said that, I am a bit nervous of making a mess of the task ahead. The cost of one handmade dress could have gone towards at least 3 or more summer dresses from the above-mentioned shops. Nonetheless, I am determined to enjoy the challenge and re-learn my sewing skills as a dressmaker.

After I have placed my order and paid for it with Pay Pal. I decide to write a few more lines in this project, before I know it, the time has flown by with the clock showing 10.30 am. I hear Geoff come in to make a hot drink and I shout "hello", but he doesn't answer. I go and find him in the kitchen and have a hug. He wonders why I have not joined him outside yet as he has brought a few of the pots onto the lawn to start emptying them and it is a slow laborious process.

I tell him that I am coming out now and will stop writing for a while. It is so sunny outside in the garden and I do not want to be inside and had agreed to help with the task after breakfast. However, once I start writing, I do find it hard to stop!!

We enjoy working together and it is an easy task albeit a long one to shake all the compost soil off from the individual plants and then search out any bulbs inside the compost soil that is now filling the wheelbarrow to the top, before we bag it up for using in the garden borders.

The time passes very quickly in sorting out the bulbs and all the leafy stems with bulbs on into a tidy order inside a polystyrene box. Finally, by 12.30 pm we have done the job together, we feel quite proud of ourselves, as we carry the box of bulbs and leaves waiting to die back into the shed for safe storage over summer. They will stay there until it is time to replant them again in the autumn season, around late September early October.

I head indoors to make us both salad sandwich for lunch with a few crisps.

After lunch, I decide to take Chumley for a long walk up the River Weaver just at the back of us, but instead of going up on our side of the river, where Chumley loves to swim, I will cross the locks and the bridge and walk up past the boatyard and along a path overlooking woodland which we call the ridge.

It is a beautiful afternoon. I meet a few people but all of us without exception, give the utmost respect to each other and stand back in the grassy areas of the walk or wait in other spaces whenever someone is heading into our own pathways. I think this courtesy will continue long after the dangerous days that we are living through.

I reach the top of the ridge near the Blue Bridge that spans the River Weaver and decide not to head over the bridge and down the other side of the river, as I know that Chumley will want to swim, and he wasn't well last week after swimming in the river which may be too full of debris and little bugs for his stomach in this hot weather. So, we head down back the way we come and all the way back.

I am rewarded with the most crystal-clear views of the river and surrounding banks bathed in a beauty that is simply breath-taking for its sharp clarity of everything I see with my eyes, the world around me bathed in sunlight and the sky above so blue that the muddy river has also turned blue.

I stop and take a few snaps on my camera to show Geoff when I get home. I reflect deeply about the blue, as this is the colour being used for the NHS and it is like a gift from heaven above that makes me reflect on just how beautiful today is. I think about how amazing our NHS is for saving thousands of lives, caring for thousands of people dying, with so much love given to all the patients by the doctors and nurses. I feel humble that I am walking in this world of blueness and sunshine being protected by everyone working flat around the clocks 24/7. It fills me with hope for all our futures to return safely. We eat tea early as I have a ZOOM meeting with my writing group scheduled for 6.30 pm UK time, our host and chairperson Bob is in Paphos where he and his lovely wife Carol have been since the 9th March, 2020 and are unable to return home as all flights have been cancelled. They had a scheduled flight booked for the 2nd May but that has now been withdrawn too. They are not sure if they will be home in the summer or will remain at their home in Cyprus until September.

Cyprus is in the same lockdown as the rest of the world, but their measures went into place much earlier and with stricter conditions where a curfew has been imposed from 9.00 pm to 6.00 am with no-one being allowed to go outside their own home. During the day, all essential travel and exercise has to have a legally signed document stating where they are going and for what purpose? If this document and/or valid reasons are not shown on the form, it is an on the spot fine of £150 euros. To date, Cyprus has a small number of deaths recorded as 10.

Our ZOOM meeting goes well, there are 16 of us interacting and catching up with each other discovering what we are all doing to fill the days of lockdown. After listening to each of us, we all agree that we have never been busier and that the days are flying by very quickly as we busy ourselves with lots of projects or try new skills out.

We are all missing our family and friends but have accepted that this is how it has to be and feel blessed that we are all safe. Five of us read a piece of work out to the group.

Three of us have pieces about COVID-19, mine is a page from my own chronicles that I am writing daily here on these pages, one is a short evocative poem of imagery from David Varley, one is a story about a holdall bag from Shauna Leishman that departs from its owner to go into service to helping the hospital, the other prose is a lively futuristic piece about having a MOGL as your personal friend at home which is loved very much at first until it becomes more skilled than its owner who decides to switch it off, fabulous performance piece written and read by Liz Sandbach.

The 5th piece of work was by David Bruce and was excellent too. My piece of work was praised for its uplifting positivity, and I enjoyed all the other readings too. My mobile phone started ringing before the end of the meeting, so I had to leave the meeting. The call was from my friend Elizabeth Ostapski letting me know that my cousin Alan Johnson in NZ has had an MI and is in hospital having stents put in. He was admitted last Thursday. We only spoke to Alan and his wife Joyce on Facetime on Easter Monday, and it is upsetting to hear such news about Alan.

We stayed with Alan and Joyce on an adventure trip to NZ in 2013 when we toured both the North and South Islands. We visited NZ in 2009 but it was a flying trip of just 10 days in which we packed a lot in and drove 3000 miles in total but had always wanted to return and see more of the North Island too. Alan and Joyce showed us a lot of places in the North Island and took us down to Cathedral Rock which is just beautiful. We have always promised to go back one day, but that may be unlikely now and given the current climate we are all living in. We pray for Alan's speedy recovery. I telephone my sister Irene to tell her about Alan, as she is awfully close to him and fond of him as they grew up together.

The night sky is so beautiful tonight. I head outside with Geoff for Chumley's last toilet break before bed to see the beautiful stars along with the satellite station flying just overhead of us too.

Tuesday 21st April 2020

This morning after Chumley's first walk of the day is over and we have eaten our breakfast. Geoff heads outside, to sand the decking fences, ready for repainting. Geoff had been able to obtain some sandpaper from Screwfix in Northwich, who are allowing some items to be purchased on-line, with a strict collection time slot.

I put some washing into the machine and then write up the rest of yesterday's events into this chronicle. I glance at the clock and see that it is already 10.30a.m. I started writing one and a half hours ago. I notice Geoff passing by the window and heading inside.

I shout 'hello' to him, but instead of answering me whilst my fingers are busy continuing to bash the keyboard, he arrives in the study with a hot cup of coffee for me, which was much appreciated. I tell him that I will be coming outside to help in a few minutes.

I finish my work, reply to an email from Bob in Cyprus about his book review.

Geoff taps the window and asks me to help him move some of the garden furniture off the decking so that he can sand the balustrades down, I go out and help with this task and then hang my washing out to dry. It is nearly lunchtime, so I head inside to make us a sandwich for lunch with some fruit for after.

I take Chumley down the river on our side of the paths at the back of the boatyard and head up towards the woods near Marshalls Arm where there are some steep steps leading to wooden walkways and wooden bridges. It is a delightful walk; the area is full of gorgeous Bluebells just nodding their heads in the gentle breeze. The shrubbery all around us is that gorgeous new spring green as tiny buds and leaves unfurl themselves. Chumley and I enjoy a leisurely walk along the woodland paths which climb through the trees and lead to Hartford eventually. It is a good 3 miles walk and we have a lot of fun climbing up the paths and crossing the bridges.

We met a couple of cyclists, a family with children and a couple of dog walkers. On each occasion we were able to stand aside and let people pass us well within the recommended social distance of at 2 metres. Most of the time we were a good 3 to 4 metres apart at the various passing points of our walk.

We head home after 45 minutes and go through a higher woodland section where unfortunately, I tripped over a tree root and landed hard on my right hip and knee, using my hands to save as much of the fall as I could. I feel a bit shaky but dust myself down, carry on the walk and head down the other side of the woods for home, via some steep steps, which take me a while to descend down, due to the pain in my hip and leg.

We arrive home and I head inside to make Geoff a drink, as he is busy painting the decking balustrades and hoovering all the debris up from around the bottom shed.

Just as I am about to go inside, my phone rings and it is my granddaughter Autumn on the screen excitedly chatting about going on holiday and at the same time her mummy is asking where Granddad Geoff is?

Autumn had been dreaming about Santa during the night and had woke up this morning wanting to see and speak to Granddad Geoff. Sarah told us that she often goes into our bedroom at their home and looks out of the window for us to arrive in our car like we used to do a few weeks ago before lockdown. I chat to both Autumn and Sarah whilst I go and find Geoff to give him the phone.

Autumn tells me all about her holiday, "how she has been packing her suitcase this morning herself, getting her passport out, but that the photo inside it, is of her when she was a baby and now, she looks nothing like that, as she is a girl of 4 years old now!!! Autumn says Nana look how I put Annabelle dolly inside my trunk. Did you know that you can either push the trunk case, or sit on it and ride it?"

Autumn has a small compact mirror that she shows to me on the phone screen, it is one that I gave her a couple of years ago when a beautician gave me two at the time, when I was buying some make-up

Autumn showed me her lip gloss which she is just putting on, as they are getting ready to go to Bedrid now and mummy has a map so that they know where they are going. They have just finished their mocktails at the airport and are looking forward to a glass of wine each on the plane.

I loved every minute of chatting to Autumn; it was just like she was with us in the garden.

I pass the phone to Grandad Geoff who continues to chat to Autumn, and she tells him that she has put a small chocolate egg in his drawer for him ready for when we next visit and one for Nana too. They chat and talk happily for the next hour, whilst I smile with happiness and leave them to talk in their own language and special bond with each other. Autumn mimics me when it is time to say goodbye, she waves lots and keeps saying "bye, bye".

Tonight, is on-line Zumba again which is great fun. After I finish my Zumba Class, Geoff and I watch the film My Mother's Son. We also go outside to see the meteorological show of stars tonight where apparently, we will see lots of shooting stars until early sunrise at 5.00 am in the morning. We do see a couple of them before bedtime.

Geoff goes to bed before me tonight, as I want to complete today's notes for this chronicle. It is 11.30 pm before I head upstairs to bed. Geoff is already fast asleep. I undress quickly without disturbing him and snuggle down for the night. However, my Fitbit watch will not synchronise with my mobile phone data, so I stay awake for another 30 minutes trying to fix the problem, so that I can set the sleep mode application to tell me how little sleep I am having each night!! I would be better leaving it off, but I am quite paranoid about checking my sleep patterns, as much as I check my daily exercise and blood pressure. The joys of owning a Fitbit watch!!!

Wednesday 22nd April 2020

I discover on waking up that I have only actually had 4 hours sleep in total which is not a good achievement at all. I resolve to improve today and go to bed more relaxed.

Geoff is out with Chumley early and so I catch up with the latest news and messages received from yesterday.

When Geoff returns, he is not happy as he was a bit later going out. He said that he met too many people, couples were out early and there seemed to be lots of people to keep dodging into the long grass to maintain the social distance from.

As a result, he ended up with very wet feet and so did Chumley too. He found the river walk quite wet and muddy in places this morning and poor Chumley needed a quick hose down before breakfast.

Whilst Geoff goes for a shower, I busy myself making us some poached eggs on toast and a refreshing glass of fresh orange to drink. We eat breakfast outside which is just wonderful. The day promises to be a warm sunny one. We decide to spend the first part of our day tidying up the Cherry Blossom confetti, before chilling out with a good book to read.

I make some chocolate brownies which turn out ok, but they are not my best results. I struggled with the mixture of castor sugar and butter this morning; it was all too solid. I try using my hand mixer to beat it all up together which worked, but the finished brownies are not as sticky and crunchy as I usually make. I used some extraordinarily strong 100% dark chocolate that Geoff didn't like from his Easter chocolate gifts which has probably not helped to make the brownie cake mixture as smooth as it should be.

I take some books back to Elizabeth and some buttons for a lady who is making masks using her crochet work and needs the buttons to be able to fasten them behind the ears.

Geoff and I enjoy a coffee and a piece of my brownie cake outside. We relax and just potter around the garden this morning.

Lunch is chicken goujons with a salad and afterwards a satsuma each. It is starting to get very hot, so I take Chumley for his afternoon walk before it becomes too unbearably hot for the pads of his paws.

He knows that the route I follow. will lead to his favourite swimming spot, it is so warm. I throw his ball into the river, and he performs his full belly splash into the water to retrieve the ball, then enjoys a lot of swimming this afternoon.

I wish I could jump in with him as it looks so cool and refreshing, but I don't fancy swallowing all that sandy water containing little fishes, possibly maggots from the fishermen along with duck and swan poo ugh!!!! Fortunately, Chumley always keeps his tennis ball firmly inside his mouth and doesn't swim open mouthed at all, not like I might do!!

Chumley has another hose down with fresh water after we return home, that is his second one of the day, he was so wet and muddy this morning that Geoff hosed him down after his first walk of the day

Geoff and I open a bottle of wine, catch up on messages and sit and relax in the garden before cooking tea which Geoff has prepared and is a Coq u Vin chicken dish with homemade spicy wedges.

Sarah sends us some photos of Autumn making raspberry buns, which look amazing as does Autumn's concentration in making them!!

I have clipped my hair back today, using one of Autumn's slides and Geoff takes a photo of me which we post to Sarah, to show Autumn what her daft Nana looks like today.

Thursday 23rd April 2020

I take my little red Mx5 for its first drive out today, to Asda for the weekly food shopping. There were queues outside Aldi and Sainsbury's, but Asda only had 4 people queuing and it did not take long to be allowed inside the shop. Customers have to follow the stringent guidance and clearly marked system for going up and down the aisles, without meeting other people, like in a one-way street system that flows in one direction.

We enjoyed a delicious fruit hot cross bun from Easter today, with our coffee and tea outside in the garden. Lunch was eating a whole fruit loaf!

I took Chumley for a short walk across Roker Park, where he could paddle in the river there as it was incredibly hot today.

Tea is a delicious salmon pasta eaten outside on our little bistro table for two.

My fabric arrived today, I am so excited it is a variety of princesses against a background of words for each of the characters, like Dreamer, Friend, Voices,

Spirit. I am going to make a summer dress for Autumn from the fabric.

No sign of the parcels arriving for the children though, that I organised to be delivered last Saturday and Sunday for Autumn and Niamh. It does take a lot longer to receive post, as there is a reduced service. Hopefully, the parcels will arrive soon.

Clapping the NHS takes place again at 8.00 pm and we enjoy the chance to shout across to all our neighbours and check that they are all doing ok.

I remind everyone that next week, we need to be outside 2 minutes earlier to sing Happy Birthday to Captain Tom who has now reached £29 million pounds for the NHS from simply walking 100 laps around his garden. Bless his cotton socks.

We take Chumley for a longer walk now it is cooler and complete the Roker Park walk. We saw the colour of the sky turn from bright orange red to the most beautiful pink and blue colours again, so magical, wonderful to see and enjoy.

We sit outside until quite late tonight with a glass of wine each, toasted the stars and all our loved ones, in this stillness of the star-spangled night.

Jokes and videos continue to arrive all day and night long to my phone. Strange how it is the women who are sending all the jokes and funny stories.

We have just swapped our weekly coffee and craft times with each other for virtual chat. It is all good fun, supportive and there are amazing stories coming through from each other about how we are helping not just each other, but the community as well in the smallest of our daily actions taken, such as looking out for neighbours, giving them small gifts, like cakes or flowers, or just chatting across 2 metres to check that they are ok.

WhatsApp with friends continues constantly. We have never spent as many hours together in

Lockdown, or have we? As often our coffee and cake meet-ups do last a whole morning or afternoon over several hours.

I telephone Cathy and chat to her for an hour, which was good to do today for a change, rather than just texting each other.

Geoff's sister is doing ok after being quite poorly with a stomach bug and Becky is pulling through too from contracting the virus.

Friday 24th April 2020

Geoff and I are up early again this morning, we take Chumley out for his first walk of the day at 6.00 am. After our return, we enjoy a quick breakfast together, then we check our finances and pay some bills including my car tax.

Our food bill is more excessive in March and April than Jan and Feb. We wonder why?

Fuel and eating out is reduced to zero and the difference just transferred into food costs, which are exceptionally high in all supermarkets and shops.

However, we are eating a lot more extra food and drinking a lot more wine!! All that we have done is moved our weekly fuel bill and eating out, whilst on our travels to Cumbria, into the weekly food bill by treating ourselves to lots more wine, beer, chocolate and other yummy foods, to eat seven days and seven nights of each week.

7.30 am and I am off out with a card and some cake for a friend's birthday to leave it on her doorstep. Traffic is very quiet; the roads are almost empty.

I called at the local butchers at 8.00 am to collect some chicken fillets and thighs, along with some lamb and mint burgers for a BBQ later the first one in 2 years, but with temperatures peaking at 33c a BBQ will be perfect. Last year it rained so much, whenever either of us mentioned a BBQ!

By 8.30 am, I am in Waitrose collecting our fruit and vegetables. I arrive home before 9.00 am with all the shopping done safely.

Geoff has been to B&Q this morning, which opened for the first time in over 6 weeks today. He found it intimidating and he could not obtain what he needed to continue with our decking repainting or the canes for his runner bean plants. Despite customers being allowed in one at a time, 30 customers in the store were all pushing their way along the aisles with trolleys, only giving 18 inches gaps in between each other, which was far too close.

Lunch is a delicious salmon salad sandwich with homemade salsa for me with mango, spring onions, red and green peppers, lime juice and fresh coriander.

I take Chumley out for a walk and as it is hot, he goes in the river for his ball and enjoys a lot of swimming, so wish I could join him.

It is far too hot to work outside, so Geoff and I read a book and enjoy relaxing on the decking and just chilling out for a change.

We receive a message from Sarah to say that the present we arranged for Autumn last Saturday has just arrived for her and she was thrilled to receive a parcel addressed to her and wondered what it was?

We light the BBQ at 5.00 pm and enjoy the smell of the BBQ and the burgers are just delicious served with fried onions, mangetout and sweetcorn sprinkled with sesame seeds, simple food and simple pleasures along with a glass of rose wine for me and a beer for Geoff.

Just as we had finished washing up, Geoff's sister rang with some heart-breaking news that her consultant had telephoned today, to tell her that she has cancer in one of her kidneys and a small stone in the other one. We are devastated and Geoff was lost for words when talking to Chris, he broke down several times after talking to her about what she faces in the next few weeks.

Chris tells us that she will have an operation to remove her kidney and hopefully avoid the cancer spreading further into her system. We are both lost for words and feel so helpless tonight. We are both finding it hard not to be able to rush over there and see them, more importantly not to be able to help them, because of the requirements of Lockdown conditions preventing us.

We pledge our help in any way possible to Chris and to Becky her daughter who has just come through 3 weeks of potential Coronavirus illness herself. We telephone our children to tell them the news about their Auntie Chris. We chat to them about what we can do as a family, to help to support them through the next few weeks. We agree to keep in touch by talking to each other and to Chris herself.

It is 20 years to the date that Christine had breast cancer and underwent a total mastectomy, followed by reconstructive surgery a year later. Life throws some cruel crosses to bear, when in a person's lifetime they have cancer not once but twice. We are lost for words tonight, with an utter feeling of tearful helplessness!

We Facetime Steve and Sue tonight to see how they are getting on with their building project and how each of our families are. We arrange to chat again next Wednesday at 4.30 pm and to use ZOOM for a Crinkly Crags catch up at some point.

We watch the 10.00 pm news and see a report live from a hospital, where the doctors and nurses are clothed head to toe in protective clothing, face masks and face shields. Their masks are connected to a machine on their backs that filters the air constantly from their airways, causing them some dryness of the mouth. Their heads are covered in protective hats too.

The overall picture is like something straight off the set of Star Wars. We comment on how difficult it must be to administer drugs, injections etc to the patients, as they are totally protected behind so much equipment and gloves. We find it hard to comprehend the patient and clinician dexterity skills required.

We think about how frightening it must look for the patient lying there, seeing these aliens from outer space looming over them, checking their vital organs and survival every second of every minute every day. The photos shown on the television news tonight, reveal the strength and love shining brightly in all the eyes of the clinical team of staff as they work around the clock to save the lives of thousands of patients across the globe.

We see and hear about the most horrendous of all situations that the clinicians and teams are working under. In some cases, the patient is put into a medically induced coma, to allow nature to heal their bodies whilst they are in this fixed state. The doctors and nurses keep turning them over, as apparently this can help to increase oxygen back into their blood system.

We learn that patients organs become oxygen starved to the extent that these organs start to shut down. This procedure causes a fine line between death and life to occur. I cannot sleep, as the images and sheer magnitude of the NHS staff makes me feel humble, proud and terrified for the safe outcome of so many patients. There is an acute awareness inside us, that the majority of the very poorly patients, might not make the long journey, back to their loved ones.

Saturday 25th April 2020

We enjoy our cereals outside on the bistro table. It looks like it is going to be gorgeous day today. The sky is a deep blue without a cloud in sight and although it is only 7.30 am in the morning, there is no breeze, and it is pleasantly warm. I put all the cushions on the outdoor furniture, for us to enjoy sitting outside later.

I decide to change my winter wardrobe over to my summer one, which means taking everything out. Then assessing whether old worn-out jumpers need to be kept for winter this year, or whether some need to go to the charity shops? I make a tentative start on sifting through the clothes to keep and the clothes to donate.

It takes me ages. I am not good at letting anything go, having been brought up to keep everything, just in case you can make something else with it.

I make a reasonable attempt and have put four items out for the charity shop. The rest of the clothes can be put away until next winter.

I end up with a pile of washing to do from the summer clothes, that I have sorted. These clothes have not been used since we went to Crete in October 2019. I could iron a few of them, but others are too creased and need a wash first.

The bright sunlight is showing lots of areas of dust inside our home. I am torn between staying in and cleaning the inside or going outside and helping Geoff as promised. I decide on the latter and think the housework can wait until tomorrow. I just need to ensure that all my cooking and eating surface areas are cleaned and sanitised constantly, as recommended.

I join Geoff outside and peg some washing out. We are going to fill the three round wooden tubs with geraniums and petunias this morning. We make a base of old compost, which gets watered before we add the new compost and position the plants. It takes us a while to complete all three pots, but we are quite pleased with the results. Geoff puts them safely inside our greenhouse and waters them generously, fingers crossed that they will be fully grown by the end of May, for their outside residence.

We decide to have quick lunch of crumpets, Geoff has best butter on his and the butter just melts through all the holes once toasted, I used some Sicilian Lemon Curd for mine, which likewise oozes through the holes on the toasted crumpets. Just delicious!!

Geoff is a bit down and quite sad today, reflecting and worrying about the news from his sister last night. I give him lots of cuddles and cups of tea. I suggest that we both should take Chumley out this afternoon, then I can pop into a shop for some hair bobbles. I also feel it will be good for Geoff to walk and enjoy being together, which it was.

We walk down the river, cross the locks and head towards Roker Park first. Then we stroll through Northwich, where I buy some hair bobbles for myself at the age of 66!! My hair is just growing too long. I have trimmed my fringe a couple of times, but I am not keen to do any chopping off the length myself just yet!!

It is now an extremely hot sunny afternoon, with the mercury in the outside thermometer showing a warm 36c. Geoff is snoozing in the garden. When he starts snoring, I head to the bottom of our garden and sit on the decking furniture. I enjoy catching up with messages and chill out too.

For tea, Geoff had prepared and cooked the most delicious Moussaka ever! We enjoyed eating it outside, with a side dish of salsa and a few too many glasses of wine between us both!! Later, we decide to head indoors and watch some TV

Sarah, Paul and Autumn facetime us, whilst we are watching the Outlander series. I am multi-tasking by ironing at the same time. The Robson family were all outside enjoying a BBQ and making S'mores (campfire cookies) which Autumn showed us.

We could not quite grasp the word, due to her Cumbrian accent which she thought was just hilarious, as we kept trying to find out what she was saying.

Geoff and I enjoyed a lovely long chat on Facetime, it was like sharing their BBQ with them albeit virtually. Autumn is just full of fun and so wise beyond her years, she is very quick at picking things up. Sarah told us that Autumn did her new jigsaw puzzle from us by memory alone today, knowing exactly where each piece needed to go.

They are all having a great BBQ, but it was getting near the time for Autumn's bath and bedtime, so we say goodnight and just before we sign off, Autumn smiles, laughs and tells us that she is enjoying using my shower gel every day. I say, "oh you mean my raspberry shower gel?" she solemnly says yes Nana then grins and says, "I use your body pouffe to wash with too!!" She blows us a kiss; we do the same and say a final goodnight to them all. They do make us feel so happy inside us.

Sunday 26th April 2020

Today was a planned family celebration day for all the Leigh Family. We were going to raise a glass to toast the memory of Granddad Harold who died 3 years ago and would have reached the age of 100 this month. I started baking for the event in February and my freezer has two apple and lemon sponge cakes in store, a box of raspberry and cinnamon tray bake cakes and lots of carrot cake, all homemade by me. I did make a Christmas Fruit cake last month for this special occasion, however, that has all been eaten. Geoff is totally addicted to fruit cake and cannot leave it alone. It is just typical that this cake is better than the three that I made at Christmas for each of us. Oh well, I can always make another one, whilst on Lockdown!!

We have arranged a family ZOOM session for 11.30 am and we are both looking forward to seeing the family and little ones later. Geoff's sister and her husband and children are not going to join us, as they are still processing the news together as a family, we wanted to cancel it on Friday, but decided that we would still go ahead as we have to remain positive, and it will be good to see everyone and support all of us together as one family unit.

I manage to do some housework, along with sanitising all surfaces, whilst we are waiting. I also help Geoff with the skin on his heels, which are sore due to dry skin causing fissures to appear. After his shower, I use some special foot cream softener all over his freshly pumiced feet, as a special pampering treat to help him.

We log on early to our planned ZOOM meeting, then notice each family member joining into ZOOM very quickly. We chat to Adam, Clare, Emily and Rosie, Sarah, Paul and Autumn first, quickly followed by Anthony, Catherine and Niamh, then finally, Rachael, Simon, Cameron (eventually when he got up and put down his Xbox!!) and Millie.

I help to adjust our hosting screen so that we can see everyone, we chat for an hour and catch up with news and watch the children play. Niamh is now crawling; Anthony was able to show us how fast she can go. Millie has amazingly long hair just like Rapunzel in the fairy story.

Sarah, Paul and Autumn look great, and Autumn is busy giving her dolly Annabelle her daily vitamins to keep her healthy!! We follow Emily and Rosie around their garden and inside their tent. Autumn shows us her binoculars, and we chat about what everyone has been doing and how they all are.

We raise a glass to Granddad Harold in what would have been his 100th year. We all toast Simon and Rachael too on their wedding 5 weeks ago and who have no chance of going on honeymoon which had to be cancelled due to COVID-19.

We all have a quick chat about Auntie Christine to reassure ourselves to stay positive and strong together, just like Auntie Chris is doing.

We keep chatting for a while longer, until we realise it is time to say our goodbyes. Geoff tells everyone to take care and how lovely it has been seeing everyone today and all the children, sharing what they are doing. The event could have been recorded but we chose not to. Geoff says he is closing the ZOOM meeting after counting down from 5. All of us wave and smile our goodbyes to each other.

I take Chumley for his afternoon walk to Verdin Park as it is quite cool, so I decide on a shorter walk, he was so tired last week in the heat and all that swimming.

For tea tonight, we are having Pork Tenderloin on a bed of Fennel with fresh carrots, cauliflower, and mashed potatoes, followed by my home-made chocolate brownies and chocolate ice-cream

As I went upstairs for my cardigan, I notice that Cathy, a close friend of 52 years, has just pulled up on our drive with some essential food for us. She leaves it by the front door. I quickly run down to thank her from the safety of our front door. Cathy stands at the top of our drive and tells me what is inside the bags for us, including a birthday card for me and something from their recent cruise before Lockdown.

It was just wonderful to be able to have a quick chat with a real friend instead of the constant phone messaging, FaceTime, ZOOM and WhatsApp! The hardest thing was not being able to go and give each other a hug!

Monday 27th April 2020

We woke up to a cold Monday morning after all the wonderful hot sunshine and blue skies of the last few days. Hmm heating back on again. Those summer clothes that have just been washed and ironed now hang unwanted again, whilst I dig out my warm snuggly jumpers.

At least we slept for 6 hours last night, which was good. We feel it is probably because we relaxed more by reading our books last night.

Geoff took Chumley out and is a bit later setting off at 6.30 am, instead of 6.00 am Our planned meal today will be a Lamb Rogan Josh for tea with Basmati Rice. The cooking process will take 10 hours in our slow cooker. After breakfast, Geoff prepares all the ingredients for the meal.

I busy myself writing a few birthday cards, sorting out a letter and photograph to post to Autumn. I enclose a packet of sunflower seeds inside the letter for Autumn to plant in their garden. I tell her in my letter, that Nana and Granddad are looking forward to seeing the plants fully grown, by the time we can next visit them.

Secretly, we hope it will be sooner than that, as sunflowers are not generally out until August, which is 4 months away. But if that is what it takes to beat this virus and we have to remain at home until then or longer, then we know that in the grand scheme of things, that this difficult time period will soon be over.

We all have the rest of our lives ahead to catch up the lost hours, days, weeks and months with all our family and friends It is this sobering thought that keeps us positive and strong not just for ourselves but for them too.

Geoff decides that he is going to sand the final balustrade on our decking down this morning and give it a coat of paint. I walk to the Post Office to buy stamps and post my letter to Autumn. I hope that it will reach its destination safely, it's hard to tell though. The post is quite erratic and not reliable at the moment, although we see the postmen working flat out daily putting their lives at risk for us. I have a note in our window thanking them all, for continuing to deliver our mail to us.

I make Geoff a bacon butty for lunch. I enjoy a salmon sandwich with a home-made salsa salad. After lunch, I take Chumley for a good walk along the River Weaver and don't pass too many people out this afternoon. The few people that I see, are all very respectable as we each step sideways, to make room to pass each other safely, within the 2metre guidance.

In many cases most of us stand further away than this. I love taking Chumley out by myself under Lockdown, although I miss the walks we did every day together with Chumley. However, I can walk much faster on my own! My walking pace today is 12 minutes to one mile again, with Geoff it usually averages 20 minutes to one mile. I kid myself that by walking fast I am burning enough calories off my waistline, to compensate for the higher intake of food including wine and chocolate, that we consume daily during Lockdown!! Well at least, I am trying to keep the scales balanced!!

After I return from my Chumley walk, I decide that I will make a start on looking at the pattern I have just bought to make Autumn a dress with for summer. The fabric I have chosen is lots of princesses with words about adventures and dreamers. I hope that Autumn will love this fabric too. Most of all, I hope that I can make her a lovely dress without being able to measure her properly or see her.

Years ago, I used to make my own dresses and line them fully. I made a few outfits for myself when the children were little, not many though, as there was only fourteen months between Sarah and Anthony. I didn't have many spare hours at all. I did make Sarah a beautiful dress with silver sequined straps as a ball gown, when she was studying at Lancaster University on her QTS and English degree course. The ball gown is still in our loft 20 years later!

I busy myself puzzling out the pattern pieces, but suddenly realise that I still don't have Autumn's up to date measurements, which Sarah promised me she would send over the weekend. However, I can make a guess and start to cut the paper pattern pieces out and will remind her later to send them to me.

I have arranged a Facetime call with my friend Jan on Wednesday morning. I am looking forward to discussing my sewing project and asking Jan a few questions as well as catching up again in a visual meet up. This telephone chat will be much better for us both, instead of my long-winded messages to Jan.

My school friends have set a group WhatsApp up. We use it throughout the day and night to contact each other. It is a fantastic support group for those days when we are feeling a bit glum and need a tonic boost. We do also share a lot of love and laughter with each other too. I find it incredible that in this Lockdown period, it is the women who are sending jokes around to each other, every few minutes, we send lovely family photos, videos, music and poems too!!

We forward the jokes to the men and all our other friends too. I have tried sending some to the family group, but they take the mickey out of me or tell me that they are inappropriate as our 4-year-old granddaughter can see the pictures pop up on her mummy's screen. My son asks me to let them know ahead and provide a quick summary. Likewise, they are not that keen to have them sent unless worth sending. I guess my children will have a constant circulation of messages including humour from their own groups of friends.

In the meantime, it is good that women have just found a way of switching our normal coffee and cake times or lunches or craft groups, into virtual meet ups together electronically!!

Geoff and I rush to watch the daily briefing from Number 10 tonight as the Prime Minister Boris Johnson has returned to work today. We are looking forward to seeing what he is going to deliver to the Nation, as the next stage to take us out of Lockdown. However, we are disappointed as the briefing is chaired by Matt Hancock informing us about the statistics and the plans of the government to help people. So many people have lost their lives in this horrible battle against the deadly virus.

The UK has reached over 20,000 deaths today. We are not out of the woods despite the statistics showing a flattening with a slight reduction in numbers of cases confirmed. We stop watching the briefing. There is nothing new that we learn at all, it is disheartening watching it.

The Lamb Rogan Josh that Geoff made, and cooked tonight was utterly delicious, and we enjoy every mouthful and even manage to save and freeze the leftovers, despite us both having a second helping and Geoff a third helping of it!

At 7.00 pm tonight we took part in another ZOOM meeting with my brother Christopher and my nephews and nieces from my genetic family. This was good fun to chat to each other about COVID-19 The pandemic is affecting each of us in different ways, with some members of the family on the frontline in the NHS.

We enjoy some good banter between us about politics, growing old and the seriousness inside the hospitals from first line accounts within the family.

The harsh reality is grim. One of my niece's husband tells us how he has to handle the COVID-19 patients every day, either transporting them around or restraining them! The chat turns to masks and the lack of PPE as an ongoing concern. In addition, the problems being faced in Care Homes is raised and just how bad it is inside the homes. My nephew is working closely for the government, but he is not able to say a lot about what is happening behind the scenes.

However, he tells us that we should prepare ourselves for the stark facts, that normal life may not begin until well into January next year. Everyone agrees that it is still a long road ahead for all of us.

Tuesday 28th April 2020

At 4.30 am this morning, Geoff is brewing us a mug of tea, I thought it was much later than it actually was, when he put my drink down beside me! We wonder who else like us is drinking tea in the early hours?

I know that Geoff is always a morning person, he cannot stay in bed once he is awake, however, this COVID-19 has made most of the world's population not able to sleep at night. and we are both no exception to this problem.

We go to bed relaxed and tired. Inevitably though, we find ourselves tossing and turning through much of the night. Our brains reflect on the effects of whatever news item, we have watched today about the virus. It just stays there with us 24/7. Although we are protected safely inside our 'bubble', people around us are fighting for their lives in every hospital and nursing home. Ordinary people just like us, are dying by this cruel killer disease. Despite the statistics showing a flattening, the end of the tunnel is out of sight. We may even see a return to the horrid beginning, for a second time around.

Today is a cold looking day, after so much warm sunshine, these last few weeks. I decide to get up when Geoff took Chumley out at 5.30 am and start some baking, rather than sit reading news items or social media stuff. I make Geoff some Mary Berry fruit scones, as he loves scones as much as chocolate!

I make some cinnamon and raspberry tray bake, followed by my famous G&T drizzle cake. I will freeze most of my baking. However, we will enjoy some of my home-made cakes, as a treat later.

After breakfast. Geoff busies himself with some painting of a bird box and a planter bicycle in the garage. I spend some time checking my pattern pieces for making a dress for Autumn to wear. I am looking forward to having a Facetime call with my friend Jan tomorrow night. I want to run a couple of things past Jan before I start cutting the fabric out. My questions include how to use fusible interfacing, check actual measurements against the pattern specifications? I have worked it out myself, but to chat it through with Jan, will boost my confidence.

At 11.00 am Geoff and I start to move the stones off our drive where the grass bank bordering our drive beneath the stones has been damaged. A lorry reversed down our drive a couple of months ago, when dropping building materials off for a neighbour who lives in the corner of our cul-de-sac.

After we complete the task. I look at the messages that have been coming through on my phone, whilst working outside.

I discover that my letter, photo of us and the packet of sunflowers has been received by Autumn who promptly has a mini meltdown in front of her mummy Sarah. Autumn misses us so much.

Apparently, Autumn could not even bear to look at the photograph of us, with our words of love written on the back of the photo. Autumn asked Sarah to put it away in a drawer out of sight.

I felt sad when I saw this message from Autumn. I had hoped it would be good for her, not make her cry that was never out intention at all. Quite the opposite in fact, as my note and words were positive, as was the gift of sunflowers for her to plant them with her daddy. In the hope, by the time they are fully grown as giant sunflowers, we will be back visiting them all again.

There is another message from my daughter-in-law Catherine who sends a picture of Niamh standing up and then sitting down and getting back up again to reach for something on the bed. It was only Sunday, when we had a family ZOOM catch up that we saw Niamh crawling and now she is almost walking!

I felt so sad for not being able to see our two granddaughters. We are missing them so very much at this time when normally, we would be with them both. It is hard missing the moments of their daily development, denied of giving our love to them at this difficult time for all families in COVID-19 Lockdown.

There is a third message from one of my school friends Jean who has just been chatting to Geoff's sister Chris, whom she worked with and who lives near her in Nantwich. Jean tells me in her message, that she has promised to help Chris in any way at all that she can over the coming months. When people do lovely things, it makes me feel humble, for all their kindness and love.

I take Chumley out for a walk just before the rain becomes heavier. I manage to complete 3 miles with him across Roker Park and Verdin Park.

Chris telephones, to tell us all about her pre-op. Apparently the cancer has been growing inside her kidney for the last 5-7 years without her knowing about it. I am staggered by her news as she had an MRI last year. I know that I too have lumps in my kidneys and liver, having just had an ultrasound which confirms their presence and the fact that one of them has blood inside the organ known as a haemangioma. I must contact my GP again who could not determine whether my lumps have increased in size, since my last MRI 6 years ago, or what action is needed to stop the haemangioma from leaking blood into my kidney or liver, where this is happening.

Chris is very strong and positive on the telephone. We chat for a long while about the operation next week to remove her kidney. The tumour inside her kidney measures 10 cm which is the same size as her kidney, so the sooner it is out the better for Chris and all of us too.

Due to the COVID-19 requirements for patient safety, Chris will have to walk into the Alexandra Hospital next Tuesday, on her own. She will be kept in for 2 days without any visitors being allowed to be present. This is causing anxiety for her husband Jim, who is not well himself. It is a difficult time for anyone being admitted to hospital. It is both frightening and scary . We offer to help in any way that we can, given that we are under Lockdown regulations and guidance too now.

Whilst Chris is on the telephone, Sarah and Autumn Facetime us, but we cannot take the call, so we message back, to say we will facetime them both as soon as possible. They are just going out for a walk whilst they wait for us.

When we facetime them after their walk, we enjoy lovely funny conversations with them both. Autumn is feeling happier and proudly shows us the gifts and letter that we sent to her along with our photo. She pulls lots of funny faces and makes us laugh so much.

We have a virtual group hug with Autumn hugging the phone as if she is hugging us for dear life. In return Geoff and I make all sorts of funny faces and show each other what we have been doing. I bring my tray of cinnamon and raspberry cakes so they can see but not smell or taste them!. They tell us that they are going to bake some flapjacks. Autumn shows us her puzzle, that we posted last week. We have such amazing fun with them both, that it makes us laugh and smile, long after we have said our goodbyes to them

I spend an hour chatting to Bob and Carol on ZOOM and Bob gives me some sound advice with my book project about my genetic mum. It is just lovely to talk to them both online. Bob suggests that Geoff could ZOOM him tomorrow night, so they can have a good natter, over a pint of beer together virtually!!

Later this evening, Sarah sends us a message to tell us that Autumn has put our photo under her pillow to sleep with, which just melts our hearts.

Wednesday 29th April 2020

Brrr, neither of us want to get out of bed this morning, it is so cold after all the hot sunshine last week.

Geoff took Chumley out as it is starting to rain. I get up to have a shower, sort breakfast out and put the card and a bottle of fizz ready to take to Elizabeth whose birthday it is today, I have baked some cakes to take as well. I will leave them on her doorstep, then knock and move myself to her gate, so that I can wish her a happy birthday within the confines of social distancing.

Elizabeth opens the door, so I wish her a very happy birthday from a safe social distance. Between us all we must post at least 20 jokes or clips a day and when we run out of jokes, we become just fun-loving schoolgirls with cheeky banter and innuendos all day long. It is so funny, as it used to be the men who shared jokes and smutty sayings. However, in these strange days of Lockdown, it is the women who have become the comedians I suspect most of the video clips and hilarious jokes have been created and designed by competitive men and women though.

It never ceases to amaze me how fast the jokes hit the streets within minutes of an event happening. For example, the birth of the current Prime Minister's son today, funny cartoons soon hit the joke scene with funny pictures of a baby with hair sticking up! President Trump has been the butt of so many jokes about disinfectant and Dettol usage this week. There has also been a lot of music circulating that is so beautiful it just gives you goosebumps and other music makes you want to get up and dance. I sent a music video to my 'Chicks' craft group and one of the ladies texted me afterwards to say how much she enjoyed it and found herself dancing to the song whilst cutting some fabric out and suddenly realised she had gone wrong with as she was dancing happily in time to the beat of the music!!

We are having a chicken pasta with white wine for tea tonight and Geoff preps the ingredients. We have a lot of mushrooms in the fridge to use up, so I make us a ham and mushroom omelette for lunch.

Geoff took Chumley out after lunch, when he got soaked to the skin, as some heavy rain arrived just as he was halfway round on his walk. They were both like drowned rats by the time they arrived home.

I was still waiting for my GP to telephone me to discuss the lumps that I have in my liver and kidney following Christine's diagnosis of kidney cancer, which apparently has been growing inside her for 5-7 years without her knowing this fact and on the phone yesterday, Chris advised me to check again with my GP as I know that one of the lumps does have some kind of blood inside it.

Whilst waiting for the call, I helped Geoff to dry Chumley off, it took a couple of towels to dry the excessive water on all his fur, including his very muddy undercarriage, which was just caked in mud matted hair.

My GP Sue Brown telephones me to discuss my questions. During our discussions, she advises that she cannot see that either of my lumps will be cancerous, they are more vascular in origin, with the terminology being an angiolipoma fatty lump one in my liver and two in my kidneys.

However, she can't rule it out without further tests to dot the I's and cross the T's which she will arrange for some time in August, when we should be far away from all the COVID-19 worries and pressures on hospitals. It is not advisable to go to hospital for anything that is not urgent or life threatening now. I agree. We chat about our families and life in the pandemic.

We enjoy a lovely tea, the chicken pasta was delicious and very tasty, including the white wine sauce, runner beans and chillies.

I am looking forward to a face-time chat with my friend Jan at 6.30 pm tonight. As soon as we have washed the dishes, I spend some time checking my dress pattern out and getting ready to sit and talk to Jan.. It is ages ago since I saw Jan, although we keep in touch with WhatsApp and our chicks' group WhatsApp, it is not quite the same as a face-to-face chat.

Jan rings me first and we are soon chatting away just like we used to. I have poured myself a large G&T however, we talk that much to each other, sharing life and family news, that I forget to drink it. Jan is such a great friend, so supportive and helpful. We discuss our various sewing projects and grandchildren. During our friendship, we are never stuck for conversation. Usually, we always manage to end up giggling about something that amuses us both at the same time.

I ask her a couple of questions about fusible interfacing and cutting layouts for my pattern, which I discover are on the other side of the instructions.

After what I thought was just a few minutes, I look at my watch and realise we have been chatting for over one and half hours. I tell Jan this and she laughs, and we decide that we had better sign off and say our goodbyes. My drink stands still, it is now too late to drink it I think just before bedtime. However, it might make me sleep better! I miss my friends, as much as I miss my family in these testing days for the whole world.

Thursday 30th April 2020

Today, it is the 100th Birthday of Captain Tom who has raised over £29 million pounds for the NHS just by walking one hundred laps, around his garden with his Zimmer frame.

After breakfast, we switch the TV on and watched the celebratory fly past over Tom's house performed by the last two spitfires that helped Britain to win the second world war. Tom was an active training officer during the second world war. We watch his birthday celebrations start to unfold with this amazing tribute, we have tears in our eyes. Tom looks so much like Geoff's dad Harold, who sadly died 3 years ago and who would have also been 100 years old had he lived. A big family party had been planned to mark his 3rd year of not being with us in 2020, but also to celebrate all that he did and gave to us. We know that he along with Tom, would have also probably walked 100 laps around his garden just the same.

The stories included a change of title for Tom by the Queen, who has decided he should be called Colonel Tom. This is in honour of all that he has done for the country, especially the NHS in these last few weeks.

Tom comes over in all his interviews as a fun-loving guy, a wise man, and a gentle soul. He is much loved by everyone. The cameras take us to a school near where he lives, that has had to organise a place in the hall to stand all his 125,000 Birthday cards containing thousands of wishes and love. Watching this story has been amazing. Tom has not only given us a legacy along with history to be talked about for years, but he has given us joy and the hope of a better life soon too.

The TV cameras pan to where Tom is sitting watching his fly over from the Spitfires in his own garden. The team interview him and ask how he feels today? He replies" the same as yesterday and tomorrow is another day," bless him. He is presented with a 3-tier cake that is layered in blue and white and has a model spitfire on top of the cake and all the icing is piped beautifully. The England Cricket Team Manager presents Tom with his own cricket cap and tells him that he is now a fully-fledged member of the England Cricket Team which is an emotional moment as Tom has been a lifelong supporter of the England Cricket Team.

We loved listening to Tom's wise words, when asked what he thought about the fly past by the spitfires, he said during the war, the spitfires were flown in anger, but today it was just lovely to hear the sound of those engines flying in peace over us.

Geoff and I feel very emotional all morning and reflect on how this lovely gentleman has brought joy and happiness to everyone today who just love him for the wise and special guy that he truly is. They do not come any better than Colonel Tom Moores who will be a legend forever!!

We join our neighbours slightly earlier than 8.00 pm to do the clapping for the NHS and to sing Happy Birthday to the Nation's Colonel Tom tonight. All of us retain our social distancing , although there is a longing to move closer and chat. We just wave and shout our hellos to everyone and check that our next-door elderly neighbour Sylvia is still ok, that she doesn't need any shopping doing by us. Then it is time to take Chumley for his last toilet break to the end of the road where the river is and we comment on how the night is so light, and that tomorrow will be the 1st May 2020.

Chapter Four
The not so merry month of May
Friday 1st May 2020

Happy 1st May, almost summer 2020 now!!
Today is cold and raining again, although it should dry out later.

Poor Geoff got a bit wet on his 5.30 am walk this morning.

I stayed inside and got breakfast ready for us and helped to clean Chumley up on his return from the first walk of the day.

Geoff is going to continue sorting some loose paint and filling needed around the edges of our stairs this morning.

I am going to attempt to cut the pattern and fabric out for Autumn's sundress, that I am going to make this morning. Oh, dear me, that did not quite work out as planned! I laid the fabric out and all the pattern pieces, checked the pattern layout, then discovered that something was not quite right with the instructions, as there was no detail to show me where to put all 11 pieces. I could only see 4 sections to put the pattern pieces on which puzzled me.

I noticed that the size I need to cut out is in the middle of the marked cutting margins for each size. This is fine when the piece to be cut is perfectly straight, as I can fold it back, but not so fine for the curved sections. So, what do I do to get round it? I cannot think straight, so I send a message to my friend Jan who is a brilliant seamstress as well as a great friend. I sent some photos of my dilemma and within minutes, she responds with the simplest of solutions which my brain had not even whirled its cogs into start mode at all!!

Jan suggested that I simply trace the pattern size I need to use onto a piece of paper, great solution. My brain whirls into action telling me that I don't actually have any tracing paper at all in the house I ask Jan the question "but what sort of paper will work to trace the patter?" Jan suggests greaseproof paper, of course, why didn't my brain cells come up with that solution? I guess my brain is too busy sleeping through this Lockdown time.   I hunt in the drawer for a market pen, then I successfully trace the pattern pieces required. I am so excited and want to start cutting out, but first I must go and do some food shopping. My first port of call is to our local market for fresh eggs, then some tiny, delicious Cheshire New Potatoes that have just arrived at our local greengrocers. The first tiny Cheshire potatoes are always the most delicious ones, especially with mint sauce and bacon. I do not flinch when I am told that my small bag of these potatoes is going to cost me £4.14. The taste and enjoyment of them far outweighs the price. I drive down the road to Asda, but after parking my car, I find that the queues are too long. I don't feel safe to wait with the long trail of people, even though I am wearing one of the filter masks, that my brother Christopher sent to Geoff and me this week.

I went to Sainsbury's and the story was just the same there with long queues. There were even longer queues at both Tesco's and Waitrose. I decide to buy some bacon from the local butcher, in anticipation of enjoying the Cheshire potatoes, just bought and make my way to the butcher's shop, only to discover long queues waiting outside. I give up and drive home, wondering what to cook for lunch and tea today?

Fortunately, we have some bread left to make a sandwich for Geoff, whilst I enjoy a piece of cranberry cheese with crackers. Lunch was followed by warm homemade scones, perfect!

I took Chumley out this afternoon on our regular walk to Roker Park, which is great, as I keep increasing my own personal walking pace up higher.

Chumley keeps step with me, which makes me smile so much at him.

A lovely video of Niamh standing in her cot, arrived on to the family group this afternoon. Niamh was saying "Mama" in such a gentle voice. She melts our hearts so much.

Tea is Fish fingers tonight with homemade potato wedges, accompanied by mushy peas. Simple and easy for a change!

Tonight, we watched Andrew Lloyd Webber's 50th Birthday party, from the Albert Hall 20 years ago. It was brilliant.

Our nephew and his fiancée are due to get married on the 15th August this year, but tonight we learn that sadly, their wedding must be cancelled along with lots of other weddings planned in 2020. They will send us a new date for 2021, as soon as they know that they can secure the same church and venue.

A bedtime story from Sarah arrives on the family WhatsApp group for us to read. It is called The Great Realisation, which will be read to children for them to learn about COVID-19. The Great Realisation is a detailed story about how the world became so badly infected before it became better by mending itself. The work portrays exactly how we have all contributed to pollution, by excessive use of all modes of transport travelling constantly, across the globe. Mobile phone usage is excessive. People young and old have lost the art of talking to each other. Everyone is permanently attached to their mobile phones, even when in restaurants or shops. This has become the 'norm'.

We are missing so much by not using our eyes and ears like we used to do. There are huge swathes of plastic in our oceans, that are literally shrink wrapping the fish and mammals to the point of extinction!

Many natural rain forests are being destroyed by the sheer volume of trees being cut down. Rain Forests are essential for the environment. This massive reduction in future timber stocks and will have long lasting consequences for the world.

We continue to build higher buildings which are jam packed into many major cities across the world. The finished result is one of a huge concrete and steel jungle towering above as it reaches higher into the skyline. It is no wonder that the sun remains obliterated from reaching out to the people walking below, in our modern world.

The Great Realisation is an absolutely brilliant story by Tom Foolery. We talk about what effects our own material desires have caused in our lives. Then we remind ourselves sternly, that despite thinking we have been quite good, the reality is much harsher! All of us can contribute so much more to our world, in many small ways, to save this wonderful planet. We need to learn how to improve the environment, not destroy it. I guess this has been simmering on the back burner for years, but like fools we have ignored the warning signs.

Saturday 2nd May 2020

Niamh is 9 months old today. Her mummy and daddy sent us two lovely photos of Niamh playing with a ball, as well as enjoying riding on her pink toy rocking horse. We just love how her hair is in a trendy looking pigtail on top of her head. The photo makes Geoff and I laugh with delight.

I was out before 8.00 am today. I queued up at our local butchers for over 45 minutes. Two people only are allowed inside with their face masks on. I know that some of the customers waiting outside are shopping for their families, or vulnerable people who have to remain indoors and be shielded from all other contact. I wait patiently, for my turn to enter the shop safely.

After I leave the butchers, I drive into Northwich to buy some groceries. I visit the fresh fish counter in Waitrose, to buy a piece of salmon, along with some tuna for meals next week. We no longer have a fishmonger in the town. Therefore, this is the only shop that we can buy fresh fish from. It is my 67th birthday on Wednesday, so we are cooking the tuna with spaghetti, accompanied by tenderstem broccoli, from the Pinch of Nom cookery book.

The queue is not too long outside Waitrose. I wait for my turn to enter the shop safely. I check to ensure that I am wearing my protective face mask. A large man with a face mask is standing 2 metres behind me. The man asks me why I am there? He informs me that this early time between 8.00 am and 9.00 am only for the over 70's and NHS or front-line workers.

He asks me if there are two queues? if so, am I in the right one? I am a bit annoyed with him, but nod my head to say yes, I am in the right queue.

I point out that there is only one queue not 2! As I edge closer to the entrance, a lady in front of me is asked to stand to one side. The manager explains to the lady within earshot of the queue, that the early opening is only for those over 70 and key workers like NHS staff. The woman accepts what the manager tells her and reassures the manager that she is happy to stand and wait another hour. However, she does point out that when she looked at the Waitrose website this morning, there is no mention of this system. The opening hours simply say 8.00 am to 8.00 pm. The lady suggests that Waitrose need to add a disclaimer to that effect and the manager agrees with her, but still doesn't allow her inside until 9.00 am.

I am next in the queue, so before he can say the same to me. I produce my NHS blue card as a retired NHS employee. The tannoy system urges us to not linger or browse, as the queue is growing bigger outside. I quickly make my purchases from the supermarket, without lingering.

These shopping trips are not in the least bit enjoyable at all. The cost of food shopping rises each week significantly. I wonder why?

My friend Elizabeth calls round with some wholemeal flour for me that she has managed to obtain direct from Williamsons bakery. There is quite a shortage of flour in all the supermarkets. Elizabeth also brings some books for Autumn including colouring books.

I am given a gift bag from Elizabeth, containing a birthday card and present, along with some flapjack cake too. She returns my cake tin to me. There is also a Mary Berry cookery book for me to keep if I wish.

I have one of Mary Berry's books that my daughter Sarah bought me for Christmas a couple of years ago, which I love using, however, Elizabeth informs me that her book is the full version of the TV cooking series. As I flick through the pages, I can see that some of the recipes do look interesting and different to my current one.

I make Geoff and I a light lunch, using bacon, toasted bread, corn on the cobs, which I bought last Friday, then forgot about them being in the vegetable tray.

After lunch, I take Chumley out for his afternoon walk and follow the River Weaver over the locks towards Roker Park. The route takes me over a lovely bridge by the arches. When I was a child playing with my friends, we dared each other to walk across the connecting pipes spanning the river. I smile to myself about the fun we had then, but which makes my legs turn to jelly now, by the memory of those daredevil days.

I catch a glimpse of the brilliant sunlight filtering through the green leaves on the surrounding trees. The trees themselves, are framed by one of the old sandstone block arches, that today are still carrying trains over this busy Northwich railway line.

I looked down at the clear idly meandering river below the footbridge.

I smile at how the azure blue sky is mirrored back to my standing position perfectly, so that I could see the sky above and below me. I stood still. I was lost in swirling thoughts, whilst watching a couple of dreamy white clouds floating high up above me. However, whilst I stand there daydreaming, a wet nose nudges my legs from Chumley, who is keen to carry on running down to the shallow water below the bridge, where I can throw his tennis ball for him. As I continue walking, I find myself reflecting about the view that I had just seen. Was this a clear message about life and the wonders of nature? I know I felt a rush of warmth and happiness, as each beautiful colour awakened my spirit with joy. It was like gazing for hours at a finished painting in the gallery of an unknown artist. I took a photo to show Geoff my husband..

Geoff has been busy repainting the ceilings in the hall and landing with white emulsion today. I noticed that already it is looking much cleaner.
He has had a shower, along with a much-needed rest, whilst I have been out with Chumley. I make us a brew, before catching up with some messages outside from my groups for a few minutes.

Geoff has a new recipe for Paprika Chicken from our Hairy Bikers cookbook that he wants to try out tonight. After a while, he wanders inside to prepare the ingredients, I offer to help but he declines saying that he finds it therapeutic. He tells me to enjoy a break from working hard all day too.

I use the time to telephone Christine to chat to her ahead of her kidney operation next Tuesday 5th May. She is extraordinarily strong and positive, which inspires me so much too.

We have a good natter about Christopher and Katey's wedding day, which has been postponed from the 15th August 2020 to 24th July 2021. Apparently it took the youngsters a while to re-organise everything again for next year. However, in view of the current circumstances, the wedding would probably have been only allowed to go ahead for a few guests. without it being the big occasion, they had planned.

They had a tentative date for April next year, but the church is already under great pressure from so many cancelled weddings, that it would be impossible to allow them to have a big wedding at this time. Chris and Katey are going to wait until next summer, when the world will be in a much better place. Chris and Jim will be stronger and better health wise too. I wish Chris much love and good luck wishes for Tuesday and tell her that we will all be thinking about her. I add that if there is anything at all that we can do to help in any way whatsoever, we will do.

Tea was outstandingly delicious, and the chicken paprika dish was so yummy, with a tasty sauce too.

We set a couple of ZOOM meetings up for my birthday next week. Then we catch up on Friday night's screening of Coronation Street which was a difficult one to watch due to the domestic abuse scenes enacted out. After the programme ended, I took Chumley for another short walk as it was such a beautiful night.

Geoff and I sat outside with a mug of tea and did a joint pictorial quiz trying to identify the countries of the world between us that a friend had sent to me earlier in the day. Geoff did really well and was much better than me, I like Dingbats, but found this one a bit tough, although once you find the answer you can see that really it is quite easy. Like Dingbats it's learning the process of the quiz that helps!! It was good fun. I posted it to our daughter Sarah and her husband Paul, who enjoyed it too once Autumn had gone to bed.

Although they did admit that they had to google some of the quiz questions. I will send it to our son Anthony and his wife Catherine tomorrow. However, with their young 9-month-old baby, they may not have the time to complete it together, as their time is limited for leisure during the evening, with a baby to feed, bath and get ready for bed.

We watch an episode of the Outlander Series before bedtime, it is excellent tonight. A great ending, with the much-deserved demise of the arch villian Stephen Bonnett!

Sunday 3rd May 2020

Hurray, we finally slept better last night and had a bit of a lie in until 6.30 am this morning. I joined Geoff on the first walk of the day with Chumley. The area around the river behind where we live was so peaceful, with far less people around in the early morning, than my busier lunchtime walks.

After breakfast, Geoff spent the morning masking the hall and stairs up ready for painting. Hopefully, we can find a store selling paint locally, or online.

I prepare the vegetables and Cheshire potatoes for tea later. I am really looking forward to eating them.

There is nothing like the taste of Cheshire potatoes, when they first come into season, from the local farms such as in the village of Little Leigh.

I spend the rest of the morning typing up yesterday's story of how we spent Saturday 2nd May 2020 in Lockdown. It takes me ages, I am really enjoying typing here every day, whether it is in the morning or the evening.

Just as we are both finishing our tasks and getting ready to have a quick lunch, before I take Chumley out, my phone rings with an incoming Facetime call from Anthony, Catherine and Niamh.

I am so happy and excited to see them on facetime.

The photos they sent to us this week, show so many rapid developmental changes in her motor skills and expressions. We watch entranced as she moves around the home and garden. Niamh is at the stage where she is either crawling or pulling herself up.

Anthony looks well and tells me that work is busy Monday to Friday for him, but he is doing ok and enjoying his weekends with Catherine and Niamh. He shows me his garden and all the herbs that they are growing this year. He is carrying Niamh with him. I wave and speak to Niamh, showing her a toy giraffe out of Chumley's toy box, she recognises my voice, and her eyes light up. I am so happy with her instant response, it's as if she is saying I know you Nana!

I wander through our home to find Geoff who is upstairs, he comes down, so that we can sit and chat to all the family together. Anthony shows us what he does to Niamh, that Catherine is not happy with!.

His fun game is to throw Niamh playfully and safely onto their bed, where she promptly rolls all over the bed, then nearly falls upside down off the bed, onto her head, but she is safe. Anthony makes sure no harm comes to her. We laugh with them both and can quite understand why Catherine is not happy with this game of adventure between Daddy and his daughter, as it could result in some bumps to the head for Niamh.

We know that Niamh will grow up in a very adventurous world with Anthony and Catherine, who are both very active adventurers.

Catherine shows us how Niamh pulls herself up and reaches for toys on the bed. We laugh when she tells us that her crawling skills are very fast. Suddenly Niamh is on our screen demonstrating to us just how quickly she moves from one room to the next room with such ease.

Whilst we are chatting to Anthony and Catherine. My phone shows another incoming Facetime call from Sarah, Paul and Autumn, which we have to decline whilst Geoff retrieves his phone and connects to them so that we don't miss the opportunity to speak with both our children and granddaughters.

This is turning into the best Sunday ever, just to be able to see them in their own homes and gardens. To chat to them and feel close again on this beautiful day. Autumn is eating some Unicorn biscuits and her hair is so long. Sarah and Paul are enjoying a brew in the garden with Autumn, who is also drinking a milky tea in her cup, whilst eating her biscuit at the same time.

We laugh about Autumn's bike riding skills, but also tell the parents, that we were a bit scared seeing her cycling so close to the cars on the road yesterday. Sarah and Paul tell us how much she has progressed with her writing, drawing, colouring, baking, craft work for VE Day on Friday and lots of other activities, where she is just advancing and growing up faster every day.

Autumn tells us a story about Princess Aurora that she makes up whilst on the phone to us. When she has finished the story, which was brilliant, she asks Granddad Geoff to tell her a story too. Geoff said ok, I will just go inside to find the story that I wrote for you last time. Autumn said not that one Granddad make a story up for me, which was a challenge that Geoff immediately accepted. His story was about Rapunzel and incorporated Gorgon and Zola into it too. Gorgan being the dragon and Zola the mouse. We enjoyed a happy time chatting with both our families today. It was hard to say goodbye, as we did not want to hang the phones up, it was just like being with them again as always.

We had a quick bacon butty for lunch. I took Chumley out for his afternoon walk, whilst Geoff went for a shower. Geoff prepared tea whilst I was out walking. Tonight, we are going to enjoy salmon with stem ginger and chilli, from the Hairy Bikers Cookbook.

On the way home from our river walk, I noticed that Chumley seems to have hurt his mouth. Small droplets of blood were dropping onto the pavement I suspect he has caught his gum on a sharp object or by holding the end of his ball thrower in his mouth too long.

This sometimes happens when we play a tug of war game I clean his mouth out with warm salty water and have a cup of tea with Geoff outside.

At 4.00 pm we have scheduled a quick ZOOM test with Cathy and Chris ahead of our scheduled session for Wednesday 6th May. It was fun and good to see them both on the screen, as well as show them around ZOOM and catch up at last again with each other.

Our evening meal tonight was very spicy hot, but also sweet with the ginger. Geoff is a superb cook, will follow a recipe but also go off piste. Our meals together, are better than any five-star restaurants. He has just grown in confidence and expertise in making meals that are divine. He enjoys it as a hobby he tells me, although I do feel guilty at not cooking as much in return for him. Although I do bake exceedingly good cakes!

Monday 4th May 2020

Chumley is still bleeding a bit from his mouth this morning. He won't let us examine it properly. It appears to be small spots of blood, nothing major. Part of us wonders if he may have bitten his tongue, or damaged his gums with his ball thrower, or a sharp stone. We will keep bathing his mouth as best we can and wait a couple of days to see if it heals on its own. If it -does not stop bleeding by Wednesday, we will contact the vet.

Chumley seems to have a bit of a dodgy tummy with a lot of poo trips during the night. However, his poo is normal in colour. So perhaps the heat may have caused him to pick up a bug, or he has foraged in the undergrowth and ate something we didn't see.

He often tends to sniff anything and everything, when exploring amongst the leaves and bushes surrounding the river. We always notice what he is doing though, so we call him out of the long grass or put his lead on, especially if it's in an area where we know there is litter and debris lying around.

We set off at 7.20 am this morning to go to the B&Q Superstore in Crewe for some emulsion paint, which we cannot order on-line or buy locally. Geoff said the shelves were quite empty in our local store, with staff not knowing when anything is coming back into stock. This will be one of our first times out together in the car since before the Lockdown in March. We are slightly nervous, but plan to be there before the opening time of 8.00 am when we do not anticipate any delays and should be able to find the emulsion paint that we have chosen quickly, knowing that it is actually in stock.

As we arrived on the car park, we were surprised to see that the car park was almost full, and that people were queuing around several cordoned off barriers, waiting to go in one at a time on the basis of one in and one out. It was well organised, and we stood more than 2 metres apart. Although we did notice that at some points, the barriers in between each cordoned off area allowed less than 2 metres between the customers weaving round these sections. We had our masks on and felt reasonably safe.

It took over one hour for us to reach the entrance, then less than 15 minutes to find the paint that we wanted. Not a pleasant experience, standing outside with everyone looking grim and miserable. Is this what our future life will continue to look like for a long time to come we wonder? Shopping for anything that is not on-line is just not a pleasant experience at all. It is one that is quite scary to say the least.

Once home, Geoff and I cover the hall, stairs and landing up with dust sheets and I make us a cup of tea, whilst Geoff starts to paint the walls with our first choice of paint Kiwi Lime Crush which looked fabulous in the brochure, but neither of us is quite sure when it is on the walls.

The colour is a very bright lime green. It will lighten up as it dries hopefully. We have a pale willow tree colour to paint the other walls with, which will add a softer overall painted finish when complete.

I quickly print out the program for the VE Day celebrations on Friday 8th May 2020. I take one to each of our neighbours living in our small close. I suggest that we could put chairs out on to our own drives, in the same way we stand on our drives each week, for the NHS clapping on Thursdays at 8.00 pm. We cannot extend the invitations to the residents living just around the corner though as it would cause too many people to mingle closely. However, I will knock on the doors of each house to ask each of them to do something similar to where we live, on Friday 8th May. The neighbours were appreciative, each of them said that they had been wondering what we could do together, on Friday to celebrate.

Whilst Geoff is painting, I catch up on this writing. Geoff finishes the painting and is quite pleased with the result. I make us some lunch before taking Chumley out for his afternoon walk.

I am just heading down the road with Chumley, when my friend Barbara and Ian drive past to give me some flowers for my birthday on Wednesday.

I cannot stop and hug them because of the Lockdown rules. I feel bad not stopping or going back home to chat to them. I miss my friends so much. It was so exciting seeing them drive up. Chumley's toilet needs are long overdue. He won't use the garden at all, his body knows when to go and at what time. This morning, he has been kept waiting to go out, so I have to keep going with him. Geoff is in our house, washing the paint brushes and roller out, so they head on up the hill to our home, to leave them in the porch with Geoff.

I return from my walk with Chumley, to find my friend Norma arriving with a gift and card for me. We stand 2 metres away on the drive catching up, as best we can, it is so hard not to hug each other.
Elizabeth pops by with some books, which she leaves on the garden wall for us to pick up later.

I decide to tackle my sewing project for making Autumn a summer dress. To my dismay, I discover that the markers for aligning the pattern pieces together, have been trimmed off. They are no longer outside the cutting line but inside the cutting line! I have a mini meltdown about this, thinking how stupid of me not to have noticed. I thought that I had been so careful when cutting the pattern out. I decided to ring a friend and ask advice, even though I think that it will be easy to just use a mark or sewing stitch, where the markers are needed to match the pieces up.

We have an early tea. I am at an online meeting tonight with my writing group. Our landline telephone ring. On the line is my sister thanking me for the small gift that I left inside the porch for her husband George, who was 80 years old on Friday. We chat quickly for a few minutes. I cannot linger as we are just about to eat our evening meal. I promise to ring her back again before my meeting starts.

The daily briefing is on the TV which Geoff listens to intently. I clear up my sewing mess, then get ready for the on-line meeting.

I ring my sister back first, however, she is eating her tea, so I promise to catch up again soon. We chat about their health and being isolated due to their vulnerability.. I ask if her children were able to pop round, just say hello from a distance on Georges birthday? My sister said they did come round on the day. She said it was good to see the family standing outside the conservatory. They were able to talk to each other but only through the glass windows.

All these celebrations getting cancelled or postponed, until we are in better health times outside Lockdown. It doesn't matter in the grand scheme of things. We are all doing really well, by adhering to the guidelines.

Our writing group commences with 20 of us participating on-line. We complete a great writing exercise for the first 10 minutes, then read some of them out, which are excellent. After listening to individual writing news from members. Our chairperson Bob announces the winners of the Tonia Bevin's Poetry and Prose awards for 3 places in each category starting with 3rd place, 2nd place and then the winner in 1st place. All six winners read their winning entries out to us, which were brilliant pieces of work. We are an amazing diverse group of talented writers, who never cease to amaze me.

Tuesday 5th May 2020

Geoff paints the other walls with our second choice of colour which is Willow Tree. This softer colour does complement well with the bright green on the other walls.. I put some washing out as it is another lovely day outside. There is nothing better than seeing washing blowing in the warm breeze. Freshly laundered washing drying outside, smells divine.

I have arranged a Coffee Buddies meet-up this morning at 10.30 am with my two friends, Jan and Trish. We connect successfully, then spend one and a half hours catching up with family news. We talk about our individual projects, that are keeping us busy, during

Lockdown. As always, we have good fun and banter, share our coffee and cakes virtually. We laughed about how we share our different cakes, by cutting them into 3 separate pieces, when we go out together to cafes. Today, on ZOOM was just the same!

I make Geoff and I a lovely lunch of bacon, poached eggs and mushrooms.

Tonight, is on-line Zumba again. I reflect how quickly the weeks are flying by, as I get ready. At the end of the session, our dance teacher Sharon asks us all to make a heart with our hands.

Sharon photographs the hearts made with love for each other tonight. We all say that they are for all the people in the world, which was just a lovely simple gesture tonight at the end of our class.

Wednesday 6th May 2020

Today is my 67th birthday. I feel so lucky and blessed to still be here in this dreadful year of the Corona Virus, which has taken the lives of 29,000 people already in the UK to date.

I reflect on my birthday, feel humble that I am still alive, my children are, my grandchildren are. The rest of my family and my friends so far ,are all still here too. This is a miracle considering the seriousness of COVID-19. The death toll is still not reducing down enough. Last night, the statistics revealed the UK to have recorded the highest number of deaths in the whole of Europe. It was such grim news!!

We went to bed feeling sad, anxious and scared by these ever-increasing figures in the UK. There are many measures could have been put into place far sooner, long before day one of the pandemic. It is disappointing and frustrating to learn about the people who have not followed the rules. The effects of non-compliance have caused the virus to spread further, along with the lack of PPE for all frontline workers, in particular the medical teams across the UK who are all putting their lives at risk daily.

I feel that my birthday is a special one in Lockdown. I think of the 29,000 people including babies and children who have died in our country to date.

They will not see their birthdays celebrated this year.. 29,000 lives gone forever. In the future, their remembered birthdays will be forever shrouded in utter despair and sadness.

Many of the deaths have occurred in total isolation, without families being able to hold their loved ones, say goodbye, or even be able to bury them with respect and dignity. They say that time is a great healer, for those people affected personally by the deaths. There will be no healing, that can mend their broken hearts. No closure or comfort when you cannot say goodbye..

The pain is a broken heart in each case that can never be fixed no matter how this all ends for each of us. I can't even begin to do the mathematics of the sum that 29,000 deaths have left behind literally millions of lives changed forever by the loss of a baby, a dad, a mum, a daughter, a son, a sister, a brother, a granddad, a grandmother, a nephew, a niece, a cousin etc.

Well, what a day! How do I begin to tell the story of this whole very emotional birthday in Lockdown territory? It is the sunniest hottest day ever, that I can remember for my birthday! Sometimes, we find a holiday abroad, for a week around my birthday.

Last year, we visited the Amalfi Coast for the first time. We stayed in a beautiful hotel called the Concazzura, which was just perfect. It was located along the Amalfi coastline, with panoramic sea views that could be viewed from every angle, of this truly romantic hotel. Unfortunately, the weather was cold and rainy. However, the rain did not spoil our first visit to this beautiful area of Italy, with its stunning scenery, fabulous cuisine and so many historic sites such as Pompeii nearby.

Anyway, back to today! My early morning cuppa in brought up by Geoff, started our day together in the normal way, with a bit of chatter about the day ahead and the weather, which through our bedroom curtains is already showing what looks like a promising blue-sky day. Geoff gave me last year's birthday card which I had kept, and he found, he then tells me a yarn about how there are no cards in Lockdown. The supermarkets have no cards either, which were as good as the one he sent me last year.

We laugh together, as this is typically something that we do at Christmas time with our saved cards from last year. I count the kisses again in last year's card, whilst Geoff watches me. I notice that the kisses are 5 times 13, which how we write it sometimes, rather than write out strings of kisses. "Hmm" I say, "Is this card from last year?" "Yes, darling says Geoff" "well 5 x13 kisses equals 65 so this card is now 2 years old". "Oh really, well here's your proper card for this year" Geoff leans over and gives me a completely different card in an envelope. We laugh and chide each other like children do.

Geoff empties half his top box on the wardrobe, he gives me two presents from Sarah, Paul and Autumn wrapped up in our saved wrapping paper. It was only a few days ago, when Geoff asked me "where do you keep the spare birthday paper these days?" So funny, the little things we do for each other. The presents had arrived at our home last week from Amazon. Sarah had rung her dad to ask him to wrap them for her, bless.

Geoff gave me a lovely birthday present bag, which was heavy and contained a few items.

He said it was impossible to shop, unless looking in supermarkets, which do not really stock the sort of gifts he likes to buy. He smiled ruefully at me and said that he had done his best to make my day special. I know that and as I give him a big hug, I say "I am not bothered about birthday presents or cards, just so glad to be safe and know that our family and friends so far are all safe too".

I do notice however, that this is a recycled gift bag, that actually has lots of trophies, ties, beer bottles and footballs on it with the words in big writing, HAPPY FATHERS DAY! I laugh, at least he tried, no need of fancy present bags. In fact, he didn't even need to put his gifts into a bag, the wrapping on them is black and yellow, it all looks a bit odd not my choice, so I guess he must have bought that, he quite proudly says "look it says Happy Birthday Hooray!" Yes Hooray, here we are in Lockdown trying to be normal and celebrate the abnormal!

Geoff is already dressed and ready to take Chumley out. I have a shower, then take my cards and presents downstairs, to open later with Geoff after our breakfast. I am so excited to put my shorts on today, together with a favourite top. It is cold now, but I can tell it is going to be hot later this morning.

My beautiful gifts from my lovely husband, include a special bottle of Chardonnay, a set of Orla Kiely notebooks, a box of Ferrero Rocher chocolates, 6 cans of ginger beer, not sure why I need these? A letterbox arrangement of flowers from Geoff, bless his cotton socks. He has done well to find and resource such lovely gifts for me to enjoy today.

I am told to close my eyes and when Geoff tells me to open them, he produces a fabulous birthday cake for me too. What more can a girl need? We hug and share our love and laughter together over another cup of tea, whilst I open the rest of my cards and presents. I open up the gifts from Sarah, Paul and Autumn which are a bottle of smoked pineapple Gin, ah that explains the cans of ginger beer, a beautiful book to read called a Dog, a Mole, a Fox a Boy which looks amazing and is beautifully illustrated, a fabulous handmade card addressed to Nana Banana from Autumn, with rainbow balloons on it and her own handwriting inside the card for me to read. I am so touched.

I have only just finished opening my cards and presents when my mobile phone pings with an incoming Facetime call from Paul, my daughter's husband. I immediately think that he is at home today, perhaps on holiday and that it will be great to see them all.

However, it is a massive surprise for me, to see that Paul is standing outside his workplace near Penrith, to wish me a Happy Birthday. Paul shows me the most wonderful clear views of the Lake District fells. We used to see this view every other week, prior to Lockdown. We miss our regular trips, to spend time with the family in Cumbria so much. I am so touched, as he pans the phone camera around, to show me Blencathra in the distance. Geoff and I climbed this fell, a few years ago with Sarah. Blencathra is where Anthony proposed to Catherine, when they climbed it on a snowy day on the 9th December 2017. What a star man Paul is doing this for me, during his busy full-time job as a Frontline worker in the distribution industry. We worry every day about the risks to him in this essential work. The company he works for, supply mineral water to millions of people! Paul made me feel so special today.

I am so happy that our daughter married Paul, who is thoughtful, kind and an amazing husband, daddy, and son-in-law too. I will remember forever, how he gave me such a wonderful feeling inside me today. I love him so much for all the little things he does, with love for his family and us.

Sarah and Autumn Facetime me after breakfast, it is just so wonderful to chat to them both on my birthday. They both sing Happy Birthday to me, Autumn is looking so happy, as she sings her heart out to me. Sarah and Autumn tell me what they have been doing this week. They have both been busy, preparing for the VE Day celebrations on Friday. Their front window has been decorated in flowers, bunting, soldiers, and spitfires. They take the phone camera outside, to show us. Afterwards they send us a photo over WhatsApp to look at. We are so proud of their amazing achievements and creative work for VE Day.

I found it amusing, when Autumn decided she wanted to sit at the dining table, then pull her chair in to talk to me. Autumn told her mummy to do the same too. It just reminded me of Sarah being exactly like Autumn is today, when she was little, quite a natural bossy person growing up fast. I watch and smile inside me, for the happy memories of yesterday and the even happier ones being made today. I say my usual goodbyes, with lots of hand waving to them both along with lots of kisses being blown to them, over the phone screen.

Anthony and Niamh have just connected to us on Facetime and say Happy Birthday to me. Niamh looks pretty dressed in blue, with her hair tied up in a tiny pigtail on top. She is such a cutie. We cannot wait for the day when we can see them again. Cuddles are long overdue for our 9-month-old granddaughter, whom we last saw in February. We chat to Anthony and Catherine on facetime for a while, which makes my day special.

I am so proud of my son and Catherine. They send us lots of photos and video clips daily. It helps us not to miss any of these early milestone days and weeks, time is just racing by. Niamh will soon be one year old . Anthony is busy working from home. We chat for a while longer, before he must return to work again, so he hands Niamh back to Catherine who also wishes me a happy birthday. I feel so touched, it is the best gift of all just to spend time with my family, even if it is in a virtual world. At least we are all safe, long may it continue!! My deepest birthday wish today, is that we all survive this dreadful global pandemic, along with the rest of the world.

It is mid-morning. I am making Geoff and I a cup of tea; I notice a black sporty car pulling up on our drive. I don't recognise the car at first, but then see our friends daughter Christina and her wife Perrie get out of the car and walk down our drive, I open the door and they are singing happy birthday to me, which is just so lovely, and I am totally bowled over.

They give me a bouquet of flowers from their mum and dad who magically appear at the same time on Christina's mobile phone screen, to wish me a happy birthday from their home in Paphos, Cyprus, where they have been locked down more severely than our country, since the 9th March, 2020.

We almost flew out with them but changed our minds at the last moment. Christina and Perrie also give me a Lily Plant and birthday card from them for my birthday. Geoff and I chat on our drive with them both. Chumley of course is the centre of attention, as he is enjoying being outside in the sunshine. He naturally soaks up all the attention and cuddles that the girls give him, he looks so handsome today and happy.

The girls are always so bubbly and happy, that we don't want them to leave. It is just great seeing them both again, to enjoy a good chat about their work, garden, house renovation and decking plans, which Geoff is happy to help them with.

A large, boxed gift from Waitrose arrives in the afternoon from Anthony, Catherine and Niamh, which appears to have been damaged in transit. The gift is a planter arrangement. All the plants are lying on top of the soil, with a box of Moet Champagne Truffles nestled amongst a lot of mess. It looks like someone has just thrown the plants on top of the soil. .I was a bit surprised , when I read the instructions, which gave the advice "to look after this planter just water". The detail was missing, that should have said " actually, you need to plant it up yourself first!"

I send Anthony a thank you. I tell him that I am busy planting my gift up from them, which is fun to do. I receive a photo displaying what their chosen gift should have looked like. The photograph resembles nothing like the tatty mix of almost dead plants, lying in ICU (Intensive Care Unit) aka our greenhouse, to recover from their bumpy ride in the big transit van that delivered them to my doorstep.

Christina and Perrie have only just left in their open top car, on this beautiful sunny day, when my friend Elizabeth walks down the drive with a big bag of flour for me that she has obtained from Williamson's bakery shop on Castle. There is a shortage of flour, eggs, and castor sugar along with other baking ingredients like yeast. Elizabeth is a wonderful friend who can resource all kinds of things for our Hartford Girls school group. Elizabeth organises our coffee times out together, lunches, theatre events, spa days. She is an amazing and very special friend, who is always positive and does so much for everyone in normal times. This year in particular, Elizabeth has covered many extra miles for each of us daily. The Hartford Girls school group is fully supported by all of us being there day or night for each other.

Whilst being locked down, baking is something that most of us in the group enjoy. However, we are all baking more each week to maintain food in our homes. Also, to avoid shopping for those little treats of shop bought cakes. I was taught to bake by my mum at an early age. I love baking. I have taught my daughter Sarah, when she was little, as did her nana who baked with the grandchildren, whenever she looked after them. Sarah now teaches her daughter Autumn to bake. I also enjoy baking with Autumn, whenever they stay with us, or at her home too.

When my children were small, they used to set up a stall inside the garage and sell my homemade cakes to their friends for pennies to spend at Mary's sweet shop down the bottom of the road where we live.

Our lovely cheerful postman is the next person to walk down the drive, he places a pile of cards on our wall for me, then with a cheeky grin he says "I guess it is someone's birthday today. He wishes me many happy returns of the day".

Geoff and I start to put the bunting up outside our home now and it is looking great. I am so glad that I went around to all the neighbours on Monday and gave them a timetable of events for the VE Day Celebrations on Friday this week. The government have agreed that it will be ok for all of us to remain in our gardens, or on the front driveways of our homes to keep the social distancing rules.

We can celebrate together on Friday, from the required distances, just like we do every Thursday at 8.00 pm. This is the time when we all go out to the front of our homes, to clap the NHS workers, as loudly as possible, with all our heartfelt thanks. The NHS staff are battling to save the lives of so many people, every second, of every minute, of every hour. Each week we stand and clap for a few minutes, every week, nod to each other, shout our hellos to everyone living in Riverside Park. It gets very noisy as the claps get louder. There are some of us who ring bells or bang with spoons on tins. It's an uplifting, reflective and poignant moment every week that helps us all to stay strong.

After lunch, Geoff took Chumley for a walk, instead of me. When Geoff returns home with Chumley, he tells me that he is a bit concerned.

During the walk, he noticed that Chumley's poo is black and tarry in colour. We realise immediately, that this must be blood loss from within his bowels. We don't panic too much, as he has had some slight bleeding in his mouth yesterday. I had bathed his mouth with warm water and salt for him. It is very difficult to see what he has done to his mouth, as he clenches his teeth down, when we try to examine the inside of his mouth. The bleeding has just been a couple of spots noticeable on his tennis ball mostly. We ring our local vet for advice, who advises us to take Chumley for assessment at 4.30 pm this afternoon. Because of the COVID19 risks, only one of us is allowed to go with Chumley to be examined by the vet. Geoff agrees that it is best if he takes him to the veterinary surgery later today.

The vet asks Geoff lots of questions, then leads Chumley away to another room, to perform a blood test. Geoff has to wait inside his car for the results, which take half an hour. Whilst Geoff is at the vets, I take some flowers to the Churchyard at Davenham, near where we live. I chat to Geoff's mum and dad who lie buried here, they are so sorely missed every day. I tell them all about Christine their daughter, recovering from her kidney cancer operation yesterday, that she is doing well and is safely through the worst of her ordeal..

At 3 pm today, we enjoyed a ZOOM birthday meeting with our Crinkly Crag friends (name given to them by Sarah and Paul when they got married. They used the names of all the fells in the Lake District for their wedding tables). Crinkly Crags is a well-known fell. The name for it has stuck ever since, between 6 of our lifelong friends. Cathy and Chris, Steve and Sue, Carol and Bob.

It was good fun to be able to chat to each other. Carol and Bob are still in their holiday home in Paphos Cyprus. They may not be able to fly home until mid-July possibly. There are no flights scheduled from the UK to bring them home. Cyprus has only had a total of 20 deaths across the island. The government have announced that the lockdown in Cyprus will now start to be eased. It has been confirmed that shops and restaurants can return to opening up again, from tomorrow. In addition, people may go to the beaches once more.

Geoff arrives home from the vet. He tells me that it is not good news about Chumley. They are keeping him in overnight for further tests including a chest Xray, ultrasound scan on his liver and more blood tests.

The results of his first blood test this afternoon are showing that Chumley has a platelet count of zero. This is dangerous for him, as his platelet count should be 200 at the minimum range. The vet informs Geoff that their test results are normally accurate. However, to be on the safe side, she is sending a further sample by courier to a specialist laboratory, who will confirm the readings and analyse in more detail. The Vet will ring us at 9.00pm to let us know when they sedate Chumley for his other investigations.

Geoff had planned to cook us a romantic dinner tonight of my favourite food - fish, we were having a Tuna Steak with lemon, spaghetti and tenderstem broccoli. I suggest that we cancel it and just enjoy a glass of wine and some cake as neither of us can settle until we know more about Chumley.

We enjoy a ZOOM Hope Family meeting at 6.45 pm tonight which was fun and interactive with Chris, Maggie, Shelagh, Cyril, Rhys, Lloyd, Becky and Lorraine. We enjoy much banter and conversation about Chris's tomato plants. Rhys and Geoff show

Chris how to grow tomato plants successfully, without over watering them. Each of us tell Chris this is why his plants have probably died on him!

Lorna the Vet telephoned us at 9.00 pm to let us know that Chumley is now sedated. He is ready for the Chest Xray and Ultrasound. Lorna is going off duty now for the night. The Vet taking over from her is called Lorraine. If everything goes well, Lorraine will ring us at 11 pm tonight, to let us know the results of Chumley's further investigations.

We spend the rest of the evening sitting together outside crying whilst we wait the long hours to pass. Eventually, we go to bed and take the phone with us, we don't sleep at all but toss and turn. The vet didn't phone us. We have a cup of tea in bed at 3.00 am, then again at 5.00 am, before getting up for breakfast. We hope that no news is good news Our telephone rings at 8.00 am. Lorraine apologises for not phoning us back last night, but it was 1.00 am this morning, before the investigations were completed.

Lorraine informs us that the Chest Xray was clear, liver is clear so no tumours, however, she informs us that Chumley's platelet levels are still low. Also, he has a small stone in his stomach. Worryingly, there is a bleed in his intestines, either high up or low down. This bleed cannot be seen on the scans as to where exactly it is located. In view of his platelet levels, they cannot perform surgery or put a camera inside him.

The plan is to start Chumley on a high dose of steroids, to build his platelet levels back up again. This will take at least 6 months. The side effects of the drug for Chumley, will be increased food and water consumption, which in turn will cause weight gain, along with extra toilet requirements. In addition, there are other effects of the drugs which could affect his GI tract, by membrane destruction. She explains that as Chumley is already bleeding internally, they will need to find a drug that can act like a sticking plaster to counteract damage and further blood loss. The plan is to discuss Chumley's case, with the medicine team this morning, to try to find a set of drugs to balance both conditions, for Chumley.

We feel totally gutted and cannot really process what is happening to Chumley. How did he become so ill so quickly? We hope that a solution will be found and discuss whether we should make our difficult decision now, to not let Chumley suffer anymore.

Thursday 7th May to Saturday 9th May

I have been unable to write on these pages for the last few days since my birthday. Our thoughts are with Chumley every minute of each day and night. We are both finding it more difficult than normal, to sleep, for feeling upset and anxious about Chumley. Neither of us can get our heads around his sudden unexpected illness.

We have both woken up with headaches, after consuming a full bottle of red wine last night. Then eating a big piece of my birthday cake, followed by consuming chocolate, instead of cooking a proper meal.

Lorna telephones us at 8.00 am with an update on Chumley. She informs us that he is bright in himself, has not done a poo yet. This is not unusual, s dogs tend to hold it in when under stress, or in a strange place without their normal walks. The plan is to try and get his combination of drugs right that will start to boost his immune system. Hopefully, the drugs but will also protect his stomach membranes. One of the vets will be back in touch later today, to advise us.

We are eating lunch, when Lorraine telephones with a request for us to consider trying a massive dose of chemotherapy, to help Chumley. I listen intently to what she is saying, but I cannot comprehend her suggestion Does this mean Chumley has cancer? The vet tells me however, that there is no evidence of cancer inside Chumley. The overriding concern for the vets, is that unless they can quickly bring his platelet levels up. He is in imminent danger of dying. Ian is a vet at the surgery, who specialises in the type of disease that is attacking Chumley.

Lorraine explains that studies of using the chemotherapy drug, can actually kick-start the platelet count faster than normal drugs. Using steroids will cause Chumley's GI tract to bleed, due to destruction of internal membranes. This other choice is an option for us to consider. The vet doesn't want to put us under any pressure, they will continue to give Chumley steroids, along with another drug to combat the effect of steroids. However, they don't want anything to happen to Chumley, without being informed of this option.

It is VE Day tomorrow and a Bank Holiday, which means the courier time slot is limited to within the next hour, to deliver this drug to the vets. But only if we do want to try this as an option.

Lorraine asks me to write down the link to an article called Thrombocytopenia, in the Merck Manual for dogs. Geoff and I need to read the information about giving chemotherapy to dogs, who are poorly with low platelets.
Geoff and I read the article together, then print out the relevant sections to keep and read. so that we understand it more clearly and can ask questions when the vet rings us back within the hour.

We discuss if we should just ask her to let Chumley die naturally? Both of us have tears in our eyes. It is hard for us to understand the article about giving chemotherapy as an option.

Our first initial thought is that this is a tough call for us to take to put Chumley through Chemo. We do not fully understand the side effects of the drug or whether it will work? We go round the houses, trying to make sense of it all. Jot down our questions after reading the article.

Lorraine telephones us before an hour has passed. We had realised whilst reading the article, that we do not have a choice. There was no pressure being put on us to make our decision. It had become very clear to us, that actually Chumley needs more help to increase his chances of survival. Our answer has to be 'yes' for the vets to proceed with the drug used to treat cancer.

Geoff and I ask Lorraine a lot of questions about the Chemotherapy. Also, what would she do if it was her dog? After a quick chat, we give the green light to go ahead to save Chumley. Lorraine feels we may already be too late for the courier to get it to them in time. She promises to let us know later in the evening.

The drug arrived in time for the vets to administer as a single injection into Chumley during the evening. There is nothing we can do now, except wait with hope in our hearts.

In the meantime, we keep ourselves busy all day. Geoff needs to go to B&Q for some new paint brushes to finish our decorating project.

I decide that I will complete the food shopping for the weekend, especially, as it is a Bank Holiday and V.E (Victory in Europe Day) celebrations tomorrow. I had already tried the supermarkets earlier this morning but found the queues to be so long everywhere I went. I abandoned shopping. Although, I did manage to obtain some meat from our local butcher in Hartford, where the queues were not too long.

I try Asda first but discover that the queue is still too long and unsafe for me to wait. I then try Aldi, Sainsbury's and drive all-round the town's one-way system to Waitrose. My good intentions were all to no avail. It is early evening. I have been trying to get into the supermarkets for over an hour. I have been driving around, parking, then discovering the queues are too long. It is time to go home and just use what we have in stock.

However, with it being V.E Day tomorrow, we hoped to have a few extra items for the social distancing celebration in our close. I am reluctant therefore not to keep trying hard to find a supermarket without a long queue! I had tried Tesco's earlier this morning, but the queue there was the longest one ever and doubled up. I decide to try once more and see if it has reduced yet. I am not hopeful, but decide to drive there, hurray, the queue has gone down. I only have to wait a few minutes to complete my necessary shopping for the weekend ahead.

Geoff and I finish the bunting preparations later after the shopping has been put away. Geoff tells me that he is going to cook the birthday meal, he had planned for me yesterday. The recipe he is using is one for Tuna and Lemon Spaghetti, with tenderstem broccoli. I am told to go and sit outside to enjoy the early evening warm sunshine, with a glass of wine. I do not take much persuasion!

We have some bunting left over, I remembered that one of our neighbours could not find any to buy. They have put an England flag up, so I take our spare bunting over to them to use. I stand socially distant away from the opening of the door when I knock on and leave the bunting by their front door.

We enjoy a delicious meal for my birthday, which tastes even better eating outside. Geoff is a superb cook! The Tuna and Lemon Spaghetti dinner is just fabulous. The memory of this type of food, transports us both back to our holiday on the Amalfi Coast in Italy this time last year. In fact the owner of the hotel gave us the spaghetti as a farewell gift. It was manufactured by him personally from his olive groves, he also gave us a bottle of pure olive oil to go with it. The lemons in Italy, were the size of melons. I hope we can return to Italy one day. It is such a beautiful country to visit, with food that is so truly delicious!

Friday morning sees us both awake at 4.00 am we are enjoying our first cup of tea in bed, whilst discussing plans for VE Day. I cannot go back to sleep. I get up to write a few more pages of this journal which I am enjoying very much. By 6.00 am I decide to bake some scones for later today. I have promised to take some to one of my school friends. I have two scone recipes one in my Mary Berry Cake Book and one in Delia Smith's cake book.

I decide to use Delia as her recipe always produces crispy on the outside scones which Geoff just adores. It does not take me long to make 16 fruit scones and 8 plain scones. They all turn out perfect.

We enjoy breakfast together with the aroma of my baking filling the air. I then shower and dress, whilst Geoff prepares to finish the upstairs painting project.

I take a scarf to Norma for her birthday. I put the scones, cream and some jam into a bag, along with a bottle of fizz for Norma and her husband Robert to celebrate VE Day. I drive to her house to deliver them to her doorstep, whilst the scones are still fresh and slightly warm.

Norma and I were in the same class at Hartford Secondary School for Girls. Our WhatsApp group organised by Elizabeth, is just brilliant for keeping all of us positive, filling our days with laughter, almost back to those happy schoolgirl days, but most of all it is keeping us focused .

We are each supporting the other in a million different ways every minute of each day, morning and night, during this difficult time of the Pandemic COVID-19 which today, stands at a death toll of 33,000 deaths in the UK alone.

I return home and find Geoff feeling down today and not himself, we are both quite stressed about everything. The emotions overcome us of missing our children, grandchildren Geoff's sister who has just come through an operation for the removal of one of her kidneys due to cancer.

The news from the vet today is that Chumley's injection of Chemotherapy went ahead last night, and he is doing ok. Only time will tell now if the drug has started to increase his platelets. The vet explains that the side effects may take a few days to manifest inside Chumley. They cannot perform a blood test to check until Saturday. Taking blood from Chumley too early could cause a massive internal bleed. This is because his blood cannot form clots. A simple procedure like drawing blood from him is highly dangerous.

We turn our attention to getting ready for the afternoon. Whilst waiting we watch some of the TV V.E day celebrations showing the UK 75 years ago in the second world war, alongside the days of now during this Pandemic.

The one thing that is so strikingly similar is how the people of the country and the world are coming together across all communities. Across the globe, there are outstanding simple acts of pure love, friendship and care for one another as human beings. The strength of so many people who are fighting this invisible war, are just too awesome for me to put into words. The history will be recorded for future generations to look back on in better times, I hope with all my heart.

Hurray let the V.E Day celebrations and community spirit begin in Riverside Park this afternoon. We take our little bistro table and two chairs to the top of the drive. Then we start to bring out our own food, wine and a couple of beers.

Our neighbours are all supportive of each other. There is a good ambience in our neighbourhood, where any of us would help each other, no matter what the task required is..

It was a very happy afternoon and evening. The families all enjoyed being outside their homes. The children were happily playing outside. There was a great atmosphere all around us, where we could let our hair down a bit, share life once more, laugh, listen to music, tell jokes, whilst reflecting on all our futures.

Sunday 10th May 2020

Not a good start to the day. Louise telephoned to tell us that Chumley has blood in his wee this morning. There is blood inside his mouth too. Louise is concerned, she sounds exhausted.

We ask Louise if Chumley is suffering any pain at all? We wonder for the umpteenth time about saying our goodbyes to him. However, Louise assures us that he still stands a good chance of making those platelets in his marrow bone. Louise reassures us both that by tomorrow, she will have a more detailed laboratory report. She is going to undertake a further blood test this morning, to send to the external laboratory, to establish the exact number of individual platelets, within the blood cells.

Louise advises us that by Monday morning, the Chemotherapy should have given Chumley a chance of a good recovery. Louise feels it is not time to give up on Chumley yet. Chumley greets her wide eyed and bushy tailed every morning. The treatment for the blood in his wee will be done with antibiotics today. Louise will also take a scan of his bladder. She promises to phone us later today, following Chumley's further investigations.

I cannot stop the tears from falling down my face, as I put the phone down on Louise. I know in my heart that this is not looking good for Chumley. I feel it is the start of our goodbye to him, either today or tomorrow. Geoff encourages me to think positively, that the glass is still half full for us and for Chummers!

I know deep in my heart it is the end of the road. I am usually the stronger one and positive, but today my heart is full of sadness. The tears fall down my face all day long. Chumley's character is just so gentle, he is so lovable and has absolute total trust in us. Chumley has gorgeous chocolate brown eyes, that look deeply into our souls every day.

Chumley is super intelligent too. He knows exactly what we say to him, when he pins his ears back, then listens intently to us saying things like, "walk, let's go out, car, where is Autumn? where is Niamh? who is coming? what's that in the garden? What shall we do today? how about on our walk we go for a swim today in the river? Shall we have a biscuit?"

The list of words and short sentences that he knows and responds to are amazing! Geoff and I often say he talks to us every day, with his facial expressions and body language. There is a deep understanding between humans with all animals. I honestly believe that our pets and animals live in a different spiritual world to us, with much higher levels of intelligence way beyond our comprehension!!

Louise telephones at 5.00 pm to let us know that Chumley has had a scan performed on his bladder. Thankfully, it is clear from infection, which is good news. However, she tells us that he is continuing to bleed with lots of clots and gunk coming through his wee. It is impossible to determine the cause of this blood other than it could be the 2 high dose steroids that Chumley is taking each day affecting his GI Tract, or a cancer somewhere in his body, or simply the bone marrow not creating enough platelets. They will consider reducing down to one tablet, but until his platelets return to normal, this is impossible to achieve

We ask if it is time to let him go and is Chumley in any pain at all? Louise assures us that Chumley is not in pain, shows no distress whatsoever when passing blood with his wee, although she did say he is passing more blood than wee, which is of deep concern. His blood count is showing anaemia which has dropped already today from a count of 35 to 27.

Louise is wondering about a blood transfusion for Chumley, Geoff is unsure, he feels we have reached the end of the road. We ask Louise if it is worth carrying on? She tells us that it will buy Chumley another 3 more days, during which time his platelets may just start to increase again. I agree it is worth a final push for him and that a blood transfusion will be helpful if it gives all us some extra time to determine why Chumley is not getting better at all..

Geoff feels we should say no to all of it, but I think yes and so we give the go ahead to order the blood transfusion for Chumley tonight if needed. To give him the blood they do need further sedation for Chumley. The cost of the blood transfusion is £500. We have spent £1,000 to date. Our insurance will cover us for a total of £8,000. The cost at this stage is fine with us. In fact, at this moment in time, we are not thinking of the financial implications, just the treatment for whatever helps Chumley. Louise said Chumley's vital signs are still good. In fact, he had the strength to pull the nurse down the corridor today on his lead, bless him. He must have thought that he was coming home to us and been so excited.

Geoff and I cannot finish our evening meal. Instead, we spend the next few hours crying and hugging each other.

We let our children know and a few of our friends too. It is not easy to process this illness and understand it. Chumley gives as much love and happiness to everyone around him, as we give to him.

He is one special guy and doesn't deserve this as he is only 6 years old We hope with all our hearts, he makes it through, that the inevitable end is not close. Our hopes are for a few more years for him and us, which sounds selfish. Chumley is so much fun to be with, his love is unconditional, he brightens all of our days, with the unconditional love that he gives to us each and every day.

Boris Johnson addresses the Nation at 7.00 pm as detailed in the extract below:-

It is two months since the people of this country began to put up with restrictions on their freedom – your freedom – of a kind that we have never seen before in peace or war. And you have shown the good sense to support those rules overwhelmingly. You have put up with all the hardships of that programme of social distancing. Because you understand that as things stand, and as the experience of every other country has shown, it is the only way to defeat the coronavirus – the most vicious threat this country has faced in my lifetime.

And though the death toll has been tragic, and the suffering immense, and though we grieve for all those we have lost, it is a fact that by adopting those measures we prevented this country from being engulfed by what could have been a catastrophe in which the reasonable worst-case scenario was half a million fatalities. And it is thanks to your effort and sacrifice in stopping the spread of this disease that the death rate is coming down and hospital admissions are coming down. And thanks to you we have protected our **NHS** and saved many thousands of lives. And so, I know, you know, that it would be madness now to throw away that achievement by allowing a second spike.

We must stay alert. We must continue to control the virus and save lives. And yet we must also recognise that this campaign against the virus has come at colossal cost to our way of life. We can see it all around us in the shuttered shops and abandoned businesses and darkened pubs and restaurants.

And there are millions of people who are both fearful of this terrible disease, and at the same time also fearful of what this long period of enforced inactivity will do to their livelihoods and their mental and physical wellbeing. To their futures and the futures of their children.

So, I want to provide tonight – for you – the shape of a plan to address both fears. Both to beat the virus and provide the first sketch of a road map for reopening society. A sense of the way ahead, and when and how and on what basis we will take the decisions to proceed. I will be setting out more details in parliament tomorrow and taking questions from the public in the evening.

I have consulted across the political spectrum, across all four nations of the UK. And though different parts of the country are experiencing the pandemic at different rates, and though it is right to be flexible in our response, I believe that as prime minister of the United Kingdom – Scotland, England, Wales, Northern Ireland – there is a strong resolve to defeat this together. And today a general consensus on what we could do. And I stress "could". Because although we have a plan, it is a conditional plan. And since our priority is to protect the public and save lives, we cannot move forward unless we satisfy the five tests.

We must protect our NHS.

We must see sustained falls in the death rate.

We must see sustained and considerable falls in the rate of infection.

We must sort out our challenges in getting enough PPE to the people who need it, and yes, it is a global problem, but we must fix it.

And last, we must make sure that any measures we take, do not force the reproduction rate of the disease – the R – back up over one, so that we have the kind of exponential growth we were facing a few weeks ago.

And to chart our progress and to avoid going back to square one, we are establishing a new Covid alert system run by a new Joint Biosecurity Centre.

And that Covid alert level will be determined primarily by R and the number of coronavirus cases. And in turn that Covid alert level will tell us how tough we have to be in our social distancing measures, the lower the level, the fewer the measures; the higher the level, the tougher and stricter we will have to be.

There will be five alert levels. Level one means the disease is no longer present in the UK and level five is the most critical – the kind of situation we could have had if the NHS had been overwhelmed.

Over the period of the lockdown, we have been in level four, and it is thanks to your sacrifice we are now in a position to begin to move in steps to level three. And as we go, everyone will have a role to play in keeping the R down. By staying alert and following the rules. And to keep pushing the number of infections down, there are two more things we must do.

We must reverse rapidly the awful epidemics in care homes and in the NHS, and though the numbers are coming down sharply now, there is plainly much more to be done.

And if we are to control this virus, then we must have a world-beating system for testing potential victims, and for tracing their contacts. So that – all told

– we are testing literally hundreds of thousands of people every day.

We have made fast progress on testing, but there is so much more to do now, and we can.

When this began, we hadn't seen this disease before, and we didn't fully understand its effects. With every day we are getting more and more data. We are shining the light of science on this invisible killer, and we will pick it up where it strikes, because our new system will be able in time to detect local flare-ups – in your area – as well as giving us a national picture.

And yet when I look at where we are tonight, we have the R below one, between 0.5 and 0.9 but potentially only just below one. And though we have made progress in satisfying at least some of the conditions I have given, we have by no means fulfilled all of them.

And so no, this is not the time simply to end the lockdown this week. Instead, we are taking the first careful steps to modify our measures.

And the first step is a change of emphasis that we hope that people will act on this week.

We said that you should work from home if you can, and only go to work if you must. We now need to stress that anyone who cannot work from home, for instance those in construction or manufacturing, should be actively encouraged to go to work.

And we want it to be safe for you to get to work. So, you should avoid public transport if at all possible – because we must and will maintain social distancing, and capacity will therefore be limited. So, work from home if you can, but you should go to work if you cannot work from home. And to ensure you are safe at work we have been working to establish new guidance for employers to make workplaces Covid-secure. And when you do go to work, if possible do so by car or even better by walking or bicycle. But just as with workplaces, public transport operators will also be following Covid-secure standards.

And from this Wednesday, we want to encourage people to take more and even unlimited amounts of outdoor exercise. You can sit in the sun in your local park, you can drive to other destinations, you can even play sports, but only with members of your own household.

You must obey the rules on social distancing and to enforce those rules we will increase the fines for the small minority who break them.

And so, every day, with ever increasing data, we will be monitoring the R and the number of new infections, and the progress we are making, and if we as a nation begin to fulfil the conditions I have set out, then in the next few weeks and months we may be able to go further.

In step two, at the earliest by June 1, after half term we believe we may be in a position to begin the phased reopening of shops and to get primary pupils back into schools, in stages, beginning with reception, year 1 and year 6. Our ambition is that secondary pupils facing exams next year will get at least some time with their teachers before the holidays. And we will shortly be setting out detailed guidance on how to make it work in schools and shops and on transport.

And step three – at the earliest by July – and subject to all these conditions and further scientific advice: if and only if the numbers support it, we will hope to reopen at least some of the hospitality industry and other public places, provided they are safe and enforce social distancing.

Throughout this period of the next two months, we will be driven not by mere hope or economic necessity. We are going to be driven by the science, the data and public health.

And I must stress again that all of this is conditional it all depends on a series of big ifs. It depends on all of us – the entire country – to follow the advice, to observe social distancing, and to keep that R down.

And to prevent reinfection from abroad, I am serving notice that it will soon be the time, with transmission significantly lower, to impose quarantine on people coming into this country by air. And it is because of your efforts to get the R down and the number of infections down here, that this measure will now be effective.

Monday 11th May 2020

Geoff and I hardly slept a wink last night. Both of us were both overwhelmed with emotions, causing us to spend the day crying. In our hearts, the harsh reality sinks in about saying our sad goodbyes to Chumley in the next couple of days. Nothing short of a miracle can save him from the journey his ravaged body is undergoing.

I got up at midnight and crept downstairs to have a little cry on my own. Geoff heard me go down and followed me too, so we both hugged and cried a bit more, then drank some water, before going back to bed. We tossed and turned until about 3.00 am, when Geoff made us a brew. We tried to catch some more rest if not sleep. We both dozed off for a couple of hours. I dreamt vividly of Chumley running along beaches with us, climbing the fells in the Lake District. In my dream he was swimming in the cool clear lakes, jumping into the river, on a hot sunny day with his funny belly flop, that always amuses us and anyone standing watching. He just loves to show his skills off, swimming is something he never tires off.

The telephone rings just after 9.00 pm, it is Andy who is the Vet for this week, he gives us an update on Chumley.

Chumley is still passing blood in his urine, but it is full of clots which is a good sign as that means he must be making a few platelets of his own. Because he is bleeding and passing blood, this is making him severely anaemic, which in turn then reduces the chance of him making and keeping his platelets building up.

Andy tells us that the plans for Chumley are to run another blood test. This will be quickly despatched to the external lab for manual platelet counting today. Andy is also going to check through Chumley's platelet results with another Vet who specialises in this field of work. Chumley's red cell count is now down to 18, from the top range of 35, which yesterday dropped to 27.

They decided not to give Chumley a blood transfusion yesterday, preferring to play the waiting game, just in case his chemotherapy and medication start to kick in to build back the levels needed for his immune system. Andy explained that giving a dog a blood transfusion carries risks. They will only perform this procedure as a last resort. Andy informs us that if by lunchtime, his blood count has fallen by 1% then the transfusion will take place. However, if his blood count stays stable and holds its own at 18 then that will be the good news we all need. The vets will continue to monitor him by physical signs, to check he is not in serious danger of rapid deterioration. Andy promises to ring us back later, around tea-time or sooner if necessary.

Lorna telephones us at 9.30 pm with an update on Chumley who is still very anaemic and quiet in himself, but she feels that this could be as a result of his anaemia. Lorna still feels that Chumley can recover. There is still hope for him she tells us. Lorna will take another sample of blood at midnight tonight. If his anaemia has worsened, then the transfusion will go ahead.

We discuss with Lorna if it is worth carrying on with his treatment?. She confirms that it is not time to give up just yet on Chumley, whilst there are other options to try. Lorna said that if they run out of options and if Chumley takes a significant turn for the worse, then she will ring us straightaway. All treatment will cease. Lorna informs us that Chumley is eating well and that in itself is a good sign. Lorna explains that once blood from another dog is introduced this can affect Chumley's own blood count. The results would cloud any issues around his platelets. It will no longer be just his own blood that is in his body.

Lorna explains that there is always a danger of giving too many drugs and options like a blood transfusion to dogs with immune system and platelet problems. So that instead of helping or curing the problem, it actually worsens it for the dog. We thank Lorna for all her care and devotion to Chumley for us. She promises to ring us back first thing in the morning with an update.

Norma called with my bag, cake tin and some flowers for me this morning. It good to chat to her on our drive

I did some washing whilst Geoff completed some gloss painting in the hall. I occupied myself with some housework in the lounge and conservatory. It is a very cold windy day today, such a change from the hot sunny days of last week.

The postman brings me a few more cards with some surprise presents, one is from Sarah my daughter. When I open it, I discover that it is a beautifully crocheted rainbow, to hang in the window. The crocheted rainbow was made by one of her NVQT teachers, who has set a business up called Crafty

Teacher. The teacher is spending a lot of time making all sorts of crafts to sell to the public. The business is donating 20% of all sales to the NHS. I feel blessed to have a lovely thoughtful daughter who posted this to me, along with my other birthday gifts last week. Their birthday card to me also arrived this morning, apparently, my card was posted at the same time, as the handcrafted card from Autumn. My birthday just goes on for several days which is good fun for me.

My friend Jan has posted a birthday card along with a beautiful gift of a make-up bag in my favourite deep pink colour, I am so chuffed with this thoughtful gift too.

More post comes through our front door from 2 neighbours who have sent lovely thank you letter for all that we did for VE Day last Friday and providing some delicious cakes and snacks too. Most of all for getting the neighbours together again as a community of friends living side by side.

We eat some toast and crumpets for lunch. Then after lunch Geoff has a sleep whilst I complete the ironing. I telephone my friend Jan, to thank her for my beautiful pink handsewn cosmetic bag, which was a lovely surprise to receive in the post today..

We walk to the post office to post Autumn some colouring books and to purchase a get-well card for Christine. There are some beautiful summery pink flowers being delivered later today for Christine to enjoy. After going to the post office, we walk into town to buy some fresh milk, plus a few other supermarket items that we have run out of. It is a long walk home without Chumley by our side.

I start some sewing this afternoon, as I am making Autumn a summer dress. I hope to finish it this year not next year!

No news from the vets. It is early evening, so we enjoy some paprika pork tenderloin for tea with homemade wedges and runner beans.

The telephone remains ominously silent. Lorna telephones at 9.00 pm and informs us that Chumley is a bit quiet today again. Although, he is still eating his food which is a good sign.

They ran some more blood tests at lunchtime, nothing has changed. Lorna is deeply concerned that his normal blood count is dropping down further.

The vets had planned to give Chumley a blood transfusion at lunchtime today if his count had fallen by another 1%. However, it was agreed to see how Chumley is by midnight tonight instead, to see if he can make it through without the vets giving him a transfusion, until they have no choice. Lorna explains that it is fine line between giving the blood to Chumley to help his blood disease or to sit and wait a little bit longer just in case the chemotherapy and steroids do start to work on Chumley. Lorna informs us again, that even with a blood transfusion, it can actually make the problem worse for Chumley as the other dog's blood could cloud the accuracy of Chumley's own blood, which is the best solution for his body to heal him naturally.

We understand and agree with Lorna, that unless his count drops drastically, to hold back from giving Chumley the blood transfusion until we are totally sure that he needs it at that crucial point in his body. Lorna explains that if his count doesn't drop any lower by midnight, this will clarify to her that he is holding his blood levels, albeit they are dangerously low for him. We agree with Lorna to withhold the transfusion until the morning handover.

We thank Lorna for all her hard work and excellent care that Chumley is receiving from the Veterinary Group.

Thursday 14th May 2020

After breakfast today, Geoff was on a mission to go and finish the supermarket shopping for the items we have run out of and could not replace yesterday, rather than be caught up in endless queues again on Friday.

The doorbell rang and it was Elizabeth my friend on the doorstep with a big bag of plain flour and some flowers for me to cheer me up with our worry over Chumley.

I was puzzled as to why Liz was giving me some flour, but she said it was to replace my bag of castor sugar which I had taken around to her last night as she had run out and there seems to be a shortage of castor sugar. I have a small box with castor sugar in and so could easily spare this bag for my friend. I didn't expect or need anything in return as it was given to her freely by me for all the lovely kind things that she does for me and my family too, like books for Autumn and all biscuits and cake treats for Geoff and me from Williamsons bakery.

I decided to go to our local butcher in Hartford called Littlers, whilst Geoff was out at the supermarket, because there is always a big queue on a Friday and only two people are allowed in at a time. It was a good decision, as I was able to walk straight in and buy some chicken fillets, some diced lamb, bacon chops to go with our Cheshire new potatoes and some of those delicious handmade lamb and mint burgers, just in case we do have another BBQ, if the warm weather decides to return to us again.

Geoff was back with everything ticked off the list that we needed to buy. Together we put the shopping away, then breathed a sigh of relief that we did not need to go out in the morning, only for some fresh vegetables and fruit for the weekend ahead.

We enjoyed a salad and ham sandwich for Geoff, whilst I tucked into a salmon sandwich and salad. We were able to enjoy our lunch outside again, just love eating outdoors.

My telephone pings with an incoming FaceTime call from Sarah and Autumn. We always find it exciting to be able to chat to them both, to listen to what they have been doing together. Autumn proudly shows off her latest baking achievements of raspberry buns. Autumn tells us all about her craft skills in making lots of cards and drawings to show us.

Sarah and Autumn make us laugh so much, it is like a double act. Autumn puts her eyes so close to the phone screen, that we are actually looking straight into her eyes, likewise she is looking straight into our eyes. It is just magical!

Today, the weather was one of those perfect blue-sky days with vivid sharp colours everywhere we looked. The trees did not look real, they were so green, almost like an oil painting to be preserved for ever. It just goes to show that without the air and car traffic, how much clearer and fresher the world around us has become.

We decide to go for a bike ride this afternoon whilst the weather is good. My bike is very old and is a trusty Raleigh Town and Country bicycle, which I love and feel it could be renovated and repainted. However, Geoff feels that it does need to be replaced with a lighter model. We both feel that it will cost me as much as a new bike to strip my old bike down and repair it. I agree with Geoff that it would probably be cheaper to buy a new one. We decide to wait and see, as once Chumley comes back home again, it is unlikely that we will be free to go out on bike rides together again. Our cycle route takes us through Hartford and down the Northwich By-pass and home again via Hunts Lock. It is warm and sunny and despite a couple of wobbles setting off from the drive, I soon master my bike again. I enjoy cycling once more, regardless of the creaking sounds emitting from my rusty 20-year-old bike.

Once home, we sit outside for a while in the warm sunshine, then I do a bit more sewing on the dress that I am making for Autumn. Geoff prepares tea which is a Chilli Jam Chicken Recipe with brown rice. I have to say it was totally yummy. I am cooking tomorrow night, which will be bacon chops with new potatoes, asparagus and button mushrooms sautéed in butter.

It's not good news from the Vet tonight. Chumley's blood tests are still too low, the steroids do not appear to be making much difference. Chumley remains lively, there is no sign of any further bleeding happening. It may be possible to give Chumley a blood transfusion, whilst they continue to look for the solutions.

We both agree that this should be ordered, then administered to Chumley, if his blood count drops any lower than is safe. We are advised however, that a blood transfusion will put the platelets back into Chumley's system but will only mask his underlying problem to keep him going for a while longer, but it will make it harder for the vets to know what the root of Chumley's problem is, without looking into his bone marrow to take a sample.

The vet informs us that it is difficult for them to progress until Chumley's immune system restarts itself. We agree that it is the right time now to order a blood transfusion. We all feel that should his blood levels drop to a dangerous point over the weekend, the next stage will be to give the steroids one more week. This course of action meets our agreement, just in case Chumley's immune system is being slow to respond. We feel sad and low tonight.

Friday 15th May 2020

We slept well, despite our concerns for Chumley. I was in a much better frame of mind than last night, when I felt so tearful. I had a few WhatsApp chats with Sarah too, who sent me the Coronavirus coaster video.

I left early to shop in Waitrose. I spent a fortune on 2 bottles of lovely wine, bread, snacks, fruit, and some chocolates for the weekend ahead.

The update from Andy the vet is unchanged for Chumley, he is bright and happy, with a waggy tail, but still no further increase in his platelet count. The good news he has stopped bleeding internally. The only option open to us is to be patient, whilst we wait with hope in our hearts.

Petrol has dropped to 0.99 per litre, which is the lowest it has been for years. I have not put any petrol in my car since February. I fill it up this morning at a cost of £11.00 in total! I normally put £25 a week into my car fuel tank.

Geoff is finishing painting the last final sections of the hall, stairs and landing. We have put one lampshade up temporarily.

We enjoy some gardening together, mow the lawns, then undertake some general tidying up outside in the garden. It soon becomes lunchtime, which is enjoyed outside once again. Later this afternoon, we prepare the kitchen for the emulsion painting tomorrow.

I spend the afternoon working on my sewing project of a dress for Autumn, there is a lot for me to learn and progress is slow. I soon discover that I need some lining for the bodice top, along with elastic for the waistband. I rummage around in my fabrics, but I do not seem to have anything suitable. I decide that I will order on-line, but I cannot find the exact lining I need to purchase. I telephone an on-line fabric shop to ask their advice. It must have been too late, as there was no answer from the number I rang. I will try again on Monday. Most shops and businesses are operating a skeleton service and working from home. The hours that the shops are open for business has changed significantly. More people are working from home and not from their normal place of work.

I cooked tea for a change tonight. We enjoyed some baby Cheshire potatoes, with asparagus, pan fried button mushrooms and bacon chops. Our meal was simply delicious.

At 7.00 pm we switched the TV on for the usual Friday Andrew Lloyd 'Webber Musical. Tonight, it is a theatre version of 'Cats on the TV, which is being streamed. As always, it is free to watch during Lockdown. We have chocolate and wine to enjoy. I have let my friend Sue Merrill know which musical it is, so that she can watch it too. After about an hour of watching, we decide we are not really enjoying the show. We do not like the story or the music.

I send a WhatsApp message to Sue; she feels the same about Cats that she is not enjoying it either. I tell her that we have decided to switch over and try the Cirque Du Soliel 60 minutes special on ice. The aerobatics of the show 'Crystal' will be performed during the first part of tonight's performance. The tickets for this were on sale earlier in the year for the Albert Hall in London. I almost bought tickets for us at Christmas. Thank goodness I didn't! Sue said she is going to join us in her home, to watch the same show with us. Cirque Du Soliel on ice, was absolutely brilliant.

Saturday 16th May 2020

Louise is now back on duty at Willows Veterinary Practice. Louise was the vet who admitted Chumley on the afternoon of my birthday on the 6th May. Then rang us on Thursday 7th May to advise us of an option to look at giving Chumley a massive dose of Chemotherapy, to help to kick start his platelet count.

There is still no change in Chumley outwardly, Louise informs us, and she thinks that he looks a bit bored today. However, he is lively when trotting out for his toilet breaks and he is eating well. They are not going to send any further blood samples off until Monday to the external lab.

If she has time, Louise told us that she will take another sample herself, then complete a manual count again. Louise is going to ring us tomorrow morning, as there will be nothing further that she can do today, to make a difference to Chumley's platelet levels.

I am quite excited this morning as I am just about to sign into a Virtual Gladstone's Library Writing Conference, which was due to take place at Gladstone's Library, Hawarden last week, but had to be cancelled due to COVID-19 circumstances. However, my writing group decided to switch the plans to a Virtual conference on-line today using ZOOM which Bill Webster has kindly organised for us. I will write up the details of our virtual day together, later today or tomorrow. The course starts at 9.15 and should finish around 1.15 pm today. It is 9.00 am already. I will make myself a coffee, then join the conference early, just in case there are any hiccups.

Gladstone's Virtual Writing Course on Saturday 16th May, 2020 .
9.15 am to 1.15 pm
Attendees

Bill Webster
Bob Barker
Joan Dowling
Linda Leigh
Mark Acton
Robyn Cain

Selina Kirkham
Stephen Morrisey

Bob will send a Zoom invitation out to ALL members in due course. So, while we will form the committed core of the meeting, hopefully others will join us on the day.

The rough agenda I suggested to Bob is as follows:

- 09.15-09.30 Gather and chat
- 09.30-10.30 Exercise 1 (including readings)
- 10.30-10.45 Coffee and cake!
- 10.45-11.45 Exercise 2 (including readings)
- 11.45-12.00 Tea, coffee, beer, or wine
- 12.00-13.00 Exercise 3 (including readings)
- 13.00-????

Wind-down, feedback, goodbyes Meeting close.

Sunday 17th May 2020

We received our early morning call from the vet about Chumley, today her news upset us both very much. Louise the vet told us that unfortunately, she had tested another sample of blood from Chumley yesterday, worryingly his platelets still remain low at a count of 3. This is not good news at all. We asked Louise what the next course of action is and if the analysing machine is accurate? The machine has displayed some discrepancies on previous tests. Louise said it is accurate. Louise has also undertaken a manual count, with the same result. Our next 2 options to consider she said, could be to try Chumley on another stronger drug for his immune system.

We asked what side effects the change in medication could cause? Louise informed us that it can lead to severe vomiting and diarrhoea. The second option for us to consider is to let Chumley be anaesthetised. Once Chumley is asleep, they can aspirate the bone marrow in Chumley to see if there are signs of cancer, stopping his platelet regeneration.

We asked what the risks of this procedure would be? Louise said that the worst-case scenario would be that Chumley could bleed during the procedure, but other than that, he should survive ok. Our next question to Louise was "if he has cancer in his bone marrow, then what would his quality of life be like? Also, what was the point of doing the procedure if cancer is suspected?" Louise informed us that he can be given cancer drugs. Both

Geoff and I were crying at this point and found the conversation with Louise difficult. We asked if we are now running out of options for Chumley and questioned once again, as to whether we should let him go, rather than prolong his suffering, or quality of life. Louise told us that Chumley is so bright eyed and busy tailed, he is eating well and is playful.

Louise told us that at this moment on the ward, Chumley is showing no signs of discomfort or pain. The only suffering they can see with him at the moment, is that he is raring to go. Understandably, he is a bit bored at times, especially with limited exercise. Louise felt strongly that whilst Chumley is showing such good physical signs, we have to keep going to help him to become well again We all agreed not to start Chumley on any more drugs, until after we have a further fresh blood sample processed and analysed by the external laboratory on Tuesday.

Louise would need to refer Chumley to a specialist vet for a bone marrow aspiration to be undertaken. We all agreed to hold back any further decision making until Tuesday. In the meantime, Louise is going to send us a little video clip of Chumley later today. It will be a good boost for us to see a video of him. It is frustrating that we cannot go and visit him. The risk of bringing him home is too great with those low platelet levels. We are told that if he bumped into anything at all, he would bleed continuously inside.

Geoff and I spend a tearful worrying day and evening. When the video clip arrived from Louise, we both could not stop crying.

Chumley looked just like the Chumley we love and miss so much. He was bright eyed and wagging his tail, whilst playing with a soft toy and having so much fun! Most evenings after tea, Chumley will select a particular toy from his box for us to play with him, exactly like Louise is doing. It causes us to shed more tears, watching the video repeatedly. The video clip gives us a strong message, that we do have to try and find a solution, that will enable us to give him every opportunity, to return back home to us.

We spend the rest of the day finishing the kitchen painting and gardening outside. It is so hard to concentrate. Both of us are under no illusion, that if Tuesday brings bad news, our decisions will be tough ones to make.

I make us a delicious salmon meal with new potatoes and runner beans for tea. I open a bottle of white wine too, which is delicious.

During the evening, I type up my scribbled handwriting from the exercises given to us at the virtual Gladstones writing group ZOOM event, which I enjoyed yesterday morning. I am quite pleased with my efforts as all 3 exercises, allowed me to stretch my imagination for each of the three exercises.

My completed exercises from yesterday are shown on the next few pages:

1.Bill's exercise

We are given 5 minutes to have a root round our own homes. Then return to the ZOOM meeting with an object to show the group. We have to briefly describe the object and how we came to be the owner/keeper of such an object?

After we have finished showing all our individual objects to each other on ZOOM. We are given 25 minutes to write a poem or story, in the first-person account of how we came to own the object. We must not be truthful in the story, or else it will be disqualified!!

My object was a hand painted boomerang bought from the aborigines at Ayers Rock Australia. This was a special trip for us when we visited Sydney for the very first time in our life. It was my 50th Birthday and we met up with our son Anthony, who was backpacking around the world. At this this point in his travels, he had reached Manley, Australia, where he was staying for the last 6 months of his travels.

My story

It is 6th May, 2003 Today, it is my birthday and it's one of those milestone birthdays. I am half a century old inside my head, but actually and physically, I am a teenager without a care in the world, who at just 18 years old, knows that I have the world at my feet!

For my 18th Birthday Celebrations. I have robbed a bank, well not a real bank, as in the high street! Let me explain. I was with my friends a few weeks ago. During the evening, we were chatting about getting out there and seeing the world, living our dreams about travelling, whilst we are young. But we needed cash to do carry out these plans, to fulfil our dreams. Well, it was quite easy really, you see my granny who is ancient, keeps a shoebox underneath her bed and every day, she adds more notes than I can count, which isn't much at all. I was always rubbish at maths. I am good at putting piles of 10 sets of notes together, scattering them around the floor of my bedroom. My brainbox boyfriend does the sums for me and takes a share of the bounty too.

My granny's notes are $1000 dollar bills, and she receives them from her rich toy boy every week. The money is for services rendered between the British and American Citizens. These people live side by side in every street, in all the towns and cities of the UK ever since the USA and UK joined forces, to become one country known as UKUSA.

Our plan is to nick a few of these $1000 notes, then head off to live our lives. We intend to live life to the full! It's not our intention to be saddled with hundreds of babies between us all. So, last week, I stashed several thousand-dollar notes in my nightdress case. How? you may well ask. I did it when staying for a sleepover at my grannies most nights, by nicking the shoebox swiftly from under the bed, during those loud snoring hours of 3.00 am, when granny was elsewhere in her exhausted physical state of mind and body. It was a piece of cake to whip in and out of the shoebox, judging by the amount of notes, someone has been having a good time, most hours of each day!! Anyway, brainbox, feels we each have enough cash now to live our dreams and travel.

My first trip is to the iconic city of Sydney in Australia, it is a 24-hour flight to get there from Manchester, but I don't mind. I will just eat, drink, read, watch a film and repeat over again.

I want to catch myself a kangaroo when I arrive, so that I can bounce around the city. Oh yes I want a real Koala Bear to cuddle. They look so cute on all the films I watch. My final mission is to throw a boomerang at the Sydney Opera House and watch it circle up high, then fly around the famous Sydney Bridge, before it returns into my thieving hands.

So, the first thing that I need to do when I land in Sydney, is to find myself a weather beaten looking genuine aborigine from the settlement at Ayers Rock. I read in a travel book, that they tend to sit around the harbour at Sydney. This is the area where the Manley Ferries depart each day, carrying tourists that are going back and to in the ferry boats, between Sydney and Manley.

If I find myself a genuine aborigine, his boomerangs will bear the hallmark of true witchcraft. A hand painted boomerang will contain enough magic within its abstract painted features, to make my boomerang a super special one, that is guaranteed to fly and return.

I know this to be a fact. I am quite a clever clog really!! I have read that to obtain a genuine boomerang . I must avoid the tempting display of boomerangs laid out for the tourists, on a cloth sack for sale on the harbour wall. Instead, I must look for the one sticking out of the aborigine's baggy trouser pockets. My plan is to nick it, then run as fast as my legs will carry me. When I am at a safe distance from the scene of my crime. I will launch my boomerang at the opera house. I will stare open mouthed, as it returns into my thieving hands, which I will then bring home to keep forever. This object will remind me of the fun I had, and I will be able to tell my story for years to come!

2. Exercise from Robyn

Look around the room you are in now and select one object.

We each listed the following objects between us.

- Red wine bottle half full
- Battery Charger
- Box of coloured pens
- Microphone
- Gecko/Lizard
- Gavel
- Biscuit Tin

Robyn told us that our family were being held as hostages and needed to escape.

They had been captured by a group of scientists and were being held captive by guards who were watching their every move including going to the toilet with them and they needed to escape. In the room, were the above 7 objects.

I cannot believe that my beautiful family have been taken hostage and are in a laboratory with a group of eminent scientists who are guarding them day and night.

How can I help them to escape, I wonder? I rapidly run through my head different scenarios!!

If I look up on Google or YouTube very quickly, I can probably get them to make a bomb using some of the items I know are scattered around the laboratory that they are being held captive in.

So here goes with my downloaded recipe for escape, but disaster to all could occur if great care is not adhered to

Ingredients are the 7 items shown above.

Methodology is as follows: -

Tuck the battery charger under your arm
Pierce the caps on the battery charger using the plastic covered colouring pens that you are pretending to use to colour a masterpiece drawing of one of the guards

Use the live lizard to bite into the guard's legs whilst they are asleep on the job

Pick the Gabble up to make lots of noisy sounds to deafen and distract the guards

Take the Microphone and shout loudly that the world's deadliest rattlesnake has just uncoiled itself from the dark corner, keep shouting "over here, over here" in a terrified voice. The guards will then saunter across nonchalantly to take a look at all the noise.

Empty the biscuit tin where your imaginary rattlesnake is moving and keep saying to the dark corner, here eat these poisonous mouldy old biscuits you little horrid rattlesnake!

To Cook

Now get ready to run as the guards bend down to see if the rattlesnake is eating the bait of mouldy old biscuits and whack the guards firmly on their heads with the half-finished bottle of red wine. If you make it sharp and fast as hard as you can on those skulls of theirs, they will fall down to the floor unconscious and as you drop the bottle it will shatter into several large shards of glass. Take the biggest piece of shard and stab the guards to death but be quick with it.

Open the door, throw down your battery charger, which will spontaneously ignite the red wine and explode into the lab, destroying the guards by melting their faces and bodies in slow agony.

Finally, don't look back, but run like hell down the stairs and escape into the warm sunshine and freedom at last!!

Stephen's Exercise

We discussed religious mystiques, magic mushrooms, mystical consciousness, cosmic homecoming beyond words

The exercise needs us to each imagine what sort of experience we would have if we participated in taking magic mushrooms or other drugs that give a controlled experience which will give you the person something like you have never experienced before.

We discussed how often opium and drugs that give the user a pleasant happy feeling are often used in patients with cancer.

The exercise requires the start of the journey, the middle and the end of the experience, it must capture sense, feeling and outcome.

Start

I enter the room and walk slowly to the comfy sofa in the corner where I can see out of the window but cannot be seen by anyone.

There is soft music playing, it is romantic piano music and as I sit there quietly, I feel the stresses and tensions of the day start to leave my body at last!! It feels like those heady days of being away on holiday when your whole body just collapses in on itself in sheer relief from the stresses and strains of everyday life, where you are pulled and pushed in all directions by the mad busy lives we all rush around in!!

I am wearing a loose flowing summery cotton dress, no tight clothes are on me, no restricting sleeves, leggings or tights, my body feels light and free, I do keep my underwear on though! Just in case you ask!!

The drink is waiting for me to take that first cool sip from the simple crystal rimmed glass etched with deep red strawberries. Inside the glass is my pale honey coloured liquid which continuously keeps bubbling happily making me reach for it and slowly allow it to ripple over my tongue with delight at its pure sweetness of tropical pear and orange blossom mingled with pineapple.

I take my time and sip each drop with my eyes closed as I drift off into my dreams.

There is no rushing sound, no drumbeat. I simply sip and smile as every single taut wire in my programmed body pings and allows me to be released from the constant grip of constricting bands onto a grassy meadow full of sunflowers waving to me with happy faces turned upwards to heaven.

I feel light and floaty as if I am a butterfly flitting around just whispering quietly to the colourful flowers everywhere telling them how much I love them.

There is a sudden rush inside my head like the feeling of tearing down a runway on a jet plane at 500 mph. It is not an unpleasant sensation; in fact, it is quite the opposite, as I eagerly anticipate the final thrust of being sent soaring high into the cobalt blue sky, with the earth below me framed in tiny specs of browns and greens, like a patchwork quilt intersected with long grey lines criss-crossing every now and then.

I sigh with ecstasy and feel elated beyond any earthly experience that I know.

There is pure joy rushing through my body at 100 mph, I can feel all the blackness being swept away and it feels like I am being cleansed in a hot foaming bubble bath that just keeps regenerating its milky warmth around me.

I have no fear, I see no danger, I am free from pain, my body is totally weightless. I am a fluffy cloud billowing across the sky and blowing my own little rainbow bubbles out around me just like the magic bubbles trip so easily from a child's wand when they are small and never cease to delight. I feel excited and happy on this journey that is mine alone!

I look down and see happy people smiling at me, I smile back at them, they wave, and I wave back blowing kisses as I drift on by.

The wind that is carrying me on my journey picks up speed as it heads out west, across an inky blue sea frothing with foam and huge waves, begging me to ride on the crest of its highest waves with my surfboard as it sends the salty spray over me with laughter and rolls itself back once more to the shore.

The horizon dips and rises just like the waves below. But ahead the hot fierce sun beckons me on, I look around at so many vivid colours from dusty pink, purple hues, to burnt orange, fiery red, for a grand finale as it sinks to the ocean alive and big, penetrating my soul with riches of light that surpass all the rainbow colours I know and sending me riches that I could not have dreamt about even if I had tried.

I wonder briefly if I have died as the tunnel of light swings open wider and carries me towards its epicentre, I cry out the pleasure is so intense, this must be heaven as all around is peacefulness and calm as two doves fly close to me, are they angels? Am I being carried by whom?

Suddenly, it is over, I am back in my old comfy chair in the corner gazing out of the window once more, where no-one can see me at all, or know where I have been this past hour or so. All is well, as I came home once more.

I thoroughly enjoyed the online virtual workshop today with my writing group colleagues.

We each said our goodbyes before signing off and gave our thanks to Bill for organising the course.

Monday 18th May 2020

We wake up early, enjoy our early morning cup of tea in bed and discuss our plans for the day ahead. Geoff has the gloss paintwork to do in the kitchen and the upstairs handrail to sand down and repaint. I have some washing to do and will clean everywhere up once Geoff has finished painting. We can then put the kitchen back together and the job should be finished by lunch time. We both agree that after lunch today, we need to go out, to have a break from the house to recharge our batteries.

Louise telephones to tell us that Chumley is just the same. He is very happy in himself is bright eyed and bushy tailed, there are no indications whatsoever, that he has any further bleeding going on inside him.

His gums are healthy, his wee and poo are all looking clear and free from any untoward bleeding.

Louise will leave it to the very last minute of the day, before she takes a fresh blood sample, for sending to the external laboratory. This arrangement should give Chumley the chance to make more platelets. Louise has already told Chumley, that he needs to produce at least 60 platelets for her later today.

We thank Louise very much for all that she is doing for our little boy. We tell her that we feel stronger today, that we really appreciated the little video she sent to us, showing Chumley enjoying some playtime. Louise told us that all the nurses and vets have fallen in love with Chumley. Everyone is working hard to make him better for us.

The kitchen is finally finished and looks great with a fresh coat of paint in Kiwi Crush and Willow tree. We do some other jobs whilst waiting for the gloss paint to dry.

After lunch, we drive to Chester to a superstore B&Q . We want to look for a few bits and pieces for the kitchen, such as the photo frame, hanging stickers, a mirror and some lampshades. It is our furthest journey since Lockdown. We enjoy the drive to Chester, the roads are quiet, which is most unusual and surreal It felt like turning the clocks back to the sixties, when very few cars were on the roads.

We arrive at B&Q take one look at the long snaking queue outside the store and decide we do not want to stand in it for hours and that it is not worth the risk to us either.

We noticed on our way into the store that across the road, Dunelm is open. So, we drive to the car park for Dunelm and enter the store. There is no queue, they have an abundance of hand sanitisers to use outside and inside the store.

Within a few minutes of being in the store, with our face masks on, we find two lampshades, the photo frame hanging stickers. Geoff picks up 2 smart plugs, which will enable him to programme our lights to be switched on and off, using voice control from Alexa in the lounge.

We drive over to the M&S food store on the retail park at Ellesmere Port. I have run out of the wildflower honey that I like. I bought 3 jars of it as we went into Lockdown, which have all gone now.

There is no queue at Marks and Spencer. It feels quite exciting to be returning to a store, that we used to enjoy a few treats from when our store in Northwich was open. Sadly, the store closed last year, due to decisions made by the company, to shut down many of its smaller town branches much to our disappointment.

Once inside the store, we feel a bit anxious as we have to follow a one-way system to go all round the shop floor. The aisles are in total darkness. We walk past many rails with lots of clothes hanging on them, with the usual underwear, bags and shoes etc. Nobody stops to look or touch, we just keep walking in single file, 2 metres apart from other customers, until we reach the food hall queue. We wait a few minutes to be allowed inside. The system in place allows one customer to enter as one customer leaves the shop, thus allowing another customer inside. We notice that the shelves are quite empty. It feels grim, no one speaks or looks at you. We learn not to go down aisles, where other shoppers are browsing. It is like playing a game of cat and mouse.

We arrive at the shelves of jams and honey which are quite empty. My wildflower honey is nowhere in sight, so I choose an acacia honey in a small plastic bottle. We buy some herbs and one of Geoff's favourite steak pies. Having completed our purchases, we make our way to the cashiers, as directed by the staff wearing protective plastic visors. We both feel that it was a complete waste to come here, we both cannot wait to leave the store and drive home. Shopping is just not like it used to be we think that it may never return to be the same. At least, we had a couple of hours away from home together, without worrying about Chumley, for a short while.

Geoff prepares our tea as soon as we arrive home. Tonight, he is cooking us a new chicken dish which is Chicken and Chorizo Rice Pot using wild brown rice. It is delicious, as all his cooking is just lately. Geoff is excellent at finding new recipes, to try out.

After tea I log onto our Vale Royal Writing Group fortnightly ZOOM catch up and reading meeting at 6.30 pm for a couple of hours. I enjoy listening to some great reading, from pieces of work that some of my colleagues have produced. Karen Wheatley who teaches creative writing at Sir John Deane's College and whose classes I have attended, arranges a further meeting for Thursday 21st May at 6.30 pm to teach us all about Scrivener. I am using Scrivener for this project and for another book about my birth mother. I am looking forward to learning more about the software on Thursday.

Tuesday 19th May 2020

We sleep better, as it is a cool morning. We decide to finish the hall and landing painting by revarnishing the top banister rail. I put some washing in the washing machine.

The weather looks promising for another dry day today. It is going to be a long day for us both, waiting to hear the outcome of Chumley's blood tests by the external laboratories.

By the middle of the afternoon, the outside temperature was starting to rise to 19 degrees with the sun coming out of the clouds too, warming our back garden up. We decide that too much work has been done by us both, over the last few days. It is time to just sit and chill in the garden, whilst waiting for the all-important telephone call from Louise the vet at the practice, where Chumley is being cared for.

I decide to cancel my on-line Zumba class tonight just in case the vet rings, whilst I am in the middle of the Zumba class.

The telephone rings at 3.30 pm and Louise tells us that sadly Chumley's platelets are still only 4 in total. He should have 200 platelets for his normal requirements. We are so disappointed and can tell that Louise is struggling to tell us this news from her voice, she sounds tearful. Louise along with all the nursing team, have not only rooted for Chumley, but have given him so much tender care, even fallen in love with him too.

We ask what the next stage is? Together we agree to give Chumley a stronger drug for one week, to see if this will help to kick-start his immune system. This final push may generate some platelets. Louise gives us the hard facts that the drug of choice for Chumley is a very toxic one. It has quite severe side effects with vomiting and diarrhoea. It may not work, or it might, there are risks, with pros and cons for us to think about.

In the meantime, although Chumley is still quite poorly,

Louise feels that perhaps a few days at home with us might help to lift our spirits and Chumley's. Louise arranges for us to collect Chumley at 6.30 pm this evening. We have to telephone her as soon as we are parked on the car park. Louise will bring him out of the veterinary surgery to us on a lead, to pass over without compromising the social distancing rules.

We are able to chat on the car park, with Louise for a few minutes. Both of us are delighted to see Chumley again after 2 weeks. He is ecstatic to see us.

Louise feels that if this drug does not help Chumley, then he must have some underlying disease which is attacking his immune system, then destroying all his platelets and blood cells. Chumley is still quite anaemic, but Louise is not too worried. The test results for 'Tick Invasion' are negative. We are relieved that he hadn't been infected by a Tic. We thought it was unlikely, as we do groom him after every walk. Both of us always check for ticks or other insects sticking in his coat.

Louise still feels that the next stage would be to perform a CT scan on Chumley, then to complete an aspiration of his bone marrow where the platelets are normally made to see if something is going astray? Or to check if he has cancer spreading rapidly within his bones. Neither Geoff nor I are keen to go down this final route. Only to discover that Chumley has cancer. Whilst there is no cure, we feel very strongly that we do not want Chumley to have a reduced quality of life. He would become a shadow of his former self, requiring cancer drugs for the rest of his life. We feel he would suffer too much.

On a brighter note, it is so lovely to bring Chumley home. To be able to give him lots of tender cuddles and play gently with him. He looks sad in his eyes and is totally exhausted too. His whole demeanour is one of lethargy. Chumley is just not himself. We realise that he hasn't got enough blood in his system, which in turn reduces the amount of oxygen circulating in his body. Coming back home is traumatic for him, as well as us, so we go to bed early. During the night we each take turns round the clock to look after him.

Wednesday 20th May 2020

Geoff and I are a bit bleary eyed this morning from lack of sleep. Geoff was downstairs at 1.30 am with Chumley making sure he was doing ok. I came down at 4.30 am and sat in the conservatory with him until breakfast time for us all at 7.30 am. I know I will not last the day and Geoff is the same.

The sun is a hot high ball in the sky this morning. We put all the cushions out and wind the Parasol umbrellas up. Our intention is to be outside all day long and enjoy the beautiful weather, whilst it is here today.

Louise our vet will be sorting out the new strong drugs for Chumley, which we will collect when they ring to tell us that the drugs have arrived.

The news today on BBC is that Colonel Tom Moore is to be knighted. He will be known officially as Captain Sir Thomas Moore under the Ministry of Defence Protocol for his fund-raising efforts after a special nomination from the Prime Minister.

The war veteran raised more than £32 million for the NHS Charities by completing 100 laps of his garden before his 100th birthday in April. The knighthood was formerly announced by the Queen today.

Boris Johnson said that Colonel Tom's fantastic fund-raising broke records and inspired the whole country. Boris said that everyone has been moved by his incredible story. Tom is a true national treasure, who has brought inspiration to millions and helped all of us to celebrate the extraordinary achievements of the NHS. Tom has embodied the national solidarity, which has grown throughout the crisis. He has showed us that everyone can play their part in helping to build a better future.

As it is such a lovely morning, I am going to walk into town to collect my prescription from Boots.

We enjoy a ZOOM meeting at 3.00 pm with Cathy, Chris, Carol, and Bob. No sign of the Suttie's. So, we message them, they ring back to say that they had gone to Derby to collect some plaster, as they want to push on with their house project.

Whilst we are talking to our friends on ZOOM, Kerry one of the receptionists at the Willows Veterinary Group telephones, to let us know that Chumley's new medication has arrived. We have to telephone her as soon as we are on the car park, so that she can pass the drugs safely, through the window to us.

The temperature outside is 30 degrees. There is not a cloud in the blue sky. We stay outside all day long. We enjoy garlic bread for lunch. Tonight, we had a BBQ for tea, consisting of minty lamb burgers with ginger and spring onion sausages, served with fried onions on brioche buns. It is just heavenly to eat outside, in the warm sunshine.

After tea, I take two birthday cards out to deliver locally through the letterboxes, the first one is for LJ who is 6 years old tomorrow. The second one is for my niece whose birthday it is on Friday. I buy a long bar of Swiss nougat chocolate with the words Superhero on for LJ and a big box of Jelly Baby sweets for his sister Seren. I knock on their door and stand at a social distance chatting to the parents Richard and Jen. LJ and Seren peep through the door too. They are so mega excited to see me, and likewise I enjoyed seeing all of them too, they are a lovely family.

It is so hard to avoid hugs, but we did and kept our distances. Their grandparents Carol and Bob remain in Paphos, Cyprus. They flew out on the 9th March 2020. Our friends had no idea that they would be locked down, unable to fly home. However, it is the safest place for them to be as Cyprus has had so few deaths. The total number of deaths is 20 across the whole Island, which is now completely free of further cases. Cyprus acted decisively and quickly at the start of the outbreak, by ensuring all tourists returned home.

No other tourists were allowed to travel and arrive on the island.

The government imposed stricter lockdown measures than the UK. It also put curfew on each person residing in the country. As a result of the measure imposed earlier, Bob and Carol can move around more freely again, within governmental guidelines.

Our friends are hoping to catch a flight home in July, when the planes will be able to fly safely again across Europe and the rest of the world hopefully.

I take a birthday card and an orchid plant to my niece Rosalyn, who lives in Leftwich with Alan her husband, who is also my nephew. I leave the card and present on their doorstep, then knock on the front door to let them know I am outside their home.

Together, they talk to me through their lounge window which remains shut. Chatting through a closed window, is strange and surreal, but the safest way of speaking to each other for now.

Thursday 21st May 2020

No sleep. I am up at 4.00 am with Chumley. I am fully dressed. We all walk down to the river, at the back of where we live, for a 10-minute slow stroll, whilst it is still cool. The sunrise is so beautiful this morning.

Geoff has gone to do our food shopping early this morning, then to B&Q for some paintbrushes that he needs to buy so that he can reach behind the radiators.

I spend the morning cleaning up, checking everywhere over, even more thoroughly, with Chumley home. We were given strict advice about the latest drugs Mycophenolate, being extremely toxic to us and furnishings. The wearing of disposable gloves is essential at all times.

We both have a lazy afternoon; it is warm enough to sit outside again, after a cloudy cool start this morning.

Tea is griddled chicken with some delicious New Cheshire potatoes, which are the best, particularly the first crops of the season, when they are small in size. Once cooked, we drizzle butter and mint sauce over them.

Geoff is feeling incredibly sad and tearful today. He feels that Chumley is just not himself at all. Geoff feels that we are being cruel by even trying the new medication. Deep down inside his heart, he feels strongly, that it is not going to improve Chumley's chances of recovery at all.

I feel more optimistic than Geoff is today. I tell him that we have to trust the vets who have prescribed this new drug for Chumley. It is a last chance for him and a potential answer to his platelet recovery.

I joined in with the online ZOOM Scrivener meeting at 6.30 pm this evening which was hosted by our Chairperson for the Vale Royal Writers Group Bob Barker but organised and delivered by Karen Wheatley, who teaches creative writing for Sir John Deane's College.

Scrivener is a piece of software which allows you to write a novel, short story or any piece of writing, similar to using word. However, it is far more sophisticated than word. I have bought the full version of Scrivener. I have been self-teaching myself about it too. But I am looking forward to being taught it by an expert teacher tonight, along with my writing colleagues. I thoroughly enjoyed the course and learnt so much from Karen, who is a brilliant teacher. She explained the features of the software and its capabilities perfectly. I was totally inspired with her clear and concise teaching methods.

My course finished at 8.30 pm. Geoff did the NHS clapping and cheering for us both, outside our front door. We have heard that this may cease next week. We have enjoyed the chance to shout across to our neighbours, whilst clapping and ringing bells, along with making much noise! We cannot give enough thanks for all the hard work that the NHS are delivering 24 hours every day, for everyone in the country, during this dreadful pandemic time.

We continue to enjoy the early evening sunshine as we sit quietly outside with Chumley, until late evening. The weather is warm and balmy. Tonight, is one of those lovely long light evenings, without any darkness. The summer season has started earlier this year. If these amazing blue-sky days continue, it should be a long hot summer in the UK.

Chumley is very happy this evening. He is quite playful too. It's as if he is just like a puppy again. We enjoy the fact that he is very tactile with us tonight. He keeps bringing his tennis ball to play with, then searches for a favourite toy from his toybox until he finds the one he wants. We laugh with joy at his funny antics. Life feels normal and good again.

Geoff took Chumley for his last toilet break before bedtime. He was concerned, as there was a small amount of fresh blood in Chumley's stools. Nothing more than the size of a small grain of rice, but it indicates that Chumley is bleeding internally. We decide to ring the vet in the morning, as it is quite late now. We nurse Chumley through the night with no sleep for us at all. Chumley is peaceful and does not appear to be in any pain.

In our imaginations, we feel that he may just suffer a lot of blood loss, this might be our goodbye to him, we hope not and that he pulls through.
Neither of us can sleep.

Friday 22nd May 2020

In the morning we ring the vet at 9.00 am. We know from the past few weeks that they are busy first thing and usually changing shifts and handing over the cases to the team coming in for the day. The receptionist tells us that she has spoken to the vet about Chumley. The vet is busy at the moment, but he will ring us back later this morning. We are both upset, we spend the morning cuddling Chumley on the rug wearing our gloves. Although he is noticeably quiet and not himself, there is a resignation in his eyes with a deep look of love passing between him and us from his gorgeous eyes. He knows, we know too. We try to prepare ourselves for the inevitable. It is an emotional morning of shedding buckets of tears between us both.

Andy one of the vets who has been looking after Chumley along with Louise telephones us at 12.15 pm. Andy listens to our description of the blood in Chumley's stools. We describe how his demeanour is low and sad. Andy tells us that he is not worried too much about the slight blood loss. Chumley has not had any further blood loss in his body since 10.00 pm last night. Andy explains that Chumley has probably been too energetic inside the home.

Andy advises us that Chumley has to have complete rest. We must continue to use the garden for toilet breaks, not go for walks as Chumley will be feeling weak inside his body. Andy informs us that Chumley is in danger of losing blood, just by walking too much around the home or garden. He may be trying to display more energy, than he actually has at this moment in time. Andy advises us to walk Chumley on his lead for no more than 10 minutes once in a morning, then once in the evening. Complete rest for Chumley is essential at this stage.

Geoff asks Andy is it time for us to let Chumley go now? Andy's response is not at all, we all love

Chumley, and we are totally smitten with him. However, we would not let our clinical decisions for Chumley fail you, or prolong his life, if we thought that this treatment was not going to help him to recover his immune system and platelet regeneration. Andy has checked with the Specialist group clinical medical team this morning, about the medication and plans for Chumley to recover to full health again. Their advice is exactly the same as the other clinical experts.

If at any stage Chumley was not going to recover, Andy assures us again that the right clinical action would be taken. Andy tells us to ring him anytime at all over the weekend. Especially if we continue to worry, or if we see any further blood loss in his stools. Andy advises us to keep Chumley totally bed rested. The two short walks round the garden each day are sufficient. We need to encourage him to use our lawn for his toilet breaks. Andy asks us to ring the surgery with any news or worries about Chumley, or further blood loss in his stools. Andy told us that the receptionists will pass our messages on to him, so that he is kept informed.

Andy promises to ring us over the weekend as he is on duty until Tuesday next week. Geoff thanks Andy for giving us reassurance. He promises to let him know how we get on with Chumley. We will be keeping him totally rested, whilst checking for any further blood loss in his stools. If there are further concerns, we promise Andy that we will report these to him over the weekend via the reception staff.

We have some lunch, pull ourselves together and breathe a small sigh of relief.

Geoff pops to the churchyard at Davenham to mow the grass and bring the flowerpots home for me to refill. He forgot to take the handle off the lawn mower though, so he is disappointed to discover this when he arrives at the churchyard. Never mind he told himself,

I can do it tomorrow when I bring the pot back with fresh flowers. Geoff drives over to Bostock for some fresh eggs and to see if there are any Salvia plants left at the farm, where we bought 6 plants a few weeks ago.

I go out to town for a few bits of shopping that Geoff forgot to collect. I also want to buy some fresh flowers to put down on the grave at Davenham for Geoff's mum and dad whom we miss so very much. We are so glad they are not going through this pandemic experience though.

It is incredibly windy today. The garden is taking such a fierce battering. There is warmth in the sunshine. However, it's not possible to sit outside in the wind, which is so strong. It is battering all our hard work in the garden, just as my peonies are about to burst into flower.

Each Friday evening, we have enjoyed watching the free musical shows from Andrew Lloyd Webber, although we didn't enjoy Cats the Musical last week. However, we did enjoy the Cirque Du Soliel show Crystal performed on ice which was just outstanding last week. We check the listings and discover that tonight the musical is The Sound of Music, which was a big hit, when re-released a few years ago. The Cirque Du Soliel show is Kurios. I let my friend Sue Merrill know what is showing tonight. This is something we do each Friday, with each other and share our views.

We enjoy an early evening meal and settle down to watch The Sound of Music with a glass of wine and some chocolate. The Sound of Music does not disappoint. It is a fabulous uplifting musical. We find ourselves singing along with the songs, totally enraptured by the two-hour musical. We loved it and went to bed singing all the songs. For the first time in ages, we enjoyed a more peaceful sleep.

Saturday 23rd May 2020

We wake up to lots of garden detritus everywhere and know that it is going to take us a while to brush up all the leaves, particularly as it is still very windy outside today.

Chumley is looking brighter today, so we feel confident, that he is getting there slowly.

Geoff takes the beautiful pink carnations that I have arranged to Davenham churchyard and cuts the grass. He then pops down to Winnington Garden Centre on his way home for some growbags, along with a few more salvia plants for the garden.

When he returns home, he busies himself in the greenhouse. potting on our tomato plants. I bake some fruit scones for us to enjoy later.

Anthony telephones us to let us know that he is currently in Northwich at his flat that is for sale. He is picking up some post from the flat. He tells me on the phone, that he is going to come round to see us at a social distance on the front, or in the back garden, without coming into the house. We are excited to be able to see him again. He can enjoy a freshly baked hot scone, with us over a cup of tea when he arrives.

We enjoy chatting to Anthony in the garden. All three of us maintain a good social distance and sit outside. Chumley is looking glum, from inside our conservatory. He knows Anthony is here and is one of his favourite people, that he likes a cuddle with. However, we are reluctant to let Chumley outside in case he becomes over excited. Also, Chumley's new drug is toxic to others.

We have to wear gloves. In the end, we allow Chumley a very quick cuddle from Anthony whom we give protective gloves to wear, when stroking Chumley.

Chumley is so happy, wagging his tail furiously. He has enjoyed lots of adventures to the beach, with Anthony and Catherine. I feel happy seeing Chumley happy with Anthony. I tell Anthony that I think Chumley is turning a corner at last. Anthony shakes his head sadly, as he tells me with tears in his own eyes that Chumley is more poorly, than his dad and I can see. Anthony fills us in about the latest activities and growth developments with Niamh, who is cutting more teeth. Anthony told us how he taught her to climb the stairs yesterday. Anthony said she only needed showing once, then she was soon off! He does make us laugh.

It was just lovely to have some time with our son. He is hoping that his flat will sell soon, as they need to build an extension to their home. They can only move forward with the plan from the architect if the sale of his flat happens. Anthony bought the flat a few years ago as an investment for his future retirement. However, these particular flats were for sale at a much higher price, than they are worth now. The reason for a drop in value, has been caused by a massive surge in increased availability, of newly built house/flats within the town of Northwich. We wish him good luck. Tell him that we hope his flat will sell at a good price, despite being on the market for less than the original purchase cost.

We spend the rest of the day tidying up the garden and brushing leaves up.

Geoff prepares the same meal, we had after my birthday which was Chilli Lemon Tuna, and Tender-stem Broccoli with Spaghetti The meal is absolutely delicious the second time around, particularly with the garlic and parsley flatbread. It just had to be accompanied by a huge glass of white wine for me and a delicious Moretti Beer, for Geoff.

I have been feeling a bit flat and sad most of the day. I think the lack of hugging, not seeing my family and friends, is just getting to me more as we head into June. It is 3 months nearly, for us still being in

Lockdown. Yet the UK death toll continues to rise without abatement on its rampant path.

I am worried about schools opening again in just over a week. It is like sending lambs to the slaughterhouse I feel. Who is going to protect the children and the teachers from contracting this virus?

No proper PPE for the NHS staff, in many areas of the UK. Absolutely nothing even planned, to help the teachers, who will be in close proximity of parents, other children and staff. It all feels so risky.

Autumn will need to return to nursery whilst her mum our daughter, Sarah goes back to school as a key worker. However, Autumn will not be able to enjoy the same experience she has had at the nursery. Instead, she has to be dropped off, isolated from friends, not allowed to mix, staff unable to hug or cuddle her, or any of the children in their care.

It seems crazy to me; the guidance is so stupid that we cannot go and look after Autumn. We are perfectly fit and well with no underlying diseases and not over 70.

Yet Sarah and Paul can employ a cleaner and a child minder to enable Sarah to return to work. How utterly crazy is that? Surely, we can fulfil those roles, rather than have complete strangers in the home! I feel so mad today, at everything that does not seem rational to me! So many people have flouted the guidelines and rules such as having several visitors at their homes, grandchildren staying over, long drives to the coast and tourist spots.

Geoff and I have not had any visitors to our home, have followed the rules properly, carefully, and safely not just for ourselves, but for our families, friends and all people that we love.

We hope that we can return to normal life one day again soon, knowing we stayed safe for our family.

We want to stay alive to tell the stories. We do not want to be dead or suffer life changing conditions, from the consequences of rule breaking to allow COVID-19 to take any of us away forever.

Sunday 24th May 2020

We were up with the lark again this morning, a brew in bed at 5.00 am after Geoff returned from his early morning toilet break for Chumley.

I stayed in bed a bit longer. I tried to go to sleep, but I couldn't settle. So, I got up and pottered around downstairs with a very forlorn, sad looking Chumley this morning. I put my gloves on and spent some time stroking and cuddling him. I kept reassuring Chumley that he is going to be ok, he will feel better soon. Chumley doesn't seem to have the energy to lift his head up off his bed. He has not even wagged his tail at all this morning or touched his breakfast.

I bring this journal up to date. Then I spend a couple of hours typing on these pages. I lose myself and become engrossed in my thoughts as I write.

Geoff and I have breakfast together. We decide to take some chicken thighs out of the freezer for a Coq-au-Vin meal, later today.

It is cool outside, but still dry. Geoff is going to wash the windblown debris and dust off the cars this morning.

I will do a bit of tidying up. I will enjoy catching up with my Hartford Girls news and plans. Tricia Harrison sent us a message yesterday, to see if any of us would like some red and green pepper plants that are spare. I order one of each from Trish along with a couple of other friends. Tricia sends us a message, to let us know that she has put the pepper plants behind the land-rover, for us to collect this morning.

I drive to their yard in Sandy Lane, Whitegate to collect our two plants. I offer to go and collect

Elizabeth's for her too, but she is going for a walk this morning, then planning to call and collect the plants herself.

I arrive at the yard down Sandy Lane and cannot see a land-rover. There are a couple of cars parked inside, so I undo the gate and walk up towards the cars. A lady is feeding her horse, I ask if she has seen Trish and Phil anywhere this morning, or if not does she know where the land-rover will be parked?

I cannot see it anywhere, so I assume that perhaps they have not arrived yet. The kind lady tells me that Trish and Phil have not been seen this morning. She checks the stables for me in case the plants were in there awaiting collection, but they are not.

I sit in my car for a while to give them chance to arrive, but I realise after 15 minutes, that they may have changed their plans. Perhaps, they are not coming to the yard this morning after all. I ring Trish's mobile, she tells me that they will be coming to the yard later this afternoon, but in fact the pepper plants are behind the land-rover at their home on Marbury Road.

I laugh and say it is not a problem. I will call round for them later. Trish tells me whereabouts her home is just past Cogshall Lane, 3rd house on the left before Marbury Hollows. I set off for home and call at the Hollies Farm Shop, to pick a few treats up for Geoff and me to enjoy today, after all it is the Bank Holiday weekend.

We enjoy lunch which consists of some delicious home baked onion bread, ham, mango salsa, a caramelised pork and onion sausage roll. Then we enjoy a yummy chocolate twist pastry each.

We decide that we will chill out and read this afternoon. I head over to pick the plants up from Tricia. I enjoy a lovely long chat to her outside her home at our social distances. Tricia is busy in the garden, adding some new plants into the front border.

We chat for a while about sewing, and my writing project. Trish's piano skills and painting project, school days, our children, our own lives when we were growing up. How we all went to work from the moment, we left school. For me, this was at the age of 15. We both had to give our parents all our salaries. It was uplifting talking to Trish, knowing that we are all so much alike, in our principles and upbringing.

Geoff is fast asleep in the conservatory when I arrive home. The sun is just starting to come out, so I put the cushions out on the chairs, so that we can sit outside with a hot drink of tea. We always enjoy the time in our garden together.

The food for our Coq-au-Vin meal tonight has been prepared by Geoff, whilst I was out collecting the plants. I peel us some Cheshire potatoes to accompany it After putting the tea together into the Le Crouset dish, we pop it into the oven, then return to sitting outside again in the warm sunshine. I sit and knit for a while. Geoff is reading a book called the Librarian of Auschwitz.

Tomorrow is Bank Holiday Monday, and the weather is predicted to be very hot

So, during Lockdown, the long Easter Bank Holiday has been and gone. The first May Bank Holiday has been and gone. Now we are at the last weekend of May Bank Holiday.

I feel slightly annoyed at being locked down so much. All around us many families are picking their lives up again, visiting each other, not just one person to one person, but whole families and friends meeting up It feels so wrong that we have to remain locked down. That we cannot move around freely, to see our children and grandchildren without fear. We miss the freedom and green light to go. We follow the rules and guidance to protect ourselves and our families. Sadly, more people are breaking out now, heading to idyllic beauty spots across the UK. Flocking in their droves to the coast too. It is all utter chaos and madness around us. We would so love to break free! It simply is not safe to do so though.

Monday 25th May 2020

Today we were awake at 4.00 am again. I came downstairs, to let Chumley out for his toilet requirements. The early morning sky was already deep blue. The temperature quite warm. The weather is going to be glorious today, extremely hot. My Fitbit recorded a total of just 4 hours sleep. We managed to stay in bed until 5.00 am, after I had taken Chumley on the grass. We enjoy our first morning brew of tea in our mugs.

I put the washer on. We had some breakfast together. I typed yesterday's entries up. It is still only just 6.30 am in the morning, far too early to be outside in the garden. The lawns and furniture are still a bit damp with the early morning dew.

Geoff and I sit in the conservatory, to read our books for a while. It is peaceful and calm.

I decide that I am going to paint the old stone teddy bear outside, who is reading a book. The teddy bear has been resident in our garden, ever since our children were little. He must be about 38 years old at least. We have lived in this house for 39 years in total since 1981.

Geoff decides he is going to paint the trellis fencing at the back of the greenhouse. We both enjoy the morning painting in the garden and yes we have our shorts on too in this beautiful hot weather.

We can hardly believe it when we look at the clock and realise it is lunchtime. I make us a fresh sandwich with onion bread and ham for Geoff, but cheese with walnut and mango salsa, for me.

As it is hot, we decide that we are going to sit and enjoy the sunshine in the garden. We enjoy reading our books. Days like this are few and far between most years. However, this year the skies and warm sunshine have been most enjoyable, particularly during this never-ending lockdown situation that shows no sign of ending. In fact the hospitals in Somerset have just announced more admissions. It is quite scary to read about all the people who are just travelling far and wide across the country, seeking the best places to visit, regardless of the risks.

Our friends Steve and Sue are helping an elderly relative down the road from us. They telephone to see if they can come and see us for a few minutes at a social distance, which is allowed on a one-to-one basis. We agree and look forward to seeing the second visitor to our home since lockdown on the 23rd March, 2020. It was good to chat to them from a distance, as we have not seen them since February 2020.

After they leave, we prepare our evening meal, which is fillet steak with homemade chips and asparagus. We give Chumley a ten-minute stretch of his legs first.

Our evening meal is eaten outside. And we consume a large glass of red wine each to toast each other, our family and friends, whilst we enjoy the warm balmy summer evening.. Hard to believe that this is now our 4th Bank Holiday spent at home just the two of us

We are happy and content to stay in our homes, to keep saving lives. Although the news about the government minister Dominic Cummins who decided to drive his children to Durham in April, instead of staying at home with his wife, is causing a bit of a stir, with some fierce debates by the public. There are a lot of people who feel he should resign for telling us to stay at home, whilst not staying at home himself, when his wife was taken poorly with the Coronavirus.

There is a lot of banter going on in the usual messages between my Hartford School friends group today and some sad stories too, where each of us immediately supports each other through these difficult days. Especially the times when one of us might be at a low ebb. We also share a lot of fun and laughter, recipes, jokes, innuendos, and plants. If anyone needs anything, we are all there looking out for each other, helping each other too. It is unconditional love and support from a strong group of lifelong school friends. I enjoy being part of this group very much.

Tuesday 26th May-31st May 2020

Today, I am not going to write as normal but instead, I will write about Chumley our amazing, gorgeous dog who is a cross between a springer spaniel and a collie, known as a sprollie. He was born on the 13th June 2013.

These few pages of writing here, may be the start of the end of this book for me.

Life in Lockdown has been a roller-coaster ride of emotions and changes to the world, that none of us could ever have imagined. Today, though marks the end of my journal book of life captured with hope in our hearts each and every hour in 2020. There were so many challenges, as we walked through each and every hour of the invisible enemy. Some of us kept behind lines as told to by the government and the scientists. The bravest of all soldiers walked right out there, to stand and work diligently and tirelessly on the front lines. Their mission was simply to save lives.

During the summer months of 2013, Geoff was busy enjoying his retirement by gardening and completing jobs on our home. to make life ahead easier.

We discussed having a dog again, as our previous dog a golden Labrador called Amber died when he was 17 years old in 1998. Amber had been with us since the children were just 3 and 2 years old.

Amber was from a farm in Antrobus and just like the Andrex Puppy Dog advert for toilet paper. .

Geoff has always loved Border Collie sheepdogs. His family had a collie dog called Shep when he was younger. I have always loved spaniels for their energy and intelligence too. Geoff wasn't too keen on having a dog again, which would be a tie. However, I felt that as our children have left home and have their own lives. It feels the right time in our lives to have another dog again.

We have often discussed part-time work or volunteer work in the hospitals, or pharmacy delivery of prescriptions to homes locally. The debate goes on between us.

Eventually, I look on the Internet and discover a litter of dogs on a farm near Choldmondley, pronounced Chumley. The puppies are a cross between a collie and a springer spaniel in black and white. There were 7 of them and all have been taken except two males who are for sale.

I decide to take Geoff for lunch one Saturday at one of our favourite local restaurants The Fishpool at Delamere. During the course of our lunch, when we are both relaxed, I talk to him about perhaps just going to have a look at the puppies, but not to commit to having one, I am interested in what they look like. It might make our minds up to be a definitive no or a yes let's have another puppy.

Geoff listens to me telling him that we could just pop over to the farm this afternoon and look at the two puppies, but not make any firm decisions. Just see how we feel about having a dog again. He agrees and we set off to Choldmondley Farm, after first ringing the farm to check the puppies are still available.

We arrive and discover that the owners of the farm are away on holiday. Their son is able to take us to the barn, where the two puppies are playing. He lets us have a look at them when they both jump up excitedly at the opening on the barn door.

The two puppies are pushing each other out of the way, as they each vie for our attention. The slightly larger one pushes his younger brother down. We instantly want to hold the one that was pushed down by his bigger sibling. We are allowed to hold them outside the barn door. I take a photo of Geoff holding one of the puppies. I know in that instant he is totally smitten. The memory of that first tender hold of a lovable black and white sprolly is etched on our hearts forever. Our little happy puppy who we named after the area where he was born. Chumley.

Chumley died today at 12.30 pm on a lovely comfy bed inside the special room at our Veterinary surgery.. His euthanasia drug was administered by the Clinical Director Vet who admitted Chumley into their hospital care on the afternoon of my birthday Wednesday 6th May. Louise, Andy, Lorna, Lorraine, Alan, Receptionist Kerry, have all done their utmost to love and care for Chumley during his sudden and unexpected illness leading to this day, which we knew was inevitable from day one on the afternoon of my 67th birthday.

Before administering the end of Chumley's last few minutes. Louise brought Chumley to the steps of the practice, where Chumley gazed at us both. He talked to us with those gorgeous dark chocolate brown eyes of his " hello again you two. What have you come back for? I haven't left you yet, so I am confused slightly. I guess you just wanted one more hug. I can't wag my tail any longer, but I can sit a while on the steps with you" I noticed immediately, how white and old looking his face and slightly open panting mouth was. He just sat down on the steps with us quietly, letting us love and cuddle him. I noticed his head was held up high.

Chumley sat in his usual upright stance. He was gazing ahead with his head held high, at the sun shining brightly above us, just north east in the cobalt blue sky above. Chumley knew exactly in that moment of his final goodbye, just where his next journey would take him. I knew that he wasn't afraid to go. He just needed us to give him his wings, to open them up for him, then set him free to soar high above, like a balloon released from its ribbons.

The three of us sat together quietly, it was wonderful to be glove free and massage Chumley's head, which he always enjoys. To stroke his back and tummy gently for him. We were obstructing the steps leading to the door marked 'staff only' but we knew we would not be here for too long.

A couple of the staff managed to squeeze past us quietly and quickly.

After a few short minutes, the door opened. A serious and sad eyed Louise wearing her gown and face mask, told us that her final preparations were now ready for Chumley. Louise informed us, that we would be going into the room on the left, as we entered the building. Louise told us that she would be standing by the door to carry out the procedure. Louise explained that she had put a cannular onto Chumley's leg, which we had already noticed. To this cannular she would administer the strong dose of anaesthetic to Chumley through the long line which is attached to the vial of liquid. Louise explained to us, that as Chumley has virtually no blood cells circulating through his body. The effects of the drug may take a little while longer than normal, to put Chumley to sleep. Louise encouraged us to sit on the large square comfy bed with Chumley, to talk to him.

We stroked Chumley gently, kept talking to him about how much we love him, that this bed is just like his own comfy bed at home. We reassured him that he was going to have a big, long sleep now, then he will be better again forever. We whispered to him that he would be able to run pain free in the wind, with his ears flapping, that wonderful tail wagging happily once more!

The effects of the drug only took seconds before Chumley fell fast asleep, with our arms around him. He just laid down his head in a deep peaceful sleep. We said, "night, night, Chumley, sleep tight and run free".

Louise told us we could have a few minutes with Chumley on our own and left the room. Geoff and I made sure that Chumley was comfy, as his head had dropped down off the bed onto the floor. We lifted his head and body up carefully, so that he was stretched out asleep in his usual position, as he does at home with us.

His eyes were still open, we both gently closed them for him, as we do in death for our loved ones. As I looked back at Chumley, for the very last time I saw that his body had somehow just collapsed into a big pile of black fur. We had noticed the last few days, that his body was becoming misshapen as the disease sapped his life blood literally. My eyes took in that Chumley was just no longer there but had somehow escaped his body.

A friend once told me at his wife's funeral that our bodies are just shells carrying us around through life and when we die, they are simply discarded. We leave them for another place, beyond what we know and cannot see. All we are made of is just physical matter. I thought that was so true when I looked at Chumley's body for one last time and saw with my own two eyes, that he had just discarded his physical form and stepped out of it, just like we discard our clothes at night, when we step out of them for bedtime.

I found it profound to see the physical and spiritual departure in those few seconds of looking back today. I know the tears will be there forever inside our hearts, but I also know that in life we receive teachings from each other as humans. And this is true for our pets too, who live in a much more heightened sensory kingdom. They can hear and smell things, that humans simply cannot.

It's hard for me to explain here on this page, the image and feelings I had, but what I felt was that he had just stepped away from his body. He took his own gentle soul and all his funny little mannerisms with him.

Just like those indignant looks on his face on Saturday when our son Anthony called round. Chumley watched us from the other side of our conservatory door not understanding why he couldn't run and play with all of us. In the end, I brought Chumley out to Anthony, who put some gloves on, then gave Chumley a much-needed hug.

My goodness that was one happy Chumley who was overjoyed to see Anthony and be stroked gently. It never ceases to amaze me how animals like humans' form bonds with some people in their own kingdoms, more strongly than with others! I guess it is some genetic instinctive aura that we all have around us, that gives an acute sense of knowing who we trust and love, likewise who to steer clear of!

It wasn't long before Louise returned. We gave our heartfelt thanks to Louise for everything she and the whole team have done for Chumley. They all worked incredibly hard to save Chumley's life during the last 3 weeks. Geoff and I said our final goodbyes. Our drive home was a long tearful one. The pain in our hearts hurt so much.

The rest of today passes in a hazy blur, through tear-stained faces, hearts that will not stop aching.

We keep looking around at our empty home and garden that no longer has our gentle soulmate sitting there beside us or running excitedly around the garden playing ball and running to us with his favourite toys.

Lockdown hours and days have created a silence around us every day, with the lack of airplanes flying over into Manchester, reduced traffic noise, no visitors, the only wonderful sounds we hear all day long are the happy birds chirping to us, our own voices when we chat, the FaceTime calls and ZOOM meetings with family and friends and of course the NHS clapping and cheering every Thursday night at 8.00 pm.

Today, however, the increased silence around our lives feels unbearable. It is so very tough as we make the calls to our children, family and send messages to all our friends who know and love us and Chumley with the same unconditional love, he gave to everyone in his short life of just 6 years and 11 months.

My lifelong school friend Barbara telephones immediately she receives the message, to chat to us and I can hear that she is crying. I cannot talk to her properly for crying so much, on the phone myself. It is so very hard and painful, but she fully understands. she gives me great comfort by just staying on the line and talking to me, until I am a little calmer.

Eventually, Geoff and I rally round and start to remove Chumley's belongings. The last drug given to Chumley for one week was Mycophenolate. We were advised it is very toxic, the guidance sheet with the drug gave strong advice about taking precautions of handling everything with gloves all the time, not letting him lick us or touch us, of disposing of his toilet waste carefully by washing it away, to wash and sanitise all bedding and areas where Chumley had lain or been.

I set to and start to clean and sanitise the home and all his belongings, so that I am kept busy through the fast-falling tears. Geoff loads everything into a pile. We had given Chumley a brand-new bed that we bought recently for summer. He always enjoyed his sleep in his new bed, as he could snuggle down deep inside it.

We had no choice, but to dispose of everything belonging to Chumley today, carefully and properly to avoid any dangerous substances reaching others or lingering in our home. The task kept us busy with less time to cry, for a while anyway.

Geoff was exhausted and went to bed early at 9.00 pm. I could not settle down at all. We had both hugged each other so much today. Shared our tears over endless cups of tea and glasses of wine.

However, we were reaching a point where we needed our own space for a while. I tried to go to bed and sleep but gave up. In the end, I sat downstairs looking on my phone and the computer at all our happy memories and adventures with Chumley since the 1st of October 2013 when he not only joined our family but lit up our lives totally with unconditional love.

I put a few photos on social media and spend the rest of the evening until 2.00 am, adding an album of Chumley to my phone and iPad so that Geoff and I can share the happy memories and stories together in the morning. Eventually, I manage a couple of fitful hours sleep at last.

It is now Wednesday 27th May and both Geoff and I are total wrecks this morning from the lack of sleep. I had eventually fallen asleep on the sofa last night as I could not face going upstairs to bed. I found myself reaching down for Chumley, but he was just not there to lick my hand and nuzzle up by my side. I heard Geoff go to the bathroom and he came down to see if I was ok? He made us both a cup of tea and we went back to bed to cuddle each other tightly. Shared our tears together in tight hugs, with our arms wrapped round each other.

If either Geoff or I could not sleep during restless nights of little worries about anything, we would always get up, so as not to disturb each other. However, whenever one of us came downstairs to wander around or make a hot drink, Chumley thought it was great that we had come down in the middle of the night to be with him. He always enjoyed sitting with us quietly, nuzzling our hands for a cuddle and looking into our souls with those beautiful deep chocolate brown eyes of his, until we were able to go back to bed again. It was as if he was our mum or dad comforting us, with the inner wisdom that everything will be ok.

The images throughout our long restless night were raw and heart breaking as we relived those last few hours with Chumley and his rapid decline into his final moments before our last goodbye cuddle with him. Both of us feel so glad that we were strong enough to be with Chumley and talk to him as Louise administered his final euthanasia drug which took Chumley out of his pain and into a deep peaceful sleep whilst we held him for one last time yesterday lunchtime.

We feel so very tearful as we come downstairs to see the empty space where Chumley would have been snuggled up in his cosy large fluffy grey bed, just waiting for us patiently with his paws crossed over, to take him out on his first early morning walk. The silence in our home is overpowering, we are totally bereft and feel so lost ourselves, as we try to come to terms with losing the best dog ever.

Eating breakfast this morning is a slow process as we try to swallow our breakfast cereals but have no appetite for the daily bowls of cornflakes with hot milk for Geoff and porridge with honey for me. Neither of us has the energy or strength to put one foot in front of the other and move forward. Grief is holding us back from living this first sad day without Chumley in our lives.

Messages of love and telephone calls continue to arrive all throughout today, our neighbours are totally devastated as Chumley was well known and loved by everyone who met and fell in love with him for not just the handsome dog he was, but the amazing intelligent and very gentle dog that made up his personality, along with his inquisitive chocolate brown eyes that just made everyone melt and his funny expressions and fantastic ways of talking to us with those soul-searching eyes of his.

Thursday 28th May, Friday 29th May, Saturday 30th May and Sunday 31st May have just merged into one empty tear-filled void, where we hardly remember what we did each hour, food and drink just stuck in our throats as grief overcame our days and nights. Geoff and I try hard to understand and comprehend how Chumley became so ill so quickly on my birthday Wednesday 6th May. I was 67 this year, Chumley was just 6 and would have been 7 next month enjoying an afternoon with his puppy school class friend Ted who is a gorgeous collie dog living just across the river from us with his lovely owners, Helen, John, Emily and Tom.

I search for answers and find none, I look for the reasons and find none, I look for what Geoff and I may have missed in looking after Chumley, I find nothing, he was a very fit and active dog, we would each walk at least 3 miles with him on his usual walks, restricted as we are by Lockdown, both Geoff and I have enjoyed our once-a-day exercise separately with Chumley on his usual 3-mile route. Under normal life we normally complete 10 miles a day with him together. I find nothing to give me peace or answers.

Geoff and I thought that Chumley would be by our side as he and we grow old together for at least another 6 years as Chumley was only so young and strong, so much so that he even had the strength to take one of the vet nurses for a walk, whilst he was in the vet hospital not the other way round, he was in charge and she commented on just how strong a dog Chumley was, we know and smile often at his strength in pulling us should a squirrel or cat run across his path ahead of him when on a lead.

I ask myself today is it time to finish writing these final pages of life under Lockdown for us since the 12th March when our unknown last trip to look after our granddaughter Autumn in Dalston, Carlisle, Cumbria ended abruptly with the speed of how the UK quickly became riddled with death and disease like the rest of the world around us.

We had absolutely no idea of what lay ahead of us as we drove home on Thursday 12th March chatting about taking Autumn to choose her own Easter Egg, which was just a very small dinosaur one.

We left Sarah's birthday present and card with Paul for the 28th March, just in case we didn't return for our planned stay with them over Mothering Sunday weekend, our planned walk and pub lunch.

As Geoff and I drove home, we chatted about the clocks going forward on Sarah's birthday and how the nights will soon be lighter again and that driving home down the M6 will be easier for us in the lighter nights ahead.

I told Geoff that cleaning Sarah and Paul's house for them had been easy to do, whilst he had entertained Autumn after lunch, then we swapped roles as Geoff took Chumley out for a walk and I spent the afternoon helping Autumn with her jigsaws and playing card games with her, she always makes me laugh and she is just so clever at times and knows when she is going to win the game, her face gives it away!!

Nothing in our wildest dreams prepared us for the hours, days and weeks ahead when life stood still, and the grim reaper took his fill as he greedily devoured so many lives and brought fear to every doorstep as he went on the biggest killing spree in our lifetime.

Saturday 30th May 2020

We met Anthony, Catherine and Niamh at 11.00 am this morning in Church Lane Mobberley. It was so lovely just to see them and be outside in the gorgeous sunny weather, we all kept our distance from each other and enjoyed a lovely walk around the wide-open spaces of the fields in Mobberley starting just opposite the church.

Niamh was in her back carrier on Catherine's back and so we were able to walk quite separately with each other and enjoy catching up. We walked for about 45 minutes before returning to our cars as it was time to take Niamh home for her lunch and afternoon nap. It lifted our spirits just seeing part of our family once more and being outside walking and chatting to each other like old times many months ago.

We have missed a great deal of developmental stages with Niamh, who has cut 3 teeth, is not only sitting up, but standing and climbing stairs too. Niamh's hair has turned a lighter shade now than the dark hair she had when she was born 9 months ago, but she is such a cutie and has the most adorable smile and big blue eyes that are just gorgeous.

I take a couple of photos with my camera of the three of them and just hope that it won't be too long now before we can enjoy the hugs and cuddles once more, 3 months is a long time not to be able to see your family and hold our second granddaughter whom we last held on the 22nd February, 2020.

We say our fond goodbyes, no hugs and each drive back to our own homes. But at last, we feel we can smile properly, with the joy of seeing them in person, rather just on a phone photo, or video.

Our children have been fantastic and consistent throughout all these weeks. But nothing can compare with the joyous feeling, of being together again as a family. The smiles on our faces, as we drive home, will sustain us for a long time to come.

Sunday 31st May 2020

A day of doing nothing much in particular. We replay yesterday over again and how wonderful it was to be with our son, his wife and our second granddaughter out together in the warm May sunshine. A perfect day with lots of happy memories, to help to move us forward into the summery month of June tomorrow.

Conclusion

I had intended to continue this short journal of 3 months (one quarter of the year) in 2020 to a longer ending. However, the virus is here to live amongst us and is not going to disappear overnight.

The loss of our beloved dog Chumley put a stop to my motivation to continue writing daily, so I felt it was a good point in time to end this story of 3 months.

A friend once told me that the best videos taken are those of short duration that capture a moment in time as a snapshot. To video anything longer would then result in something boring. I have applied his advice to this short journal of mine. I know that there will be thousands of words and stories written about the COVID-19 Pandemic of 2020.

This is my snapshot of 3 months in 2020 and I hope you enjoy reading my work.

This has been a good time to reflect and re-align ourselves during 2020.

We will all learn to live slowly again in this different world and gain confidence, as we slowly overcome our own fears and the dangers, we all face in each day.

During Lockdown of the UK in 2020. Geoff and I learnt to enjoy our time together, to cook new recipes, to sew, to read, to write, to learn new skills and challenges that tested our brains and mental capacity.
We enjoyed taking delight and pleasure in the smallest of things, like the birds happily chirping all day long. The gorgeous blue skies and vivid spring colours of the trees and flowers this year, as nature healed the earth.

We worked hard in the garden along with others doing the same as us. We used our greenhouse to keep us busy and fed with tomatoes, runner beans and chillies. Instead of walking every day together, we learnt to enjoy our separate walks with Chumley. We kept our eyes and ears open each minute of every day so that we could help to support friends and family wherever and whenever needed with words of encouragement, no matter the hour of the day or night.

We learnt that not rushing about was good for us and the chance to slow down became a bonus we hadn't anticipated! Going out and holidays would be something of the past, which will return in the future, but for now this is no longer a priority. Staying safe, hearing that our family and friends were safe was all that mattered to us.

Our greatest loss in life during Lockdown was the inability to see, touch and be with our children and granddaughters. One of whom was just a baby of 6 months old, the other granddaughter a girl of 4 years old, whom we have journeyed to spend every week with on a round trip of 300 miles each week since she was born.

This was the toughest part of all for us to bear daily. However, we had no choice as they are the next generation that needed to be saved not us!

The rules were designed to keep us all apart, so that death on a plate did not reach our tables through unknowing transmissions!

Chumley Leigh

You burst into our lives one warm autumn day,
and right from the start, you just wanted to play.
Born in a barn on a cold windy farm,
but sleeping on hay, you came to no harm.
One of eight siblings that nipped here and there,
you jumped at the barn gate, not having a care.

It came down to two – how would we decide?
But we couldn't resist those Malteser eyes.
The energy, excitement, were all so appealing.
We were smitten – you gave us a warm happy feeling.
Take me home please, I promise I'm fun!
I'll be yours to adore, will walk slowly, won't run.

Now you're part of our family, life's started anew.
So much love, so much joy is the gift that is you.
That adorable ball of soft black and white,
those long floppy ears that shook sometimes with fright,
especially when things loomed up in the dark,
you'd be scared in the night, but still up with the lark.

You loved your long walks, ran like the wind,
through overgrown grass, a crazy whirlwind.
We laughed at your antics, walked even in rain,
side by side, the three of us, again and again.
Down to the river, relaxing, taking time out,
unconditional love is what a dog's all about.

Last spring, you left us, while still in your prime.
A year on, it still hurts that this was your time.

Acknowledgements and citations

To all my family without whom I would not be the person I am today

To all my friends for their love and friendship throughout all the days of 2020!

To Vale Royal Writers Group for all their supportive encouragement.

UK Government daily briefings

BBC and ITV daily updated news articles

Castle and Winnington Community Group Social Media

WhatsApp messages, stories and information

Gemma Peacock author of the Rainbow Poem

The Times Newspapers on-line COVID 19 article

Lucy Watts MBE MUniv FRSA
Independent Advocate, Support Broker
Consultant, Trainer, Speaker and Business Owner.

(I'd love for you to include my blog in your book, which would give me great pleasure. I'm happy with how you've shared it too. Thank you for keeping the emotion in the piece as people need to understand my emotions behind it.)

Wikipedia definitions of COVID-19

About the Author

Linda Leigh was born in Liverpool in May 1953 but grew up in Northwich, Cheshire, with the family that adopted her in 1954.

From an early age, she enjoyed reading books and writing short stories during her academic years at school.

After leaving school, Linda studied at Mid Cheshire College to obtain her business management qualifications, whilst working for ICI (Imperial Chemical Industries).

After changing her career to join General Practice for her next career, an opportunity arose for Linda to study at Macclesfield College where she achieved the highly acclaimed Practice Manager's Diploma for General Practice.

The circumstances that brought about Linda's adoption, have been a huge gap in her life. Writing about the facts of how each of our lives are shaped, has given Linda the inspiration, to continue writing the history of our lives.

linda_leigh@btinternet.com

Printed in Great Britain
by Amazon

67381391R00163